THE SPIRIT OF A TEAM

Successful CEOs and Coaches Share Their Strategies for Achieving Excellence

Achieving Excellence

1. "I look for three things in leaders: self-awareness, emotional intelligence, and intellectual integrity." —Carl Johnson
2. "If a team is going to make that investment of time, you have to match it." —Larry Kehres
3. "I've always lived on the edge. It just felt like I was chasing something. That's always been my makeup." —Charlie Frye
4. "Everybody should want to be challenged. Comfort isn't the greatest thing in the world." —Luke Fickell
5. "It's not just talent that gets you where you need to be." — Steve Clinkscale
6. "If you harness your mind, this is what you want to achieve, and you live it every day. Every day will create an opportunity for you to take a step in that direction." —Dwight Schar
7. "Be a better student because you want to be a better football player. The things that make you a better student are the same things that make you a great football player." —Nate Moore
8. "Coaching is holding people to standards. Some guys you have to push harder than others." —Matt LaFleur
9. "I know that you either continue to grow or you begin to die. You just can't sit stagnant." —Matt Kaulig
10. "Giving [the employees] ownership, we did it because they are our most valuable asset. If we're going to grow, we can't do it without people." —Dan Niss
11. "I looked at myself in business as more of a coach than a manager. I felt more comfortable doing it that way." —Bob Sebo
12. "Bring your best every day and you will have no regrets." —Sue Ramsey

THE SPIRIT OF A TEAM

Successful CEOs and Coaches Share Their
Strategies for Achieving Excellence

LEE OWENS
with
LARRY PHILLIPS

TUCKER
DS
PRESS

The Spirit of a Team: Successful CEOs and Coaches Share Their Strategy for Achieving Excellence ©2025 Lee Owens and Larry Phillips

All Rights Reserved.
Reproduction in whole or in part without the authors' permission is strictly Forbidden.

Cover design by Hannah Fortune
Edited by David Bushman
Book designed by Scott Ryan

Published in the USA by Tucker DS Press
Columbus, Ohio

Contact Information
Email: TuckerDSPress@gmail.com
Website: TuckerDSPress.com
Instagram: @Fayettevillemafiapress

To every team, to every athlete and coach, to every staff member and team supporter, I thank you for a lifetime filled with the *Spirit of a Team*.

CONTENTS

Foreword by Jim Tressel..viii
About Lee Owens..x
About Larry Phillips..xii
Book Outline...xiii
Illustration: Building Blocks to Team Excellence......................xiv
Preface: Making a Difference..1
Introduction: Motivation 101...6

Part One: The Foundation—Blueprint Basics

Chapter 1: Finding Your Tom Brady..14
Carl Johnson: Warren Equity Partners— Partner, Head of Operations
Chapter 2: Paying the Price..35
Larry Kehres: Mount Union Head Football Coach
Chapter 3: Poor Timid Souls..57
Charlie Frye: NFL & College Football Coach, Cleveland Browns Quarterback
Chapter 4: One Heartbeat..79
Luke Fickell: Head Football Coach, Wisconsin Badgers

Part Two: Focus on the Process

Chapter 5: Dare to Dream...104
Steve Clinkscale: NFL Coach, Los Angeles Chargers
Chapter 6: Have a Plan..122
Dwight Schar: Founder NVR
Chapter 7: You've Got to Believe..139
Nate Moore: Head Football Coach, Massillon High School

Part Three: The Pursuit of Excellence

Chapter 8: You've Got to Love It..164
Matt LaFleur: Head Football Coach, Green Bay Packers
Chapter 9: Never, Never, Never, Surrender......................................184
Matt Kaulig: Executive Chairman, Kaulig Companies/LeafFilter

Part Four: Sustaining Excellence

Chapter 10: Sharpen the Edge..208
Dan Niss: President, Charter Next Generation
Final Word: Lasting Legacy...230
Sue Ramsey: Motivational Speaker, 2013 Division II Basketball National Champion
Acknowledgments...250

INDEX OF MOTIVATIONAL MESSAGES

It Doesn't Matter 9
Effort 49
Never Forget 56
Man in the Arena 68
Risks 70
Don't Be Afraid 71
Little Eyes Upon You 77
Teamwork 90
Paradoxical Commandments of Leadership 101
Climb 'Till Your Dreams Come True 120
Opportunity 138
State of Mind 160
Commitment to Excellence 162
Enthusiasm 175
Passion 177
Don't Quit 201
Winning Is How You Play the Game 205
The Edge 222
The Road to Anywhere 228
Beginning of a New Day 248

—FOREWORD—

The proud tradition of building championship TEAMS is truly a point of pride, particularly with football in the great state of Ohio. Championship TEAM builders such as Paul Brown, Woody Hayes, Bo Schembechler, Don Shula, Earle Bruce, John Cooper, Bob Stoops, Ara Parseghian, Urban Meyer, Mark Dantonio, Chuck Noll, Lou Holtz, Lee Tressel, Nick Saban, Larry Kehres, and the Harbaugh family (Jack, John, and Jim) all had a great deal of their training in Ohio high school football, intercollegiate football at all levels, and the National Football League.

Lee Owens earned his "PhD in team building" by coaching with, learning from, and competing with the above legends in his storied high school and collegiate coaching career. Not only did Lee study and work with these extraordinary coaches, but he also was a student of the likes of John Maxwell, Bob Sebo, Carl Johnson, Matt Kaulig, Dwight Schar, Bob Archer, Jack Miller, Dan Niss, Don Graham, Zane Gross, and many other highly successful CEOs and leaders.

In my forty-eight years in higher education as a coach and administrator, Lee Owens was as accomplished as a team builder as any. In *The Spirit of a TEAM*, Lee shares his exhausting research on TEAM building and lessons learned from experiences with his championship TEAMS, along with the bonus of an array of proven leaders and their team lessons.

Whether you are building your TEAM at home, your business, your no-profit organization, your sports TEAM, your community, or serving this great nation, the lessons shared in *The Spirit of a TEAM* will be extremely valuable as you seek to reach your full potential.

Dive in, soak up the knowledge, and then see how you can apply it to serve your TEAM today!

Jim Tressel, Lt. Governor of Ohio
January 2025
Former Head Football Coach, Youngstown State University,
Four-time National Champion
Former Head Football Coach, The Ohio State University, 2002
National Champions, Seven-time Big Ten Champion
President Emeritus, Youngstown State University

−ABOUT LEE OWENS−

Ohio Hall of Fame football coach Lee Owens is a motivational speaker and team culture coach. Coach Owens is a leader and a winner. He has built winning teams and won championships everywhere he has coached.

In 2023, Lee retired from coaching after winning his sixteenth football championship. During his career, he took over struggling football programs at six different schools and led them to championship seasons. His football coaching stops included the legendary Massillon Washington High School, Mid-American Conference member The University of Akron, Ashland University, and Big Ten powerhouse The Ohio State University.

His résumé also includes coaching NFL Hall of Fame football players Jason Taylor and Orlando Pace. Owens was recognized seventeen times as Coach of the Year and three times as a finalist for the NCAA Division II National Coach of the Year. In addition, he was selected as the Ohio High School Coach of the Year 1985 at Galion High School and the Ohio College Coach of the Year 2012 at Ashland University.

"Lee Owens is one of the finest collegiate coaches in Ohio history," says former national championship-winning head coach Jim Tressel.

Beyond the gridiron, Owens became one of college football's truly impressive and inspirational speakers. He remains a popular speaker at meetings, luncheons, banquets, and conventions.

Joel Braun of AT&T can attest to that contention. "Coach Owens is not only an enthusiastic speaker with a positive message, but he is also entertaining and fun," Braun says.

Coaches Playbook LLC

Coaches Playbook LLC was started by Lee Owens in 2023. Coaches Playbook is dedicated to advancing team excellence. Using his many years of coaching experience, Owens has developed effective strategies to turn struggling units into successful teams.

In 1997, as the head football coach at the University of Akron, Lee Owens wrote the book *Blood, Sweat, Championship: A Team Guide to Winning*. Following the blueprint outlined in that book, Coach Owens led Akron to its first football championship in one hundred years during the 2000 season.

Lee and his wife, Dianne, have four married children and twelve grandchildren.

—ABOUT LARRY PHILLIPS—

Larry Phillips is an author, editor, and writer with more than one hundred writing and editing awards at the international, national, and statewide levels. He has been selected as Ohio's Sportswriter of the Year and Sports Columnist of the Year by both the Associated Press and the Ohio Prep Sports Writers Association.

Today he is the editor of three online news agencies: Richland Source, Ashland Source, and Knox Pages. Each is a hyper local online news agency in North Central Ohio.

Larry is a thirty-five-year veteran of the newswriting industry who graduated from Ohio University with a journalism degree in 1989. He has worked as a news reporter, sports reporter, city editor, news editor, sports editor, lifestyles editor, and local editor in the Thomson and Gannett newspaper chains.

He has authored two books, *Ohio's Autumn Legends, Volume I* and *II*, on a topic that is a personal passion: Ohio high school football. Larry and his wife, Laura, live in Mansfield, Ohio, with their two children, Bryan and Sydney.

−BOOK OUTLINE−

Part I THE FOUNDATION	FEATURING
1. Recruiting Your Tom Brady	**Carl Johnson**, Warren Equity Partners-Head of Operations
2. Paying the Price	**Larry Kehres**, All Time Winningest College Coach Mount Union College
3. Poor Timid Souls	**Charlie Frye**, Former NFL Player, College Coach
4. One Heartbeat	**Luke Fickell**, Head Football Coach Wisconsin
Part II THE PROCESS	
5. Dare to Dream Defensive	**Steve Clinkscale**, NFL Coach- 2024 Michigan Coordinator, National Champions
6. Have a Plan	**Dwight Schar**, Founder NVR- Former NFL Owner Washington
7. You've Got to Believe	**Nate Moore**, Head Football Coach- Massillon 2023 National HS Coach of the Year
Part III THE PURSUIT	
8. You've Got to Love It	**Matt LaFleur**, Head Football Coach Green Bay
9. Never, Never, Never Surrender	**Matt Kaulig**, Chairman Kaulig Companies and Founder, LeafFilter
Part IV THE SUSTAINABILITY	
10. Sharpen the Edge	**Dan Niss**, President of Charter Next Generation
Final Word–Lasting Legacy Champions	**Sue Ramsey**, Motivational Speaker; 2013 Women's Basketball National Champions Division

−ILLUSTRATION: BUILDING BLOCKS TO TEAM EXCELLENCE−

IV THE SUSTAINABILITY
      Excellence

III THE PURSUIT
    Passion   Commitment

II THE PROCESS
  Goals   Plan   Belief

I THE FOUNDATION
  Ability Effort Courage Leadership

Team Excellence
Teams that realize their God-given talents and abilities, working as hard as possible to go as far as possible. Teams that compete with an unselfish spirit, trusting one heartbeat, building relationships that will stand the test of time.

−PREFACE−
MAKING A DIFFERENCE

I have been writing this book for the past forty-five years. But it wasn't until 2016, when I attended the American Football Coaches Association dinner in New York City, that I realized why. At that time, I was the head football coach at Ashland University in Ohio and serving as president of the AFCA. The banquet's guest of honor was David M. Cote, chairman and CEO of Honeywell Inc.

Another attendee was Carl Johnson, Honeywell's president of industrial safety. Carl played high school football for me and has always had a special place in my heart. He shared with Cote how I had been a positive influence on him and made a difference in his life.

Carl didn't have a chance in life without football. As a sophomore in high school, he had already faced more adversity than most will face in a lifetime. Carl finished his football career at the University of Cincinnati and went on to earn an MBA at the University of Houston.

I believed in Carl. I cared about him as a person, not just an athlete, and I was there to support him and watch him grow throughout high school. As my quarterback, Carl led us to the state championship.

In an interview at the end of my coaching career, I was asked about my coaching legacy. Was it being part of a Big Ten championship at Ohio State? Was it winning the first-ever Mid-American Conference East Division championship at the University of Akron? Was it 266 victories as a high school and college head coach? Which win or championship was my greatest accomplishment?

The answer was none of the above.

My greatest validation as a coach was believing in Carl Johnson. Seeing what Carl has done in his life and how he has impacted so many people in a positive way, that's my legacy,

I coached to be a dealer of hope, to use my power of influence to help others reach their full potential.

In my career I had the opportunity to lead six different high school and college football teams. Each one was struggling to win and looking for a new coach to lead it in a new direction. I can still remember walking into the locker room or auditorium and meeting each one of those teams for the first time. I still have printed copies of the agenda for each one of those meetings. I can still see Carl Johnson more than forty years ago sitting in the back of the room at Galion High School with an uncertain look on his face.

Each time the challenge was different, but the message was the same. I told each team we would win, and they would be winners both on and off the field—and each time it happened!

This blueprint for team excellence works in the locker room—but it can and should be applied as a basis for excellence in the boardroom too. Motivating a team of football players is no different from motivating a team of salespeople or motivating your "team" at home.

Everyone is part of a team, and everyone wants to be successful. The leader of the team must be constantly selling the vision and the value of winning to everyone on the team. Only then can the team be motivated to make the climb.

Unfortunately, the vision or the value of winning is not always clear or strong enough to motivate the team to make the sacrifices necessary to get to the finish line.

Winning can never be solely about money or diamond-studded championship rings. No question, there is a lot of money in football today. Maybe too much money? High school football players are signing name, image, and likeness contracts for millions of dollars before they even get on a college football field.

It has been proven repeatedly that money alone is not an absolute motivator. There will never be enough fame or fortune to fuel the motivation needed for a team to achieve excellence. For a team to achieve excellence, the team must be motivated to win for the right reasons.

My experience and stories in this book are outlined in a step-by-step, tried-and-true journey on the path to team excellence. It is not only possible but critical to learn how to motivate your team and be successful without compromise or collateral damage.

Winning and success without excellence is an external, out-of-control experience. Often, the significance of a team's success is lost. Team excellence is becoming a team of significance, a team of purpose, and a team of destiny that becomes a lesson for everyday life.

For Carl Johnson and so many of his teammates on the 1985 state championship team, this experience was a life lesson in the spirit of a team that had achieved excellence.

Team Owens

I'm reminded of a Christmas card sent to our home from my son Andy and his wife, Julie. The card was signed "Team Owens."

All four of our children have amazing families. All four of these families have a team culture in their home—a team culture that includes discipline, accountability, hard work, and shared values. All the parents in these homes are role models for their children and lead by example. They love their children and always put the interests of their children before anything else in their lives.

Today the stress level for parents with children in their home is extraordinarily high. Financial strain, time demands, children's health, social media, and cultural pressures make it more important than ever for the family to work as a team.

Parents in all walks of life too often sacrifice or neglect the team at home. This compromise of family should never be justified by career ambitions or professional success.

As a head football coach, I was driven to go as far and as high as possible, to win as many games as possible, and to earn as much respect as possible in my profession.

My greatest fear was not falling short of these goals. My greatest fear was not being there for my family. I know there were times when

I made selfish decisions. I remember more than one long ride home, buried in guilt, after missing one of the children's events. I can still hear my youngest daughter, Molly, telling me on the phone, "Come home right now," after several weeks of working away from the family when I started my coaching position at Ohio State.

I coached eight different teams. That included buying and selling eight different homes and moving into eight different communities, all with new schools and new friends. My coaching career spanned forty-five years, 1977-2022. In thirty-seven of those years, I was a head coach.

When my career officially ended, Team Owens presented me with a memory book and shared these thoughts about our family:

"Oh, what a ride it's been the last 45 years. We lived in so many great places and met so many awesome people. Ben, Andy, Leanne, and Molly have all grown up in a football family and we were fortunate to experience many fun times."–Dianne Owens.

"Football has been a key part of our family's life starting with my earliest memories; however, you ensured that family was never a second priority. Family always had a critical role, and you showed Andy, Leanne, Molly, and me how to have both a successful career and more importantly how to raise a great family."–Ben and Elizabeth

"Dad, it has been a privilege to witness your career as one of your players, one of your coaches, and one of your biggest fans from the sidelines. We are beyond grateful for the countless memories your career has provided our family."–Andy and Julie

"Through coaching, you've given us so many unforgettable memories. Riding in a convertible in the Massillon parade and having my classmates scream my name. From OSU bowl trips to running around the Rubber Bowl with friends, you filled our lives with experiences we'll never forget. You were a great role model to us growing up, and now we get to teach our kids the lessons you taught us."–Leanne and Jake

"I've always been proud to be your daughter. Growing up, your profession has given us so many lasting memories. You have taught us so much as we witnessed the respect people have for you wherever we go. Most significantly, you've impacted my family so much. I will be forever grateful that you have been a mentor to Robby in his coaching career over the years. My childhood provided me with the strength to handle the comments in the stands, the ability to learn from the losses and celebrate the wins, and the understanding of how many memories we will share as a family. And I thank you for that."–Molly and Robby

As I concluded my football coaching career, "Team Owens" was—and continues to be—my greatest legacy.

"When all the dust is settled and all the crowds are gone, the things that matter are faith, family, and friends."–Barbara Bush

—INTRODUCTION—
MOTIVATION 101

For the past twenty years, I taught Foundations of Coaching 170 at two Ohio colleges: the University of Akron and Ashland University. I would always get behind on the syllabus and end up spending the first half of the semester on just two topics: winning and motivation.

Philosophy of Winning
"There is no substitute for victory."–Douglas MacArthur

It should be easy to define winning. If a team scores more points than its foe, it wins and the other team loses. One team succeeds and the other team fails. Winning and success are one in the same, just like losing and failure.

I would often ask the students in my class to debate the following question: "Is it possible to have a successful losing season?"

Most would rationalize that it was if the team improved or gave its best effort. I disagreed.

The students were confusing winning and success with excellence.

So here is how I explained my reasoning during a speaking engagement at the Rotary Club in Canton, Ohio, before the 1989 game between Massillon and Canton McKinley. The Massillon-McKinley series is one of the longest and greatest high school rivalries in America. While giving this speech I was head coach of the Massillon Tigers:

"If you think I'm going to propose a substitute for winning this game tomorrow, forget it! I love to win, our team loves to win, our community loves to win. But this classic Massillon-McKinley game is much more than winning and losing. This game is the standard for excellence. A competition between two worthy opponents. Two teams with willful determination, a rugged tenacity, and a belief in the spirit of the team."

With 959 wins, Massillon High School is just two wins short of being the winningest high school football team in America. Valdosta, Georgia, is first, with 961 all-time wins.

However, winning and excellence are not the same. Excellence grows within a person, within an athlete, within a team, within a community, and its meaning lasts. Success and winning are external, and often perish in a community, a school, or a team. Excellence will endure.

The goal is to go for the win with the team's best shot. This alone assures excellence. I want a team hungry for excellence, not success. I want a team in pursuit of excellence that has the same standards if it's playing for one dollar or $1 million, if they are playing in front of one hundred fans or one hundred thousand fans.

The Value of Winning

"I firmly believe that man's finest hour, his greatest fulfillment to all he holds dear, is the moment he has worked his heart out for a good cause and lies exhausted on the field of battle, victorious!"–Vince Lombardi

I am a pretty good winner, but I am a terrible loser. In several interviews as a football coach, I was asked what's the best part of my job? Winning! The worst part? Losing! Winning strengthens all that is taught in sports. There is no better feeling than calling for victory formation at the end of the game and taking a knee. That feeling right at that moment is priceless.

Winning, especially winning big games, keeps mediocrity from settling into your team.

Mediocrity is the opposite of excellence.

Winning helps pay the bills and is good for job security. Winning keeps a team healthy. I love walking through an empty training room after a win. Winning builds confidence and morale. Everyone loves a winner.

Notice how your phone blows up after a win and how quiet it is after a loss? Society loves a winner. The adage is true: "To the victor belong the spoils."

Many sports scientists believe losing builds character better than winning. I couldn't disagree more. Nothing good comes from losing. Every season we welcome our championship teams back to campus to celebrate their accomplishments. How many losing teams reunite to celebrate their seasons?

I'm not preaching to win at all costs, like "Winning is everything" or "If you're not cheating, you're not trying." But striving to win is everything. Losing will always hurt. I die a little after each loss. After a loss, I would be sick to my stomach and unable to sleep.

For me, as a competitor, the pain of losing has always been a curse. As a leader, it has always been easy for me to sell the value of winning.

Winning Is a Decision

"Not everyone gets to be a winner unless they choose to be."
—Valentin Chmerkovskiy

The 1999 season was do-or-die time for my coaching career at the University of Akron.

After our first four years, we had only twelve wins. This was year five. We were lucky to have a year five, and if we didn't win there would be no year six. We worked hard on our plan for the first four years. We knew we were close. We knew at this point it was from the eyebrows up.

We had to decide to win.

During the offseason, I gave the book *Permission to Win* by Ray Pelletier to every player and staff member on the team.

I lectured to the team from the book every night in preseason camp. I read this excerpt from the first chapter to the team:

IT DOESN'T MATTER

"It doesn't matter where you may be in life. It doesn't matter who you are or what troubles you have. It doesn't matter if you are black or white, homeless, locked away in a prison or brought up in a ghetto or in a castle. It doesn't matter if your business or marriage has failed or you have been diagnosed with a terminal disease. It truly doesn't matter. There is a champion inside you that cannot be defeated. If you're alive, that champion is in there. You didn't create it. It was given to you at birth. It is part of you."

At the end of the book, Pelletier asks his readers to take five seconds to go to the mirror and tell themselves loudly and firmly, "I give you permission to win."

I took this request a step further and designed a Decide to Win Certificate for every player on our team. It read: "Let the world know I have decided to win. I am fully dedicated to my personal mission statement, and qualified for all the rights and privileges this world has to offer. I have freed myself from self-imposed restrictions and opened my mind up to unlimited capabilities."

Everybody signed it.

Unfortunately, we lost our opener to Penn State, ranked number two, 70-24. The only other time I had coached in Beaver Stadium was in 1994 when the Nittany Lions beat the Buckeyes 63-14. Like Ohio State in 1994, our team still had high aspirations. We had decided as a team that this season was going to be different.

We went on to win five of our next six games, and we had a 5-2 record going into Annapolis to play Navy. Navy had the third best rushing team in the country. It was their homecoming game, and Ohio native and former Heisman Trophy winner Roger Staubach was back to deliver the game ball as the Midshipmen marched onto the field during pregame.

Navy held a 23-0 lead midway through the second quarter. But we scored 35 of the next 41 points for a 35-29 victory. This was the largest come-from-behind win in school history and the largest blown lead in 121 years of Navy football.

We ended the season with a 7-4 record, which included the

program's longest winning streak in fifteen years. It was our first winning season, and only the second at the University of Akron as a Division 1A team.

Motivational Paradigm

Motivation is the result of different types of beliefs: the belief that one's effort will result in performance, the belief that one's performance will be rewarded, and the belief in the perceived value of the reward.

In other words, if the team works hard, the team will perform better and win more. In turn, when the team wins more, the team will be rewarded.

The difficulty is selling the team on the idea that the rewards of winning and success will justify the time, effort, and sacrifice it takes to win.

It must be clear that winning is not easy. Indeed, as Tom Hanks's character says in the film *A League of Their Own*, "If it was easy, everyone would do it. The hard is what makes it great." There is no debate: winning is a difficult, uphill climb with many setbacks. Just winning more than you lose or turning a few losses into wins is a good place to begin.

A 6-5 season will never be good enough. No one on the squad will be excited with this as the team goal. But a team can build on a 6-5 season. When a team starts to string together a few winning seasons, eventually the stars will align, lightning will strike, and your team will find itself in the middle of one of those magical championship seasons.

I heard Zig Ziglar lecture at our coaches' convention in 1997. He told five thousand football coaches that they could have whatever they wanted in life by giving others what they need. We all have needs in life. Determine what the needs are for your team. Find a way to meet these needs and you will have a highly motivated team.

I've never had a coaching staff in greater need of positive motivation than the 1999 Akron staff. The coaches worked hard and made many sacrifices in our first four seasons at Akron. It was a real challenge, and I had asked them to spend a lot of time away from their family.

They knew we needed to have a winning season to keep our jobs, but fear is not the best motivation in the long term. The staff's salaries were not very competitive, and there were few benefits. So before the season, I went out to a few donors/boosters and raised enough money to take the entire staff on a trip after the season. All we had to do was have a winning season.

I have never experienced a group of coaches working so hard with such a positive attitude. We finished with a seven-win season. The coaches and their wives had a great time celebrating our first winning season on an all-inclusive trip to the Bahamas.

You win with motivated people, and you lose if you don't motivate well. The first job of a team leader is to motivate team performance. It is an everyday job that can never be neglected.

If you want to win, you cannot manage. You manage livestock; you motivate people.

Motivation is the ability to inspire and move people to a higher place. This ability comes from the attitude "I can make a difference." Motivation is setting and selling higher and higher standards.

Motivation is creating purposeful action, 100 percent focused. Motivation is the passion to help others learn, grow, and perform.

To be able to motivate, one must be motivated. To motivate a team, a leader can't wait for those who are not motivated or refuse to be motivated.

If you want to motivate, set goals that are challenging yet realistic. If there are conditions that keep a team from meeting team goals, then adjust the goals or adjust the timeline for meeting the goals. Continued failure to meet goals will eventually lead to losing motivation, giving up, and quitting the team.

Another part of the motivational paradigm is having a well-planned system of extrinsic and intrinsic rewards. These rewards must be appropriate, on time, consistent, and well deserved if they are to reinforce positive performance.

I was a young football coach who took over several teams that were struggling to win and needed to learn how to win. Each team I coached was a lesson in how to motivate. Along the way, I read every book I could find on motivation, leadership, and team building. I listened to every motivation tape I could get my hands on. I attended every clinic and visited every successful person who would talk with me. And in the end, not only did all these teams win, but they all won championships. If you are a team leader committed to excellence at home, in the workplace, or in the world of athletics, this book is for you.

PART ONE:
THE FOUNDATION—
BLUEPRINT BASICS

Building team excellence takes a solid foundation. There are two cornerstones to this foundation. The first is to recruit the right people; the second is to develop a winning team culture.

The first football book I purchased was written by the legendary Ohio State coach Woody Hayes. It is titled appropriately *You Win with People*. I worked for Hall of Fame Coach John Cooper at Ohio State; he said it this way: "You can't win the Kentucky Derby on a mule."

Later in my career, after a few days on the Akron job, I got a call from the former coach of the Cleveland Browns, Sam Rutigliano, who said, "Coach, if you want to win, you need to do three things: recruit, recruit, and recruit."

These three great coaches all expressed the same principle but all in their own unique styles. Coach Rutigliano also shared this thought on leadership: "A winning team culture will be in direct proportion to the leadership on the team.

The heart of the foundation for a team of excellence is sacrifice and courage. Regardless of how talented a team may be, or how strong its culture is, it will not win without a blue-collar, punch-the-clock, arrive-early, stay-late work ethic. Without a go-for-it, play-to-win, no-fear, seize-the-moment attitude, a team will never win the big one.

This foundation to build a winner is always under construction and constantly must be reinforced.

–CHAPTER ONE–
FINDING YOUR TOM BRADY

"We are told talent creates its own opportunities. But it sometimes seems that intense desire creates not only its own opportunities, but its own talents."- Eric Hoffer

Photo of Carl Johnson

Bio Box: Carl Johnson—Warren Equity Partners, Head of Operation
Background: Reared in a Galion, Ohio, home with poverty, incarceration, addiction, and abuse.
Athletic Achievement: State championship quarterback.
Scholastic Achievement: Master of Business Administration, University of Houston.
Business Achievement: President of multiple divisions at Honeywell International Inc.
Accolades: Carl has been hailed by *Fortune* and *Business Weekly* as an international manufacturing thought leader.
Professional Achievement: Warren Equity Partners, Head of Operations

If you are a football fan, you probably have not heard of Carl Johnson. If you are a businessperson, you should have heard of Carl; he's led multiple divisions at Fortune 500 multinational conglomerate Honeywell International.

I am proud to have coached Carl in high school. This story is about his natural ability to lead and motivate others to their peak performance.

Finding and cultivating leaders to elevate a team is perhaps the trickiest task for any manager, or coach. It is also imperative. No amount of talent can overcome a lack of leadership within a team.

One must be able to recognize the "It" factor." Sometimes the adage comes into play: I can't define "It," but I know "It" when I see "It." Carl Johnson had "It." In fact, he oozed "It."

Carl Johnson just might have been the most important athlete I ever coached, in more ways than one. Yet in his case, "It" came in a unique package, not easily seen, and dangerously elusive too. Carl is one of those kids who could have gone either way, growing up on the wrong side of the tracks.

"The way I grew up has everything to do with who I am now," Carl said. "I was always a dreamer, and I always recruited a circle of influence. Whether people knew it or not, they were always part of my circle of influence.

"Because I didn't have the most functional family life, I had to think outside the box. So it started early on with me, surrounding myself with the right people, the right families."

I first met Carl when I became the head football coach at Galion High School in 1983. His father had been in prison, and his mother remarried a man who was abusive. To escape his home life, Carl was forced to find refuge with friends, aunts, and others willing to take him in.

Yet from that background, Carl Johnson rose to the heights of the business world, becoming a division president at Honeywell International Inc. Carl was so impressive in his twenty years with the company that Honeywell CEO David Cote described him as his "Tom Brady" in his book *Winning Now, Winning Later*.

Carl was my "Tom Brady" too, albeit fifteen years earlier and on the football field.

Like so many athletes I coached, Carl was struggling with his identity. He was a sophomore when I arrived in Galion. With little to no family attachment, he was withdrawn and in need of positive role models.

Many teachers and coaches had given up on Carl. But I saw another side to this charismatic youngster. He was likable and fun to be around and had a good heart. He was also a quality athlete who loved to compete, and he wielded an important trait: he was coachable.

Most importantly, I trusted him. Carl was mentally and physically tough. He was committed to becoming the best athlete on our football team, and indeed the best athlete in the school.

"High school is where things kind of started transforming for me, because I never thought that I was going to be doing what I'm doing now," Carl said. "The friends that I grew up with, that circle of influence that I gravitated toward, they not only shared their time with me, I mean sometimes they even shared their lunch money. Their families, their time, their love, it started off with guys like that who really impacted my life."

Carl was getting practice time with the varsity as a freshman football player under my predecessor, the popular and successful Harry Beers. I was an outsider. My last team, at Crestview, had gone undefeated, and I was taking on the Galion job that could've gone to one of Harry's assistants. I had to prove myself to the staff at Galion as well as the players, and Carl was one of them.

"I kind of watched," Carl said. "I've always believed you learn by osmosis, where you just step back and watch people, and so I just watched how he handled himself. And I mean he was so young; he could've been my older brother."

So Carl and I were watching, observing, learning about each other. After playing junior varsity as a sophomore, Carl became our starting quarterback as a junior, and we began to build a connection.

That 1984 season, we went 7-2-1, and Carl was the leading passer in the Northern Ohio League. He played well, but when we played the best teams on our schedule and had those pivotal moments, we just couldn't finish the must-win situations that season.

In Carl's senior year, the first game was at Ashland, which featured quarterback Matt Underwood. Incidentally, Matt went on to become a broadcaster for the Cleveland Indians/Guardians.

The Arrows had beaten us the year before, and that was really in our heads leading up to that game. The 1985 opener at Ashland was tough. We were trailing 7-6 late in the fourth quarter, and they had really taken the air out of the ball with a time-consuming run game. When we finally regained possession, I huddled with Carl on the sidelines. I knew this was it. If the Galion Tigers were going to improve from the previous year, this was the moment it had to happen, the moment we had fallen short in 1984.

I looked Carl right in the eyes and told him many of our goals were on the line right here, right now. He responded immediately and took us down the field. We went 58 yards in six plays, and he threw a 16-yard touchdown pass to Mike Smith with 2:30 showing on the clock. Carl also fired the two-point conversion pass, and we won 14-7.

Although it was only the opener, I knew we had turned the corner. I had seen Carl grow up right before my eyes.

That victory propelled Galion to a 10-0 regular season, and we earned the first playoff berth in school history. Our defense was superb, and Carl was leading the offense with fullback Rob Monnett. We outscored opponents 424 to 84 and won the Northern Ohio League title.

It had taken us three years to build the foundation of this team. We had great players, including our Tom Brady at quarterback, Carl Johnson. We developed a blue-collar work ethic and one of the best lifting programs in the state.

We had a culture that was developed by the leaders on our team. We were a big family and lived in a community that loved us, supported us, and became our twelfth man. Our 1985 theme was The Year of the Tiger.

We called our offense in 1985 the "Run N' Boot." We combined the misdirection of the Wing T and the sprint-out passing of the Run N' Shoot to develop an explosive and balanced offense that was a perfect fit for our personnel.

We also rolled the dice. We totally committed to two-platoon football, something unique at that time for a school our size. It was a calculated risk.

In the playoffs, we disposed of Toledo DeVilbiss, Avon Lake, and Cincinnati Greenhills to reach the state championship game. In our four playoff games, we outscored our opponents 33-0 in the fourth quarter. This was because of two-platoon football, which kept our players healthy and fresh.

The Division II state championship was played on a frigid day at Ohio Stadium against Youngstown Cardinal Mooney. They were so much better than us that I wouldn't let our players see their film. They were bigger and faster than any team we had ever played. They were a four-time state champ and had never lost in the championship game. Their coach was Don Bucci, who had been there for nineteen seasons and compiled a 159-37 record.

Galion had never been in the playoffs before, much less a state championship game. I knew we needed to be as fresh as possible to have a chance of winning. So I cut practices way down that week. I wouldn't let the players practice in pads, and I took them down to Columbus to stay in a hotel, and the night before the game. I enforced a tight curfew to keep them focused.

In the pregame that day, the Mooney players tried to intimidate our team. They came out with baseball hats on and the words printed "1985 State Champs." It backfired. Our Bruise Brothers defense hit and pursued with vengeance the entire game.

Cardinal-Mooney had several players committed to play major college football, including their star quarterback, Mark (Bo) Pelini, who was committed to Ohio State and later would go on to become the head coach at Nebraska. We hung tough thanks to our defense and caught a break in the fourth quarter when they failed to down a punt inside our 5-yard line. The ball trickled into the end zone with four players watching to give us possession at our twenty—not great field position, but not in jail either.

Again, much like at Ashland, we had reached the do-or-die moment of the game. Carl again rose to the occasion. We methodically moved down the field on a 16-play, 80-yard march that included Carl's 26-yard pass to Monnett and a 19-yard completion to Jeff Remy.

Time after time on that drive, when we got into a crucial third- or fourth-down situation, we rolled out Carl and let him make a play, run or pass to convert. His competitive nature came through each time.

"They started hitting our right side with those rollouts," Bucci said in his postgame press conference. "Johnson really hurt us."

Finally, Carl finished it with a one-yard plunge with 3:36 left, ending in a 6-0 victory. The triumph concluded a storybook season. As of this writing, it remains the only state football championship ever won on the field by a team from North Central Ohio.

"That hurt really bad," Pelini said, "especially when we felt we lost to a team that shouldn't have been on the same field with us."

That culminated a three-year climb for the Galion football program and really launched Carl. He was selected to play in the North-South all-star game for the best senior football players in Ohio the following summer. In that game, Carl was splitting snaps with Shawn McCarthy, who went on to Purdue and briefly played for the New England Patriots in the NFL.

I was a part of the coaching staff in that game with Thom McDaniels of Canton McKinley, father of future Broncos and Raiders Head

Coach Josh McDaniels. Carl started in a rotation with McCarthy. It was a tight game, and McCarthy rallied us in the fourth quarter to send it into overtime.

It was Carl's turn in the rotation to go back in the game when we started overtime, but he went to Thom and said, "No, coach. Leave Shawn in the game. He's got the hot hand." We won in overtime, and McCarthy was the MVP of the game.

"It was an incredibly unselfish thing for Carl to do," McDaniels told the media afterward.

As I reflect on that moment, it was just amazing to think about Carl's journey. Was this the Carl Johnson I had first met three years earlier? The maturity he had gained in that short span of his high school career was stunning.

The maturity he gained, the confidence he developed transformed his life. It still resonates with me that I got to see it all up close.

"Coach was that guy that came in and gave everybody a fair chance," Carl said. "If you're going to do it, you had to earn it. It was loyalty, it was trust, it was respect, it was discipline. That's when all those pillars came into my life.'

"Coach became a role model for me. If somebody that charismatic, that successful believes in you, then you believe in yourself."

Our whole team believed in Carl. His toughness willed us to the game-winning drive in the championship game, and it was only fitting that he finished it. Later, his selfless gesture in the state all-star game was the perfect capper.

In high school, Carl's primary concern was survival and finding a place to sleep. He didn't have the proper home environment to study, so his college journey was unconventional.

My responsibility as a coach was to support not only current student athletes but also graduating student athletes. Carl was a first-generation prospective college student, and I wanted to do everything possible (including leveraging relationships) to give him a chance to achieve a better life and live the dream of attending college and playing football.

So with the help of fellow Crawford County native Mike Gottfried, then head coach at the University of Pittsburgh, Carl attended Delta

Junior College in Stockton, California. Carl's leadership qualities were again featured when he led them to their winningest season in the 1980s. From there he transferred to the University of Cincinnati.

Carl's athletic career stalled at UC, but he still impressed his coaches, including Bearcats Assistant Coach John Harbaugh, who became yet another important role model to him. The seeds for Carl's future success were planted.

Carl and I lost the proximity of our relationship after he left for junior college, but we never lost the special bond we shared in Galion. He soon discovered other role models, finding inspiration from them just like he had from me.

"Athletically, things didn't go my way at Cincinnati, but getting to know Coach Harbaugh, we just connected. I really put him on a pedestal," Carl said.

Carl instantly recognized someone else who had the "It" factor, which John Harbaugh later proved by winning a Super Bowl as the head coach of the Baltimore Ravens.

Although his athletic career ended at UC, life would never again put a harness on Carl Johnson. In 1998, Carl went to work for the Pittway Corp. and earned his MBA from the University of Houston, perhaps his proudest personal accomplishment. At Pittway, Carl gravitated toward another role model who shaped him, John Hakanson.

"John, like you, Coach, was a big influence on me," Carl said. "He was financially brilliant, one of the best business leaders I've known. He was Bill Belichick of the business world. This was never a guy who told me that I did a good job, but he developed me, and frankly, I think a lot of who I am today in the business world is because of John. It took Coach Owens and his athletic background and John, his business background, and the combination of the two molded me into who I am."

When Honeywell International Inc. purchased Pittway, Carl came to the attention of David Cote. Carl immediately shot through the ranks to the upper reaches at Honeywell.

"In 2006, we put him in charge of our gas detection business, which was then minimally profitable and beset by terrible quality control problems—customers would routinely receive defective products,"

Cote recalled in his book.

"Over the course of a few years, Carl worked hard to implement the Honeywell Operating System. His organization fixed the quality issues, developed some great new products, and focused on pleasing our customers. As a result, the business grew rapidly: over 50 percent organic growth over a three-year period and achieved operating margins of over 20 percent. Today it remains highly profitable."

Beyond the bottom line on a spreadsheet, it was Carl's personality and leadership capabilities that stuck with Cote.

"Carl exemplifies the success we had developing and retaining leaders as well as tremendous contributions those leaders made toward our success," Cote said in his book. "He was one of those Tom Bradys in our midst and we never would have found him had we not focused so consistently on our leadership pipeline, with an eye toward developing leaders from within. We also never would have kept him for as long as we did had we not incentivized him both financially and by providing him with a great work environment in which he could thrive.

"Today, our leaders are constantly being recruited for jobs elsewhere, but many of them stick around—and for many years Carl was one of them."

Carl quickly learned that building high-functioning teams was a crucial part of becoming a business leader. Frequently, he was tasked with finding leaders who had the qualities others discovered and nurtured within him. Now it's Carl who is constantly seeking the "It" factor.

"You've got to be able to connect with people. IQ is one thing, but the EQ [emotional intelligence quotient] is critical," Carl said. "You must be able to motivate, to mobilize, and work with people. It's just so important to understand the DNA of people. So I spend a lot of my time focused on that."

While Carl acknowledges that different leaders must be able to specialize in specific roles, in general he tries to focus on some common traits.

"I look for three things in leaders: self-awareness, emotional intelligence, and intellectual integrity. Then I measure the success of a leader. Is their leadership impact making people better, effective communication, and delivering results? You've got to be an independent thinker who knows how to manage.

"Second, you must be able to make people better—that has everything to do with succession planning development. The next thing is effective communication. One thing I've learned is you must have a consistent message to be an effective communicator and connect with people. If they don't understand what your expectations are and you don't understand how to motivate them, then you've got a serious problem.

"And finally, it's all about delivering results."

I doubt I am prouder of any former player than I am of Carl Johnson. His belief in me no doubt helped my coaching career at a critical time. It is rewarding that I played a small part in his future success too.

Carl and I reconnected because of family. He was the president of a Honeywell Division in Chicago when he called and asked me to speak to his leadership team at a retreat in Ohio. I was obviously impressed with the group he put together and the success he enjoyed. But I was most impressed when he talked about his wife and two daughters.

Carl asked me about my oldest son, Benjamin, who was in kindergarten when he left Galion. I shared that Ben was a West Point graduate who had completed his commitment with a recent tour of duty in Iraq and was about to begin his professional career. Carl said he had an opening and was interested in hiring my son. I thanked him but noted that Ben had already interviewed with several Fortune 500 companies.

Less than a week later, Ben called and said he was going to work for Carl Johnson at Honeywell. Ben later partnered with Carl at Warren Equity Partners. I could not be prouder of both of them.

In his career, Carl has led multiple business units at Fortune 100 multinational conglomerate Honeywell. The company features a $2.5 billion P&L and thirteen thousand members worldwide. Carl Johnson has been hailed by *Fortune* and *Business Weekly* as an international manufacturing thought leader.

I thought David Cote best summed up Carl's leadership qualities in his book:

"To win both today and tomorrow, your business needs more leaders like Carl. It's up to you to find them, nurture them, and create an environment in which they're inspired and empowered to perform. As I think you'll find, doing so creates a virtuous circle. Put great leaders in the right culture and you'll drive performance, which in turn will give you leaders in the monetary and emotional incentive they need to take performance even higher. Who knows how much or how fast your business will grow?"

Only One Thing

"I'm convinced that a team of good character—and by that I mean a bunch of guys who are morally sound and who really care about each other—will win the close games and perform well under adverse circumstances."–Terry Bradshaw

Carl's incredible journey reminds me of another true rags-to-riches story that college football fans will never forget. For me, this story started in the spring of 1996, when I drove to Evanston, Illinois, to see Northwestern Head Football Coach Gary Barnett.

The Wildcats had just concluded one of the biggest fairy tale seasons in the history of college football. They won the 1995 Big Ten Championship and went on to the 1996 Rose Bowl game for the first time in forty-six years.

As I sat in Coach Barnett's office that day, I listened intently to this great turnaround story. It was fascinating. Northwestern was the doormat of the Big Ten for nearly a quarter century, from the early 1970s until that magical 1995 season. The Mildcats, as they had been called, transformed into their true nickname, Wildcats, rolling to a 10-2 season, including an 8-0 mark in the Big Ten, and finishing the campaign ranked number seven in the final coaches' poll.

Northwestern beat an impressive array of perennial powerhouses, including Michigan, Notre Dame, and Penn State.

It was a season of firsts for Coach Barnett's purple-clad warriors. It was the school's first Big Ten title since 1936, first Rose Bowl appearance since 1949, and first ten-win season since 1903.

Celebrities who attended Northwestern came out of the woodwork, including Charlton Heston, who did a memorable promo for the Rose Bowl game explaining the Wildcats stunning season (while imitating his iconic portrayal of Moses) in one sentence: "Never underestimate the power of God!"

To be sure, Northwestern had some unlikely heroes, including linebacker Pat Fitzgerald and running back Darnell Autry, who became a household name for college football fans. It was a heady time for a program that had endured a bleak stretch of football, and everyone involved reveled in the success.

I listened to Coach Barnett discuss his program's remarkable turnaround for quite a while. He talked at great length about the total team concept, building a team that shared a vision, from the equipment manager to the president of the university. It just so happened that Northwestern's equipment manager, Bill Jarvis, was a good friend of mine and an alumnus of Ashland University.

Coach Barnett beamed with pride when he talked about Bill, how he took care of the staff and the players and how much the players and staff appreciated his effort. Coach Barnett was also aware of how much "Jarv" was doing to help Ashland football with its equipment needs. Fortunately, both wore purple uniforms.

We also discussed how Bill Jarvis was helping young equipment managers in football advance professionally. The current Wisconsin equipment manager, Jeremy Amundson, was one of his students—and there are many others.

After his thirty-five years of service at Northwestern, Bill Jarvis passed away in 2020. The equipment room at Ashland University was named in his honor.

After a few Pat Fitzgerald stories, I interrupted Coach Barnett to ask him a specific question: "If there is one thing and one thing only you would share with me as a young struggling coach at the University of Akron, what would that be?"

Coach Barnett sat back in his chair, thought for a few seconds, and gave me the following advice:

"Find a quarterback, not just *a* quarterback but the *right* quarterback. He must be talented of course, but with great character as a base." This person is a leader, a competitor, a winner, tough, and a team player."

He shared with me how his quarterback, Steve Schnur, had all these qualities. Although he was not a star, Schnur provided exactly what Barnett's team needed.

"Most importantly, have his back, stay with him, make sure he knows you believe in him and will be there for him. No one on a football team gets more credit than the head coach and the quarterback, and no one on the team gets more criticism than the head coach and the quarterback. For these reasons, the relationship between the head coach and the quarterback is the most important relationship on a football team."

One can assume this is the reason great dynasties in professional football have been defined by these coach/quarterback pairings: Otto Graham (also a Northwestern product) and Paul Brown with the Cleveland Browns; Bart Starr and Vince Lombardi with the Green Bay Packers; Chuck Noll and Terry Bradshaw with the Pittsburgh Steelers; Roger Staubach and Tom Landry with the Dallas Cowboys; Tom Brady and Bill Belichick with the New England Patriots; Patrick Mahomes and Andy Reid with the Kansas City Chiefs.

With that in mind, punctuated by my own experience, particularly with Carl's journey, bolstering Coach Barnett's advice, I set about focusing on that vital relationship with the most important position in sports.

Most Important Person in the Building
"We believe when the right talent meets the right opportunity in a company with the right philosophy, amazing transformation can happen." –Reid Hoffman

If a team has the good fortune of finding its Tom Brady, he will immediately become the most important person in the building. And then the person who backs him up will become the second most important person in the building. A team must make its biggest investments in its most important people. Always commit as many resources as possible in recruiting, training, and retaining as many superstars as possible.

Keeping more than one quality player at the quarterback position was not always easy. But it was critical for our team. The only promises we would make are that we would be honest and that we would play the best player. This worked because we recruited players who had great character, were confident of their own abilities, and liked to compete.

Early in my tenure at Ashland University, we had a Division I quarterback, Billy Cundiff. He was a transfer from the University of Connecticut. Bill was originally from Ohio, and we had recruited him hard before he committed to UConn. He arrived at camp that season and competed with a returning senior quarterback, Nick Strance, and another Division I transfer, John Ferguson.

After a difficult season in transition, Bill Cundiff won the position. John Ferguson almost left the team but decided to stay and prepare everyday just like he was the starter. Later that season, Bill Cundiff was injured, and John was ready to play. He led our team to a big victory at Ferris State and kept our playoff hopes alive.

Bill Cundiff went on to rewrite the record book at Ashland University. He led our team to two consecutive Division II championship appearances and our first playoff win, versus Minnesota State. He was the AFCA All-American quarterback in 2008 when he passed for nearly four thousand yards. Bill was also a two-time Harlon Hill Finalist. The Harlon Hill award is the Division II version of the Heisman Trophy in Division I football.

The next most important person in the building is the guy who is responsible for your quarterback.

Charlie Frye was a third-round pick for the Cleveland Browns out of the University of Akron. I remember him telling me that his quarterback coach at Akron, Tom Stacy, had better prepared him to play than a couple of his NFL coaches.

Bill Cundiff in his record-setting year had Matt LaFleur as his quarterback coach, currently the head coach of the Green Bay Packers.

Recruit Good People
"Great vision without great people is irrelevant."–Jim Collins

How do you find your Tom Brady and the people around him? First, surround yourself with good people. These must be people of high character and high intellect, people with ambition and a strong sense of purpose. They should be people who have their priorities straight and know where they are going in life.

Surround yourself with the right people—people who bring out the best in you, your best attitude. These are people who encourage you, support you, and help build you up. Greg Gillum was on my staff for nearly twenty years. Coach Gillum is the perfect example of surrounding yourself with good people, the right people. As of this writing, Greg is working with Luke Fickell, the head coach at Wisconsin. I always would have Greg in positions where he could do a lot of our recruiting. He just seemed to attract good people. He embodied the John Wooden phrase *"Good values attract good people."*

Anytime a leader is trying to build a team, he must ask three key questions of the people he brings onto the team. To achieve excellence, the answer must be yes to all three of these questions. 1. Can I trust you? 2. Are you committed to excellence? 3. Do you care? Coach Lou Holtz emphasized the importance of these three questions throughout his Hall of Fame career. Whether in business or in coaching, the people around us must know that we care about them. Care about people and you can't help but be successful.

When recruiting staff, I first look at the potential staff member's technical knowledge. I wanted bright, creative students of the game. They had to be good teachers and good communicators, poised and disciplined. I wanted them to be enthusiastic and passionate, with a strong work ethic. They needed the ability to evaluate and recognize talent. They also had to project a vision for talent development.

Perhaps the most important traits are character and conviction. These individuals need to be honest, loyal, and compassionate, yet demanding with their players. I was looking for a person with family values, a good role model.

Recruiting players starts with assessing their physical ability. Can they play? Do they have the size, speed, and skill? Are they productive? Do they make plays? How are their fundamentals and execution? Do they play smart? Are they coachable? Do they love the game? Are they a team player and a leader?

One of the most important considerations in recruiting is fit. To help determine the right fit, I developed a profile for the people that have been most successful on our teams. I would study past rosters to find background characteristics that were common to both the players who struggled and the players who excelled. I would use this research to sharpen our evaluation process. Fit becomes very important to recruiting the right people.

Recruiting the good people, the right people, most often came down to their toughness and their character.

Toughness & Character

"If you can't fly, then run; if you can't run, then walk. If you can't walk, then crawl, but whatever you do, you have to keep moving forward."
–Martin Luther King Jr.

I was blessed with the opportunity to coach many quarterbacks who led our teams to championship seasons. They were all different, but they all fit. They were all special, and it was our responsibility to adjust our teams to their strengths.

Tim Yunker was the quarterback who had the tough assignment of replacing Carl Johnson. Tim was a defensive back on the great 1985 Galion defense that shut out Youngstown Cardinal Mooney in the state championship game. Tim accepted the challenge and led the 1986 Tigers to a conference championship and a trip back to the playoffs.

Lee Hurst was the quarterback/kicker at Massillon who made his first and only field goal of the season to beat Canton McKinley in 1988. He went on the next season to lead our team to a regional championship. Although Lee Hurst was a very talented quarterback, he struggled at times with confidence. I made sure Lee knew that I never lost confidence in him.

The 1991 Massillon Tigers were quarterbacked by a 155-pound

senior, Nick Mossides. Nick loved Massillon Tiger football. He waited for his turn to play and then led the team to one of the biggest wins ever over Canton McKinley, 42-13. If not for a PAT kick hitting the uprights versus Cleveland St. Ignatius, Nick Mossides would have led the Tigers to their first playoff state championship.

Bill Cundiff graduated from Ashland in 2009 as an all-American quarterback. He set the standard for Ashland quarterbacks and was followed by two future all-Americans: Taylor Housewright and Travis Tarnowski.

Taylor Housewright was a local high school star in Ashland. He was the most popular quarterback in Ashland University history. With the hometown fan base the chant started, "Housewright for Heisman."

Taylor was big, strong, and athletic. Most importantly, Taylor was a great leader. In 2012, he led the Eagles to an 11-1 season and their first-ever Great Lakes Intercollegiate Athletic Conference championship. He was the player of the year in the conference and a Harlon Hill finalist.

Travis Tarnowski, out of North Royalton High School, was not as highly recruited as many of our quarterbacks. But by the end of his career, he had the best résumé. Travis was not a very imposing athlete on his recruiting visit, but after his first scrimmage there was no question about his toughness. He was leading the JV team down the field against the starting defense and took a shot from 300-pound defensive lineman Jamie Meder. Jamie ended up playing in the NFL for the Cleveland Browns. Travis picked himself up and finished the drive with a touchdown.

Travis had a career of making courageous passes under pressure. In his four years, he passed for more than 11,000 yards and 100 touchdowns, both school and conference records. Most importantly, he led the Eagles to championships in 2015 and 2017. He also led Ashland to its biggest playoff win in school history, a 21-18 victory over defending national champion Northwest Missouri State.

I have been asked many times about what makes a quarterback great. Is it his size or arm strength? Is it his quick release or pocket awareness? Is it his accuracy or athletic ability? Maybe it's his intelligence or leadership?

I would agree with all the above, but I have coached all-Americans who didn't have all the above. But they all had "it." I define "it" as Toughness and Character.

To achieve excellence in life you must have the toughness required to persevere through anything and everything. It is a toughness of mind and spirit that leads to physical toughness. Toughness is grit and determination. It is the heart and soul of a man.

True toughness comes from within. It comes from the core of a person. True toughness starts inside an individual and works its way out. Physical toughness is the manifestation of a person's strong mind, will, and spirit.

Being tough is when your back is to the wall and the game is on the line and you find a way to win. Tom Brady is the best when defined by game-winning drives. Toughness is a common denominator of team excellence. The factors that separate excellence in people and in teams include toughness and character. When it comes down to crunch time, what separates contenders from pretenders is not talent or ability, not scholarships or paychecks, and not experience or expertise. It is toughness and character.

The great teams, great athletes, and great quarterbacks all have a superior toughness about them. I always felt that if my quarterback was better/tougher than your quarterback I would beat your team 90 percent of the time. Because if my quarterback was tougher, there was a pretty good chance my team was tougher than your team. Like cream rising to the top, the tough teams rise above the rest.

Ultimately, toughness is a matter of mind, will, and spirit. It is giving your all in all things. It is battling in the face of adversity or success. It is about courage and exercising that courage in a competitive test.

All great competitors are tough. What is a competitor? He plays every play like it means the championship. He never gives up. He is never beaten mentally. He is consistent. Setbacks do not discourage him. He is never satisfied with his performance. He goes full speed play after play. He is aggressive. He attacks and is more interested in the team than personal glory.

In 1982, Rod "Bernie" Bernhard was the starting quarterback on one of the best football teams in the history of Crestview High

School. He set records with his passing, and he would function as the lead blocker after pitching the ball to our star running back on the off-tackle play. He was also a starting linebacker on defense and owned the team's highest GPA.

Jeff Pica was the starting quarterback for the 1987 Lancaster Golden Gales. In week eight of that season, Lancaster beat third-ranked Fremont Ross 35-27 and won a share of the conference championship. It was also on that night that Pica passed for 168 yards to eclipse Rex Kern as the all-time passing leader at Lancaster. Rex Kern was an all-American quarterback who led the Ohio State Buckeyes to three consecutive national championship games, winning it all in 1968. Later, he played in the NFL as a defensive back with the Baltimore Colts.

Prior to the start of the season, Pica suffered a complete ACL tear in his left knee. He had two options: immediate surgery and miss the season or wear a brace and play with limited mobility. Pica refused to miss the season. With opposing teams knowing Jeff had no lateral movement, they could sit back and play pass or go after him with an all-out blitz. By the end of the season, Jeff was physically beat up. He showed great courage and competed with his team for a playoff spot until the very last game. He had surgery the Monday after the season ended.

Butchie Washington is the only quarterback ever to lead the University of Akron to back-to-back winning seasons (1999-2000) in Division I football. The Zips also shared the conference title in 2000. Butchie was an athlete playing quarterback when he left Columbus Beechcroft. He turned down the opportunity to be a defensive back at Michigan State, believing in his ability to play quarterback at the Division I level.

Throughout his college career, Butchie worked on his physical skills as a passer, but also on becoming more of a vocal leader. There is more to this story which often is the case. Butchie lost his older brother, Derrick, from a tragic shooting when he was only fourteen. His brother's death left a hole in his soul.

With the help of family, teammates, and coaches, Butchie slowly healed and became a more vocal leader. He started thirty-six consecutive games for the University of Akron and at that time held most of the Zips' school passing records.

Quarterback Charlie Frye went on to break Washington's records. Never have I witnessed a tougher quarterback. Charlie's first start was in Ohio Stadium against the Buckeyes in 2001. He was the best quarterback on the field that day.

Charlie put together a near-upset performance versus the Wisconsin Badgers that was so impressive Coach Barry Alvarez looked him up to congratulate him after the game.

I witnessed what may have been the most courageous comeback ever by a quarterback. Because of an injury and the COVID pandemic, Austin Brenner had waited three long years for the 2021 football season to begin. It was going to be his year. After a 4-0 start, Brenner was leading all NCAA Division II quarterbacks in total yards. Then, on October 9, just four minutes into a game versus Ohio Dominican, Austin was severely injured.

He suffered an open fracture of the tibia and fibula. The stadium was stunned and silent. Austin was the heart and soul of the team—and like that, the season was over. Austin was taken to the hospital for emergency surgery that night. At that time, it was not a question of if he would ever play again; the question was would he ever walk again.

The comeback story of Austin Brenner inspired the entire team, school, and community. His recovery and his return to the championship season of 2022 was possible only with his belief in God and his spiritual toughness.

All these quarterbacks had one additional commonality in their background. They all had family who were there for them. Family who taught them right from wrong, family they loved and respected. This was their beginning to a solid character foundation.

For Carl Johnson, the credit belongs to those families in Galion, Ohio, he adopted as his own.

While both talent and ability are vital, ultimately it is toughness and character that drive winning teams. It is toughness and character that separate excellence from success. The destiny of any team is ultimately controlled by its character. All teams committed to excellence must recruit people who have a strong character in all aspects of life.

Character is defined by people who cannot be bought; their words are their bond. They put excellence above wealth and fame. They do not hesitate to take chances, nor do they compromise on what is right. They will not lose their individuality in a crowd. A solid character foundation includes honesty, loyalty, respect, and unselfishness.

> *"Fame is a vapor, popularity is an accident, money takes wings, "Those who cheer you today may curse you tomorrow. The only thing that endures is character."*–Horace Greeley

Key Points for Finding Your Tom Brady

1. The cornerstone for the foundation of team excellence is to recruit talented people. No amount of talent can overcome poor leadership.
2. Finding your most talented leader, your quarterback, is not an easy task for any manager or coach. Every team is looking for its Tom Brady.
3. Building a trusting relationship with your quarterback is critical to team excellence. No one will get more credit when you win, and no one will get more criticism when you lose.
4. Achieve team excellence by finding, cultivating, and advancing talented leaders within the team or the organization.
5. All teams must invest their greatest resources in identifying, recruiting, and retaining as much talent as possible.
6. Recruiting talented leaders who are competitive and confident in their own abilities creates a culture and environment that will drive team performance and, with the right motivation, achieve team excellence.
7. The most important coach on the team is the coach responsible for the development and the productivity of the quarterback of the team.
8. Recruit and surround yourself with both talent and character.
9. Develop a profile to assist in the evaluation and fit of talent to your team.
10. The "It" factor in recruiting talent to your team is most often toughness and character.

–CHAPTER TWO–
PAYING THE PRICE

"Work hard, have fun, make history,"–Jeff Bezos

Photo of Larry Kehres

Bio Box: Larry Kehres—Mount Union Football Coach

Background: Larry Kehres was born September 7, 1949, the second of five children to James Robert (Bob) and Helen Kehres, who had three sons and two daughters. Bob worked at a factory making rubber products in Ravenna. Helen picked up odd jobs along the way but was mostly a homemaker. Larry grew up in Diamond, a town of fewer than three thousand people nestled in the southeast corner of Portage County.

Athletic Achievement: Kehres played football, basketball, and baseball at Ravenna Southeast High School. He was quarterback of the football team and led the Pirates to the Portage County League championship in 1966. He went on to play quarterback at Mount Union College and was a three-year starter. As a senior, he set the record for the longest touchdown pass in school history, a 95-yard strike to Bruce Carthwright in 1970 against Ohio Northern.

Scholastic Achievement: A graduate of Ravenna Southeast High School in 1967, Kehres earned a business degree from Mount Union College in 1971. He studied for a master's degree in health and physical education at Bowling Green State University and later became an associate professor of physical education at Mount Union.

Professional Achievement: Kehres is a member of the College Football Hall of Fame and earned the American Football Coaches Association Amos Alonzo Stagg Award in 2024. Kehres established the highest winning percentage (.929) in college football history with a 332-24-3 mark in 27 seasons at Mount Union College (1986 to 2012). He won an incredible eleven national championships and pocketed twenty-three conference titles. Kehres racked up twenty-one undefeated regular seasons, by far the most in the history of the sport. He also established and coached the Mount Union swim team from 1974 to 1986 and was selected as the school's athletic director in 1985.

Over the years I've frequently attended coaching conventions where Larry Kehres is asked to speak. Introducing him by going over his record was a demoralizing exercise—so remarkable, so unbelievable—that former Texas Coach Mack Brown offered a suggestion:

"We need to stop [citing Larry's record]. It's too intimidating to the rest of us. What they have done at Mount Union puts them in another universe."

It's true. Larry Kehres was inducted into the College Football Hall of Fame after coaching twenty-seven seasons at Mount Union College (today known as the University of Mount Union), where he lost only twenty-four games. Kehres finished his career with a stunning .929 winning percentage. He won eleven national championships and twenty-three conference crowns, all at the Division III level. His dynasty lives on at Mount Union, where the Purple Raiders finished national runner-up in 2024 under Coach Geoff Dartt. In Alliance, Ohio, where Mount Union is located, they say there are three certainties in life: death, taxes, and Mount.

Yet building a juggernaut didn't happen overnight. It took years of hard work. Larry Kehres paid the price with sweat, study, and sheer determination.

His story began in rural southeast Portage County in Diamond, Ohio, about thirty miles directly east of Akron near Interstate 76. Diamond is a blue-collar community that was once a stop on the New York Central Railroad, but the depot was abandoned in the early 1970s.

Larry was one of five children born to Bob and Helen Kehres. He was second in a line of three brothers and two sisters, the "overlooked one," he chuckles. Bob worked at a Ravenna factory that made rubber products, while Helen managed the home. Larry grew up an avid baseball fan and organized teams and games from a young age. It was his mother's relative, Herman Weber, who took him to college football games at nearby Mount Union College, about fifteen miles south.

"I came to the games here with my mom's uncle, who lived in Alliance," Larry remembered. "He didn't have a son, but he loved football. He would come out and get me and drive me down to watch the Mount games. I remember going to an Alliance at Massillon high school game too, when I was in like eighth grade. I thought it was like a pro game."

In this era, Ohio was the epicenter of football at all levels. Paul Brown, the godfather of football coaches, was just up the road sixty miles driving his Cleveland Browns machine in a dominating run through the NFL. Woody Hayes had already won three national championships at Ohio State. The influence of football success was everywhere in the state, and Larry grew up in the midst of it. By the time he reached high school, Kehres was playing football, basketball, and baseball.

"Baseball was my favorite, but I liked playing football the best in high school because of the teammates I had," Kehres said. "They were my best friends. But the game I always loved my entire life until right now is baseball. A bunch of us played summer baseball, and I was always organizing some type of summer baseball team until we were probably about twenty-two years old or so."

Yet football was his destiny. As a senior, Larry was the starting quarterback at Ravenna Southeast High School, where he led his team to a share of the 1966 Portage County League championship.

"But we beat the team we were tied with, Windham, so we always considered that our championship," Kehres laughed.

As a high school sophomore, Larry also began dating his future wife, Linda. When he went off to college at Mount Union, Linda attended nearby Malone, and they continued their relationship. In his senior year of college, they were married and lived in Alliance.

By this time, Larry was also in his third year sharing the quarterback job at Mount Union. He played a bit as a freshman under Head Coach Ken Wable, and during his senior year the Purple Raiders completed an 8-1 season. Kehres also has the distinction of throwing the longest touchdown pass in school history, a 95-yard bomb to Bruce Carthwright in 1970 against Ohio Northern.

"You know that record is not allowed to be broken," Kehres joked. "I called the plays when I was coaching, and I just wouldn't call a play that would go longer than that."

With a business degree in hand and a wife to support, Larry wasn't sure about his next move. That's when Terry Parsons, a former Mount Union basketball coach and then a professor at Bowling Green State University, called him. There was an opening for a graduate assistant on coach Don Nehlen's staff. Parsons thought Kehres would be a strong candidate. So a meeting was arranged with Nehlen in Bowling Green, Ohio.

"I'm wearing my best," Larry said. "I had on my best sports coat, probably my only sports coat at that time, and I'm sitting out there waiting to meet Coach Nehlen, and finally his executive assistant called me to go in. He comes out from behind the desk and goes, 'Man, I like that sports coat!' He opens it up to look at the label, and I'm thinking, Wow, I'm glad I wore this sports coat. That got the day off on the right foot."

The interview must have gone well too, because Nehlen hired Kehres to be a graduate assistant. He was part of a staff that guided the Falcons to a 6-4 record.

"There were seven or eight of us graduate assistants, and we were all assigned to a coach," Kehres said. "I was assigned to Ray Dempsey, who had been the head coach at Canton Central Catholic, and Ray was the offensive line coach [at Bowling Green]. His organization and his recruiting, the daily work, was just outstanding. I learned that if I wanted to coach football, I'm going to have to get my ducks lined up a whole lot more than I had ever considered at that point in time."

Larry also recognized what he described as a very upbeat culture on Nehlen's staff, preaching positivity. While learning the operation of a Division I football program, Kehres earned his master's degree in health and physical education. He pondered going for his PhD but was a bit burned-out on taking classes. Then, in the spring of 1972, he was hired as the football coach at Johnstown High School in western Licking County, near Columbus.

"I saw a little sign on a job board that said football opening at Johnstown," Kehres said. "It didn't even say head coach or assistant coach. So I called the superintendent, and he said they had already interviewed most of their candidates, but I could come out and see him on Sunday. So I went to see him, and about a week later, I ended up getting the job. I tell you what: it was a great, great experience."

The twenty-three-year-old had gone from graduate assistant in the Mid-American Conference to high school head coach in the Licking County League. The Johnnies finished the 1973 season with a 6-4 record, and with Linda teaching in a nearby school district, it looked like the Kehres family was ready to put down roots.

In fact, they were, but it wasn't in Johnstown. Larry's college coach Ken Wable called. One of Wable's three full-time assistant coaches at Mount Union had resigned.

"Ken Wable called me in February when one of his assistants left, and he offered me a job," Kehres recalled. "I said no because I didn't feel right about leaving Johnstown after only one year. Then he called me back again in April when a second assistant resigned. I thought, Man, two of the four coaches on that staff left. If I don't take it, they probably won't have an opening again for years. So I went ahead and took it. But I loved that [Johnstown] job. You know 6-4 was pretty good considering we weren't very good. I mean if we were, would they have hired a twenty-three-year-old? I didn't know what I was doing, but I loved that job."

He would like the next job even better. In 1974, Larry and Linda moved back home to Alliance, and they've been there ever since. Larry was an offensive coordinator under Wable and was also asked to start the school's swimming program. So Kehres became the first Mount Union swimming coach in 1974, a job he would maintain until 1986.

"I could barely dog-paddle," he said of the assignment. "But when I got here, the AD said they needed me to be the swim coach or a tennis coach. There was no swim team, so I thought, Well, at least if I lose every swim meet, I can't be worse than anyone else they've had, because they haven't had anybody else. I didn't even know which end of the pool to start on."

Larry simply resolved to Pay the Price. He plunged in with hard work, learning and especially recruiting "guys who could swim." Kehres scouted out the best swimming prospects in the region. In those days, off-campus recruiting was verboten in the Ohio Athletic Conference. That meant burning up the phone lines in the Akron, Canton, Cleveland, and Youngstown areas to bring in the best athletes available. It was the same philosophy he had learned and perfected in football.

For eleven years Larry remained a stalwart on Wable's football staff and the head swimming coach. During that time, he once interviewed for the football head coaching job at nearby Hiram College but didn't get it. Imagine being the athletic director who passed on hiring Larry Kehres as your football coach? That's a career killer and a punch line both.

Then, in 1985, Mount Union asked Larry to become the school's athletic director. That meant he had to resign from the football staff before the fall. The athletic director couldn't toil as an assistant coach under the head football coach while also evaluating his boss from the athletic director's chair.

Kehres simply couldn't help himself. He had to stay busy. Grinding away and Paying the Price was hard-wired into him. As athletic director, Larry put together an undergraduate studies program in sports administration, something that had been kicked around at the school for years.

Meanwhile, the Mount Union football team was having an outstanding campaign. With three games left in the 1985 regular season, Wable confided in Kehres (his new boss) that if the team won its final three games, he planned to announce his retirement after twenty-four years on the job. The Purple Raiders did indeed win those last three games, and the Ohio Athletic Conference championship, before falling in the Division III national playoffs to complete an 11-1 swan song.

Now it was time for the school to hire a new head football coach.

"When Ken stepped down, I talked to the academic director about what the school wanted to do," Larry remembered. "He said they wanted to do a national search, and I'm thinking, I don't think anybody in Oregon ever heard of Mount Union. So I ended up saying, 'If you want to do a national search, I'm going to drop out of the running, because I've been here for a long time, and after eleven years on the sidelines with Ken, I'm either good enough to be the head football coach or I'm not.' You know, I had recruited the quarterback Ken had just won eleven games with.

"Well, the interim president stepped in and said, 'I think you'll have to be the football coach.' But minus him stepping in, I'm not sure how things would have gone for me."

Dynasties tilt on just such decisions. Without Larry Kehres, there would be no Mount Union dynasty. Still, it took time to develop.

In his first year as head coach, the 1986 Purple Raiders turned in an identical season to Wable's final year. Mount Union went 11-1 and was bounced by Augustana College from the Division III national playoffs.

"One of the things I learned from Ken was the importance of planning carefully, discussing what you're going to do and being well prepared to do it," Kehres said. "We had to work on it. We planned well. We planned for the season. We had a plan for the week. We had to plan for each day."

From 1987 through 1989, Mount Union was good, but not great, falling just short of the OAC championship each year. In 1990, the Purple Raiders won the conference and posted a 10-1 record. The 1991 squad was 8-1-1 and finished second in the conference. His teams were solid, but Larry was still learning his craft. One of the things that helped boost the program was Kehres surrounding himself with veteran high school coaches who taught him a thing or two.

"There were a lot of good coaches who retired from their high school jobs at fifty-three, fifty-four years of age who still had a lot of juice left," Larry said. "I had some great high school coaches on my staff: Joel Cockley, Rudy Sharkey, Bill Coldsnow, Keith Wakefield. They looked at our players as mature guys. I didn't always think like that, but they were used to dealing with fifteen- to eighteen-year-olds, and here they were dealing with nineteen- to twenty-two-year-olds. That was a great perspective to add.

"Then, I was the offensive coach, and sometimes I came up with some wacko ideas. I was a playground-football guy. Well, a lot of those guys had been head coaches before, and they could say, 'Wait a minute. Let's rethink that a little bit.' You must be willing to listen to that."

Larry also wasn't tied to a specific offensive philosophy, except winning. Some of his teams threw the ball constantly. Others featured power running games. Still others found a balanced blend. Whatever his talent dictated, Kehres would focus on it, honing it to the finest edge. His mantra was "Players, Formations, Plays"—and members of his coaching tree still spout PFP as the Mount philosophy.

The first part of that formula falls on recruiting. Getting the best players available was step one. Kehres was fortunate to recruit players who often fell within a geographic hotbed of football talent. Akron, Canton, and Youngstown were all minutes away, Cleveland a bit further, with Columbus and Pittsburgh a couple of hours away; even Buffalo was within a full tank of gas. Those youngsters with a passion and a talent for the game weren't always the right size or blessed with the necessary speed, agility, or strength to compete at the highest levels. But if they had a passion for the sport, and the ability to compete, Mount Union was an attractive landing spot.

Putting those players in position to succeed was step two. That comes with designing an offense to accentuate the best Purple Raiders in that season. If the team's best player is a quarterback, what does that individual do well, run or throw? What formations set that player up to create a mismatch on an opposing defense? If it's a running back, is he a blazer that excels in space? Is he a bruiser that wears a defense down in the fourth quarter?

That leads to step three: plays. It's often said that playmakers make plays. But coaches must give them those opportunities by dialing up the right call at the right time against a defense's vulnerability. Take the 2024 national semifinal, for instance. Ohio State had less than thirty seconds remaining before the half in a tie game with Texas. Stuck on its own twenty-five, the Buckeyes called a screen pass to their lightning-quick tailback TreVeyon Henderson. The Ohio State offensive staff caught the Texas defense in a blitz. It was the perfect call if the quarterback could get the ball out in time to beat the pass rush. That's exactly what happened. Henderson followed his blocking expertly for a 75-yard touchdown that eventually led to a 28-21 victory. That's a Play, and Mount Union athletes made hundreds of them for Larry Kehres and his staff over the years.

In fact, beginning in 1992, Kehres would never again fail to win a league championship. From 1994 until 2005, Mount Union rolled up one hundred consecutive Ohio Athletic Conference victories. The streak was stopped by Ohio Northern, who pocketed a 21-14 victory on October 22, 2005. The Polar Bears were coached by one of Larry's former players, Dean Paul.

"[Coach Kehres] took a good program and made it dominant. No one can come close to what they've been doing," Paul told Terry Pluto of Cleveland.com. "[After the game, Coach Kehres] gave me a hug and told me that we had a great plan. He was so gracious. He could not have been better."

Paul was just a freshman during Larry's first year as head coach, in 1986. It wasn't until 1993 that Mount Union won its first national championship. And to this day Larry can point to a loss as the key moment when his program went from very good to beyond compare.

"We went up to play Wisconsin La Crosse in the 1992 national semifinals, and we had an excellent team. It was in terribly tough conditions. The field was frozen, but it was bright. I needed sunglasses. There was snow everywhere except on the field, and I could barely see. Well, we lost a tough game (29-23), and afterward we're in this small room with just a few people, and a young reporter slides the quickie stats to me across the table and says, 'How does it feel to gain 601 yards, not punt, and lose?'

"The reason for that was that we had a lousy red-zone offense. Roger Harring was coaching La Crosse, and they went on to win the national championship. He had the game taped, and he said before we left campus I could take the tape home. So when I went over it, I saw that when we got down in the red zone, I'm sending in a couple of guys, an extra tight end and a running back. The tight end is like 210 [pounds], and then there's the skinny little running back. Roger is sending in two guys that are six foot three, 240 pounds. Now how are my guys supposed to block those guys?

"I told the staff and everybody else that I was the one who got us beat that day. I've told the guys on that 1992 team that if I'd been a little smarter, they might have been national champions. But I tell you what . . . I got better at red-zone football after that. In fact, I got a lot better at it after that."

A change in outlook helped too. In his first couple of forays into the playoffs, Larry said, he often felt fortunate to be there and frequently considered his opponent to be the favorite in a postseason matchup. After a few playoff appearances, though, Kehres knew his teams belonged. So did his players. Expectations were slowly but surely rising based on success. After that 1992 semifinal, Larry knew his teams were good enough to go all the way.

In 1993, after losing to the Division III national champion in each of the previous four seasons, the Purple Raiders broke through with a 14-0 record. Mount Union's offense averaged 47.1 points per game, and the defense allowed just 7.7 points per contest, with five shutouts. Quarterback Jim Ballard won the Gagliardi Trophy (the Division III Player of the Year) after completing 321-of-458 passes (.701 completion percentage) for 4,572 yards and 54 touchdowns.

Ballard was never better than in the national championship game. Playing against Rowan in Salem, Virginia, the Purple Raiders trailed 24-21 entering the fourth quarter. Ballard, who threw for 387 yards, led his team on two lengthy drives into the teeth of a thirty-mile-per-hour wind to earn a 34-24 victory.

That opened the floodgates, and the talent flowed in from all over the country. The Purple Raiders soon fielded teams with youngsters from Florida to New York, and later some from California. The player who was outstanding in high school but a step slow or a bit slight for the Division I level could still gain national notoriety by playing for the undisputed powerhouse of Division III college football—Mount Union.

"I don't think I went there to say, 'I'm getting my master's degree in football coaching,' but that's exactly what I did, and that's exactly what put me in the position I'm in today," Philadelphia Eagles Head Coach Nick Sirianni told NFL Films in a short documentary on Coach Kehres.

Sirianni won three national championships as a receiver at Mount Union in 2000, 2001, and 2002. He distinctly remembers catching a touchdown pass in a national semifinal, running out of the back of the end zone, and hugging his brother just beyond the end line. That move drew a 15-yard unsportsmanlike conduct penalty from an official he later saw in the NFL, and Coach Kehres was waiting for Nick on the sidelines.

"He really let me have it," Sirianni said. "I did not live up to the standard on that play. There's a how to win and a how to get people better, and he definitely did that for us."

Success fed on itself. Great players, combined with Larry's work ethic, his willingness to Pay the Price, meant he and his staff would put those talented athletes in a position to succeed. Mount Union's football roster grew to an incredible number. At one point, nearly two hundred youngsters were on the squad—10 percent of the student body was on the football team. Those kinds of numbers necessitated planning four separate practices, from 8:00 to 10:00 a.m., 10 a.m. to noon, 2:00 to 4:00 p.m., and 4:00 to 6:00 p.m. Now that is "Paying the Price."

There was a freshman team, a junior varsity team, and a varsity team. I also had a junior varsity squad at Ashland, and we frequently scrimmaged against Mount Union. Even though we were Division II and they were Division III, their junior varsity would frequently beat our junior varsity.

"If you're going to keep that many on the team, you have to keep them engaged; you have to show them you care about them and what they're doing," Larry said. "That's why we went to so many practice sessions, to give them as much attention as we could. If they're going to make that investment of their time, you have to match it."

Those players included talents like Cecil Shorts and Pierre Garcon, who went all the way to the NFL from Mount Union. Matt Campbell, the head coach at Iowa State, was once one of those players too. While visiting the Mount Union campus in high school, he saw more than eighty players working out on a nearby field during a hot June day. He was in love.

"For me, it ended up changing my life," Campbell told reporter Michael Weinreb of Grantland. "It's not until you step out of Mount Union and step into the real world that you realize what he's done, because we never really considered Mount to be the real world."

The volume on the roster created spectacular depth, and the Purple Raiders became a national story that drew attention from football coaches coast-to-coast.

After that first crown in 1993, Mount Union went on to win

ten more national championships under Larry's direction, in 1996, 1997, 1998, 2000, 2001, 2002, 2005, 2006, 2008, and 2012. From 1996 to 1999, the Purple Raiders won fifty-four consecutive games. From 2000 to 2003, they won fifty-five straight. From 1995 through Kehres's retirement in 2012, Mount Union never lost more than one game in a single season.

Their relentless pursuit of success had everyone scrambling with the same question: how was Larry doing it?

"Since I've left Mount Union, that's probably the number one thing I get asked," former Mount Union player Erik Raeburn, then the coach of Wabash College, told Grantland in a 2012 story. "People want it to be this one secret thing, so they can just copy that.

"But the reason they're so successful is that [Coach Kehres] is better than all the other coaches at *everything*. He's a better strategist. He's a better recruiter. He's a better evaluator of talent. He's a better teacher. He just sees everything better."

Only once did Larry consider leaving Mount Union as head coach for a different job. After the 1997 season, Kent State Athletic Director Laing Kennedy called. The Purple Raiders had just won their third national championship. Kent was so close in proximity, the Kehres family wouldn't even have to move. Larry gave it long consideration but eventually passed.

"In the end, I just couldn't see myself leaving Mount," Kehres said at the time.

But upon reflection, he told NFL Films in 2024, "I may not have had the courage to take the risk. I realized that looking back I've encouraged the young men with me not to lack the courage to take a risk."

In our interview with him for this book, Larry said it's only natural to wonder if he would've found similar success on a bigger stage. Yet after the NFL Films minidocumentary was released in 2024, Kehres had multiple coaches approach him who thought his comment about why he stayed at Mount Union really resonated with them. Sometimes the grass isn't greener. If you've found happiness, is bigger, better, or more always the answer? For some people it may be.

But Larry Kehres was comfortable with his station. Certainly no one has ever been as successful.

Larry is one of my favorite friends in the coaching profession. His accomplishments will never be equaled, yet his demeanor remains incredibly humble. This is a guy who grabbed a shovel in winter and started working to keep the snow off the coaches' parking spots. When you're working for a guy like that, you grab a shovel too.

It obviously helps that he has proof of concept. Larry Kehres established the highest winning percentage (.929) in college football history by going 332-24-3 in 27 seasons at Mount Union College (1986 to 2012).

Top Division I coaches frequently visited Alliance to meet with him. He became a regular on the national coaching clinic circuit. He's earned the respect of coaches at the highest level of football. It's enough to make an impression on those who are not easily impressed, like former Auburn football Coach Terry Bowden.

"My father [Bobby Bowden] was a football coach. My brothers have been football coaches. Our family has won more than 620 games, but I've never seen anything quite like Mount Union," Bowden told Terry Pluto of Cleveland.com. "I've met other Mount guys. They are all out of this mold. They have that culture of winning, of hard work. They've been doing it so long . . . it's just incredible."

Through it all, Larry and Linda have been married for nearly fifty-five years as of this book's publication. They have three children, Vince, Faith, and Jan, and nine grandchildren. Vince played at Mount Union and then took over for longtime defensive coordinator Don Montgomery.

"I didn't coach him because he was on defense, and he was on my defensive staff as a coach here too," Larry said. "The defensive coordinator makes all the defensive calls. Well, I always thought the safeties played too close, so one time I said we should push the safeties back. When we did that, they started completing short passes, and I said something to him like, 'Are we going to stop the short passes?' That's when he fired back, 'Are you going to let me coach the defense or not?' And he was right."

Vince proved the apple didn't fall far from the tree by succeeding his father at Mount Union and winning two more national championships with the Purple Raiders. Today he's an assistant coach at Toledo, and the father revels in his son's success.

"He's an excellent coach," Larry says proudly.

Today Larry is retired, but he still sneaks over every fall in his golf cart to watch Mount Union in action.

"Retirement is an adjustment when you're a coach. I find it difficult," Larry said. "The football game that I was in control of for all those years, I'm just a spectator. I want to be there, let them know I want them to do well. I still miss that feeling that I'm the coach. I will always stay involved with Mount Union and football. Those are the two things that I do best."

Blue Collar Work Ethic

"A dream doesn't become a reality through magic; it takes sweat, determination, and hard work."–Colin Powell

EFFORT

"It is effort that turns ability into accomplishment. It is effort that breathes life into ideas and carries dreams toward reality. Effort is the cornerstone of achievement, the crucial factor in nearly every success. If you make the effort to complete the task you are given to the best of your ability, you will not fail at anything for very long."–Author Unknown

In John Wooden's Pyramid of Success, the first cornerstone is industriousness, and he wrote, *"There is no substitute for work. Worthwhile things come from hard work and careful planning."*

Great teams and organizations all have one thing in common, a work ethic that is second to none: a blue-collar, punch-the-clock attitude. One of the mistakes made in team building is recruiting talent with little regard for work ethic. A team will never achieve excellence by recruiting talent that refuses to come early, refuses to stay late, and refuses to put in the extra effort. It is said, "The difference between ordinary and extraordinary is that little extra effort."

There are far too many talented teams not willing to make the sacrifices needed to win. Teams that are talented with championship potential that consistently underperform are frequently lazy and not dedicated.

Make sure you are the hardest-working athlete on your team or the hardest-working employee in the organization. Make sure you recruit not only a talented team but, more importantly, a team that outworks its opponents.

Woody Hayes won five national championships at Ohio State, but he wasn't considered a great tactician, nor an innovator, and he knew it.

"They may be smarter than me. They may outcoach me. But no one will ever outwork me," Hayes said.

Make sure your organization is outworking the competition. Nothing will destroy a team faster than half-hearted efforts and nice tries. Teams that win championships and reach excellence are teams committed to hours of sweat and hard work. Blood, Sweat, Championship was my title for an earlier book, taken from the battle cry of a team I once coached.

It's from the heart that I say I have never coached a harder-working team than the 1982 Crestview Cougars. Crestview is a rural school bordering Richland and Ashland Counties in the Amish country of North Central Ohio. The football team was small, and support for the team was limited. Most of the players had to play both ways, every down of every game. They battled for eleven weeks.

Often beat up with broken bones and pulled muscles, they fought each week to become the hardest-working, best-conditioned, and physically toughest team on the field. Together this squad fashioned a perfect 10-0 undefeated regular season. They recorded eight shutouts and outscored their opponents 269 to 13. They virtually rewrote the record book on Crestview Cougar football.

It would appear logical that after such an excellent season, they would be invited to the playoffs to compete for the Class A state championship. But football, like life, is not fair. With Ohio's new computer selection process choosing teams for the postseason, the Cougars were left out of the postseason. It was beyond their control.

A computer may be able to add wins and losses for a team and all its opponents. But a computer will never be able to recognize superior performance, extraordinary dedication, or team excellence.

The players on this team represented excellence because they worked hard, competed hard, and played for the right reasons. It was never about fans or scholarships or rings. It was always to honor their families, to honor their school, to honor their community, to honor their teammates, and to honor their faith. Because these young men loved the game and played for the right reasons, they were always highly motivated to work hard and never quit.

As a head coach, my greatest fear was that someday my players would return and tell me I didn't push them hard enough. I didn't know how much they were willing to give or how far they would go to be great. I never worried about this with the Crestview team, because I never pushed a team harder.

Never lower the bar! Raise it! Taking your people where they can't go by themselves is coaching, is leading, is motivating. It demands more from them than they can demand of themselves.

I grew up in a small town in the heart of Ohio. Both my grandparents found work at the Westinghouse factory in downtown Mansfield. One was a plumber there and the other was a buffer. They both worked their entire lives for this company and never cheated Westinghouse out of a good day's work. They would get up early every morning, pack their lunch, and grind for eight hours, day after day. My grandfathers taught me the greatest lesson in my life: nothing is ever given to you, and nothing ever comes easy. Life is about hard work and sacrifice. Earn it.

Neither of my parents graduated from high school, nor understood the significance of my desire to play football in junior high school. As long as I can remember, both my parents worked full time to make sure that my brother, my sister, and I had what we needed. They said it was okay for me to play football, but I would have to find my way home after most practices and games.

It didn't matter. I started playing, and the long walks home after practice seemed like a small price to pay for the competition, the camaraderie, the physicality, the grind . . . and most importantly my coaches, who became my role models. It was a turning point in my childhood. I truly learned to appreciate the things in life that I had to work hardest to obtain.

As a football player, I also learned the importance of discipline and how it relates to a good work ethic. Early in life, I thought discipline was what happened to me when I was in trouble, which was quite often in junior high school. But discipline is not what someone does *to* you; it's what someone does *for* you. Discipline is from the Latin derivative *disciplina*, which means "teaching."

Great teams define discipline as "doing what must be done, as well as it can be done, and doing it that way all the time." Or, as I can still hear my grandfather telling me, "A job not worth doing right is a job not worth doing at all."

So what is more important: talent or hard work? I believe both are needed, but I also believe hard work is more important than talent. Talent without a work ethic is a waste. There are many talented individuals on the street who lack the work ethic to develop their talents, fail to reach their potential, and are unable to be productive citizens.

Hard work even without talent can be productive. There is a saying: "Hard work beats talent when talent refuses to work hard." I believe hard work always beats talent. Team leaders like coach Larry Kehres who are both talented and willing to work hard end up in the College Football Hall of Fame. That same chemistry of talent and hard work can also be a ticket to the Heisman Trophy.

Eddie George

"I can't imagine another college football player in history having a better work ethic."–John Cooper

One of the greatest players I ever went to recruit was Eddie George at Ohio State. Eddie won the Heisman Trophy in 1995 after his senior season. He went on to an outstanding career in the NFL, where he gained more than 10,000 yards rushing.

When Coach Cooper hired me to coach for the Buckeyes, he and Recruiting Coordinator Bill Conley needed a coach to make a trip to Fork Union Military Academy in Virginia to make sure Eddie's commitment to Ohio State was still solid. The plan was for Eddie to join the team midyear, after he finished the fall academic semester at

Fork Union.

My trip was to meet Eddie and assure him of Coach Cooper's promise to play him at running back. Eddie was from Philadelphia and always dreamed of being a running back for Penn State. But Penn State wanted Eddie to play linebacker. Eddie's heart was at running back. His father's favorite football players were big, physical backs like Jim Brown. Eddie was quoted in his video, *A Football Life*: "I thought if I could become a running back and my father would see me being successful, he would be able to get off drugs."

So my first recruiting trip as a college coach was to see Eddie George at Fork Union Military Academy, ninety miles west of Richmond, Virginia, in the middle of nowhere. The staff seemed excited when they talked about Eddie, so I decided to do some homework. I grabbed a couple of the tapes he had sent for us to evaluate. At six foot three, 220 pounds, Eddie averaged over two hundred yards per game. He was the real deal. Mess this up and my first recruiting trip could be my last.

I gathered up all the Ohio State credit cards I had been issued, climbed into my new coach's courtesy car, and drove to the airport to catch my flight to Richmond. Before I left, I asked one of the staff members about the recruiting budget. The response: "This is Ohio State, there is no budget."

As soon as I arrived at Fork Union, I went to see Coach John Shuman. He was quick to point out Eddie's success both on the field and in the classroom and made a point to credit the teenager's work ethic for this improvement.

When Eddie's mother, Donna, put her fifteen-year-old son into her orange Mustang and drove him seven hours from Philadelphia to Fork Union, he was six feet, 178 pounds, with a 1.3 GPA. Two and a half years later, he was finishing a semester of postgraduate school and headed to Ohio State to play running back.

Eddie has admitted many times that it was the military academy culture of hard work that changed his life. "Chores, studying, working out, sweeping, waxing, buffing the floors, cleaning the bathrooms, marching in place, even hospital corners on the bed sheets," Eddie told Shannon Sharpe on his podcast, *Shay Shay*. "It was a culture of working hard for good grades, coming in early, staying late."

I finally had a chance to visit with Eddie. On the ride from Richmond to Fork Union, I played over and over in my head what I would say to make a good first impression, "So, you ready to be a Buckeye?" Eddie smiled big and said, "Ready. Any chance you can break me out of here today?" Eddie was grateful for his experience, but he had enough marching and was ready for his next challenge, in Columbus, Ohio.

From 1992 until 1995, Eddie competed against five future NFL backs, including Robert Smith and Raymont Harris. From the time Eddie George first arrived on campus, he separated himself from the competition by being the hardest worker on the team.

During summer workouts run by our strength coach, athletes could schedule their training regimen in the morning or evening. Eddie would come in the morning, run all the sprints and win all the sprints, even against faster players like future Biletnikoff Winner Terry Glenn, a first-round NFL draft pick of the New England Patriots. But Eddie would come back in the evenings to run again, and he'd still win most sprints. It was that extra effort that separated the extraordinary Eddie George from the ordinary college running back. No one ever outworked Eddie.

That same work ethic and a commitment to excellence earned him the opportunity to be our goal line back in his first season with the Buckeyes. In just his third game, we played eighth-ranked Syracuse on the road. In this nationally televised game, Eddie scored three times on sweeps after catching the toss from quarterback Kirk Herbstreit. But a few weeks later, it was a completely different outcome.

Against a good Illinois team at home, Eddie fumbled twice inside the ten-yard line. One of those fumbles was scooped up and carried all the way back for an Illinois touchdown. Eddie was deep in the coach's doghouse. He barely played the rest of his freshman year and was seldom given reps in practice. It wasn't much better during his sophomore year.

Most players would have quit or transferred. Eddie worked harder. He told me once it was these two years that enabled him to win a Heisman Trophy. He studied martial arts and took ballet classes because he wanted to get swifter and shiftier in the hips. He studied the running styles of backs like Emmitt Smith as he tried to sharpen his own ability at the position. He would stop in my office and ask me to teach him blocking schemes so that he would better understand what we were doing up front. That would help him read the defense and understand what to look for in the timing of his cuts.

By the time Eddie was a senior, he was the best running back in the Big Ten. On his march to the Heisman Trophy, Eddie ran for 207 yards and two touchdowns against a good Notre Dame team. Later, against his old nemesis Illinois, he set the school rushing record with 314 yards in windy, snowy, miserable conditions. During his 65-yard touchdown run in the second half, ABC broadcaster Brent Musberger bellowed, "Hello, Heisman!" Those same fans who were booing Eddie three years earlier against this same team were now chanting his name.

In the video *A Football Life: Eddie George*, Coach Jeff Fisher tells several stories about how Eddie's strength and conditioning would wear defensive players down. The body punches of 3 and 4 yards a carry would become long runs later in the game. Fisher said the Tennessee Titans were best when they played, "Eddie left, Eddie right, Eddie up the middle."

Coach Fisher remembered a game versus the Oakland Raiders played in a heat index of 120 degrees. Eddie had to go into the locker room to get an IV for dehydration but returned to rush for over two hundred yards. The next day Coach Fisher looked out his office window and saw Eddie on the field running one hundred-yard sprints.

Eddie George and his Tennessee Titans finished one yard short of winning Super Bowl XXXIV. Eddie stopped in the office to see Coach Fisher the day after their parade in Nashville. Eddie informed his coach that he had turned down the opportunity to play in the Pro Bowl, "He wanted to start getting ready for next season right now." That was typical for Eddie George.

In 2024, Eddie was in his fourth season as the head coach of Tennessee State. His Tigers tied for first place in the Big South-Ohio Valley Conference and earned a postseason berth. Eddie George was voted the Big South-OVC Coach of the Year. Eddie George was hired by Bowling Green as the new Head Coach in the winter of 2025.

NEVER FORGET

"How far have you come? Remember everything you have gotten through, all the times you have pushed on even when you felt you couldn't. All the mornings you got out of bed no matter how hard it was. Those are individual tests of character. All the times you wanted to give up, but you got through another day, they matter. Never forget how much strength you have learned and developed along the way."–Author Unknown

Key Points for Paying the Price

1. It is effort that turns ability into accomplishment and dreams into reality.
2. There is no substitute for hard work. All things worthwhile take hard work.
3. Great players and great teams have a blue-collar, punch-the-clock work ethic.
4. Recruit talent and work ethic. Talent is a waste without dedication and hard work.
5. It is the responsibility of the team leaders to demand more from the team than they can demand by themselves.
6. Nothing is ever free in life. Living a life of success and significance is about hard work and sacrifice. You must earn it.
7. Discipline is doing what must be done as well as it can be done and doing it that way all the time.
8. Hard work always beats talent.
9. The culture of a consistent and disciplined work ethic is critical to achieving team excellence.
10. One of the best responses to adversity is "work harder."

–CHAPTER THREE–
POOR TIMID SOULS

"Courage is the resistance of fear, mastery of fear—not absence of fear."
—Mark Twain

Photo of Charlie Frye

Bio Box: Charlie Frye, former NFL player, NFL and college football coach

Background: Charlie Frye was born August 28, 1981. He is the third of four children (Mandy, Clayton, Charlie, and Elizabeth) born to Dave and Sally Frye of Willard, Ohio. Dave worked at R.R. Donnelley Printing, and Sally was a teacher's aide. Charlie and his wife, Lenette, have two sons and a daughter while living in Florida.

Athletic Achievement: Charlie played football, basketball, and baseball at Willard High School. He was an all-Ohio football player who led the Flashes to a Northern Ohio League title as a senior in 1999. Willard High School retired his jersey, No. 3. He earned a scholarship to the University of Akron, where he was a four-year starting quarterback from 2001 to 2004. Frye was inducted into the University of Akron Hall of Fame after setting fifty-four school records. He completed 913 of 1,436 passes for 11,049 yards and 64 touchdowns, all school records. He ended his career ranked number eleven in NCAA history with 11,478 yards of total offense. Charlie was a third-round NFL draft pick by the Cleveland Browns. He played five years in the NFL with the Browns, Seattle Seahawks, and Oakland Raiders.

Scholastic Achievement: Charlie graduated from Willard High School in 2000 and from the University of Akron in 2005 with a degree in sports science.

Professional Achievement: Charlie worked as an assistant coach of wide receivers at Ashland University and as a director of player development at the University of Florida from 2015 to 2017. He became an offensive coordinator at Central Michigan in 2019, then quarterbacks coach with the Miami Dolphins in 2021. In 2022 he was an offensive analyst at Penn State, and in 2023 he took over as offensive coordinator at Florida Atlantic, where he remains at the time of this book's publication.

One of President Theodore Roosevelt's most famous speeches was titled "Citizenship in a Republic." It was delivered in Paris on April 23, 1910, and became known later in popular culture as "The Man in the Arena." Within TR's stirring words is one of the most famous quotes ever attributed to a United States president.

> *"It is far better to dare mighty triumphs, even though checkered by failure, than to dwell with those poor and timid souls knowing neither victory nor defeat," Roosevelt said.*

Charlie Frye would never be classified as a poor timid soul. His background wouldn't permit it. His personality wouldn't tolerate it. His upbringing wouldn't consider it. The future NFL player grew up in an environment where a blue-collar work ethic was simply expected.

Charlie was born in Willard, Ohio. Tucked away in the corner of rural Huron County, Ohio, Willard has a population of just over six thousand people and sits thirty-five miles south of Lake Erie. It has a long history with railroads and farming. Because of the large number of trees in Willard, it is known as the City of Blossoms. For years Willard High School fielded powerhouse basketball programs under local coaching icon Bob Haas. For Charlie, like most Willard boys, basketball was the favorite sport. He grew up dreaming of donning Willard's crimson uniform and racing onto the floor to star in front of a packed gymnasium.

"I loved hoops. For one thing, you didn't need anybody else to practice it," Charlie said. "I remember my dad, I had to shovel, dig out the court, and [Dad] paid for the cement, but we put up a hoop there at the house. I just loved basketball. But it turned out I was better in football."

Charlie also grew up across the street from Willard Football Head Coach Terry King, a longtime family friend. Beginning in the second grade, Charlie was a ball boy, and a water boy. Every Friday night he was on the varsity sidelines until he donned the pads himself. Frye played for King in his first three years in high school, including as the starting quarterback his sophomore and junior years.

"I was just drawn to the sport. My mom tells the story that I wrote a poem for her when I was in [elementary school] that I was going to be an NFL player and start for the Cleveland Browns. It was like I had a vision."

Rarely do such visions come true, but it did for Charlie—after a ton of hard work, dedication, and true grit.

In addition to shooting baskets in the backyard, he hung a tire from a tree branch and began peppering away with a football for target practice. When he got tired of chasing down the balls, he cut a square hole in the back of the shed and again took aim, hauling a bag of footballs back and forth, inside and outside the shed, honing his accuracy.

As a high school senior, playing for new Coach Chris Hawkins, Frye led the Flashes to a Northern Ohio League championship and a playoff victory over Bellevue. Willard was knocked out of the postseason in a second-round game, but by then Charlie had earned all-Ohio honors, and his Number 3 jersey would eventually be retired in the high school trophy case.

Still, Willard didn't attract many scouts. In those days, before social media exploded, there was no way to upload video highlights for the world to see. So Charlie used his lawn-mowing money to pay for trips to summer camps at Ohio State, Notre Dame, Tennessee, etc. It was the price he had to pay to increase his exposure to college coaching staffs.

"We had four kids, and it costs like $250 to go to the Ohio State camp," Charlie remembered. "I'm coming home from two-a-days [at Willard High School], and I have something like seven lawns to mow. One day I came home, and I asked my mom, 'Where's Dad?' She said, 'He's mowing your grass.'"

Charlie had the requisite size at six foot four, arm strength, and accuracy. He was a good athlete, and yet most Division I schools questioned his level of competition. I used the word "most" because happily, we didn't at Akron. I grew up in Mansfield, about thirty miles east of Willard, and knew the region intimately. I coached a state championship team at Galion High School in 1985, winning the same conference Charlie won fourteen years later at Willard in 1999.

When Charlie came to our seven-on-seven camp at the University of Akron, I saw him lead his team down the field for a game-winning score and celebrate with his teammates in the end zone. It was just a camp setting, but I was drawn to those competitive juices and impressed by his play, and I climbed down from the bleachers to formally extend a full scholarship offer. When Charlie accepted, it turned out to be one of the most important things to happen to the University of Akron football program. Still, that didn't mean he got a free ride at home.

"My dad had a rule that once you finished school, you're not staying at home unless you're working," Charlie remembered. "So that summer before I leave for Akron, I took a job at Domino's, and I might have lasted forty-eight hours, and I was like, 'Nah.' I'm thinking, 'Pops, I've got a full-ride scholarship.' But Dad said, 'You know the rule.' So I called Coach [Tom] Stacy and said, 'Do you guys got any rooms up there in Akron?' I ended up staying in one of the older [player's] attic with some boxes and no air-conditioning. That was my first summer in Akron. But I was able to work out and do the things that I needed to do to learn my craft."

Charlie redshirted his true freshman year while senior quarterback Butchie Washington finished his fine career. The Zips went 6-5 and tied Marshall for the East Division championship of the Mid-American Conference.

"That was a great learning experience because I saw the way Butchie interacted with everyone in the locker room, not just his friends," Frye said. "He really had control of the entire locker room as a leader. He was just a great guy to learn from."

As a redshirt freshman, Charlie competed for the starting quarterback job with Nick Sparks, a transfer we brought in from West Virginia. Nick started the first game against Ohio University but got hurt. Charlie took over and led us to a 31-29 win at Akron's Rubber Bowl. Nick was a great athlete, but Charlie was the better quarterback, and you never know what a player can do until you see them under fire. Charlie started every game for the rest of his career, including the very next week at Ohio State. It was the first game for the Buckeyes' new coach, Jim Tressel, and with one hundred thousand people at Ohio Stadium, the setting was crazy.

"I think I threw up twice in the locker room before we went out onto the field," Charlie said. "I felt pretty good about the way my first game ended the week before against OU, but this was a whole different level. They had just finished the addition to the stadium, and that place was rocking. It's funny, but I always liked to get hit early in the game. That's what always settled me down and made things go quiet for me. Then it became the same game that you've played since high school. Your emotions leave you, and it's time to make the best decisions you can."

Ohio State had a three-year starter at quarterback that year, Steve Bellisari, but Charlie was clearly the best quarterback on the field. We hung in there for three quarters and were driving late in the fourth quarter down 21-14. A field goal did us no good, so we went for it on fourth and medium. We were in trips right and threw a crossing route to our tailback Brandon Payne. Ohio State all-American Michael Doss made a play on the ball that looked like pass interference to me, but the Big Ten officials didn't agree. After that stop, Coach Tressel "took the air out of the ball" and ran power football down the field for a touchdown to win 28-14.

The most impressive thing was the way Charlie handled that situation. His last start had come at Willard High School, and then he was playing in Ohio Stadium for his first college start. It didn't overwhelm him at all. He was not a poor timid soul.

"You just have to be willing to put yourself out there and just go for it," Frye said. "I had a vision of getting to the highest level and wanting to be put in those situations. I've always lived, played on the edge. It just felt like I was chasing something. That's always been my makeup."

That 2001 season was a rebuilding year for us at Akron. We went 4-7 overall, but 4-4 in the Mid-American Conference. That autumn featured one of the toughest losses of my career. Just five weeks after the Ohio State game, on October 13, 2001, Charlie led us down the field and we scored in the closing seconds at Miami University in Oxford to take a 27-24 lead. There were only three seconds showing on the Yager Stadium clock when Miami's redshirt freshman quarterback Ben Roethlisberger took over at his own 30. The future

Pro Football Hall of Famer was making just his sixth collegiate start, but his potential was off the charts. He was a huge player, at about 6-foot-5, 240 pounds, and he had a bazooka for an arm. Miami was in a desperate situation and really had only one clear path for any chance. Roethlisberger dropped back and heaved a long pass deep into our territory. All we had to do was knock the pass down to win. But two of our defensive backs dropped back to our 15-yard line and tipped the ball up into the air. The pass would have fallen incomplete if not tipped; it was nowhere close to a receiver. But the ball went straight up in the air and came down directly into the hands of receiver Eddie Tillitz, who was in a full sprint toward our goal line. It was a 70-yard Hail Mary pass as time expired, giving us a crushing, 30-27 loss. I fell face-first into the turf, and to this day, I have not recovered.

But as this chapter notes, the world is no place for a poor timid soul. Putting yourself out there means sometimes we must endure dramatic, even unbelievable disappointments. That game certainly represented just such a situation.

The next year we won four of our last six, and Charlie was firmly in control. Our best win of the season came in a 34-20 upset of Marshall and its star quarterback Byron Leftwich.

The Thundering Herd began the season ranked number nineteen and got as high as number sixteen. They were 6-1 when Coach Bob Pruett brought his team to the Rubber Bowl. In the second quarter, Leftwich injured his left leg, and he wound up playing most of the second half with a severe limp. The game was broadcast by ESPN, and Leftwich's teammates began to carry him between plays as his limp worsened. It turned out he had a broken leg. Meanwhile, Marshall's outstanding team was really beating us up front. Still, Charlie hung in there and threw a 28-yard touchdown pass to Mike Brake to give us a 24-10 halftime lead. The Thundering Herd rallied, but Charlie's 26-yard touchdown run in the final minute of the third quarter gave us enough cushion to earn a 34-20 victory: Akron's first-ever win over a nationally ranked opponent.

A lot was made about Leftwich's courage, playing on a broken leg—and it was certainly a tremendous example of grit. But Frye was no less heroic. Charlie was getting the crap beat out of him, but he kept getting back up and led us to a victory against a more talented opponent.

Things were pointing up for the 2003 season. Charlie entered his third year as the starter, and although we lost our first two games, our offense was humming. We won five of the next six and were averaging well over 30 points per game. Unfortunately for me, Akron had just hired a new athletic director, and I was firmly on the hot seat. We finished the season with victories at Central Michigan and against Ohio University, and yet I was fired.

It wasn't from lack of effort by Charlie and his teammates. We finished that season 7-5 overall, 5-3 in the Mid-American Conference.

Charlie had completely rewritten Akron's record book. He completed 913 of 1,436 passes for 11,049 yards and 64 touchdowns, all school records. He ended his career ranked number eleven No. 11 in NCAA history with 11,478 yards of total offense. From there, he went to the 2005 Senior Bowl and performed flawlessly. He completed 10 of 12 passes for 138 yards and a touchdown to lead the North to a 23-13 win over the South. Charlie was selected as the game's MVP and cemented his stock on all NFL draft boards.

"I just came in here to have fun, and I just look forward to having a chance to play in that league," he told the Associated Press after the game in Mobile, Alabama.

Frye's vision was right on track. His courage, toughness, all the intangibles were in place. Charlie also scored a thirty-eight on the Wonderlic intelligence test. That grade placed him among the top twenty-five players ever tested by NFL teams.

"When it came time for the draft, I was pretty sure I was going to Green Bay," Charlie said. "They had two second-round picks. They sent me a hat. They even sent a TV crew to my parents' house in Willard. That would've been ideal, sitting behind Brett Favre, playing for Mike Holmgren. But they picked Aaron Rodgers in the first round, so the TV crew packed up their stuff, and I mean they zoomed out of Willard."

Instead, Charlie was taken sixty-seventh overall in the third round by the Cleveland Browns. His vision had indeed come true.

"When it happened, it was a dream come true," Charlie said. "But as you continue your journey, you see things differently. In the NFL, it really is all about where you go. Aaron was able to sit and learn from Brett [Favre], and when he got his chance, he had a Hall of Fame career. Now I'm not saying that would have happened to me, but instead of that, I'm playing my rookie year. I'm starting six games into my rookie year and we're not very good, and I'm taking a beating. That was probably the worst part of it."

Charlie had landed with one of the worst-run, if not *the* worst, franchises in the NFL, and I say that as a lifelong Browns fan. He was rushed into a starting quarterback job as a rookie behind a makeshift line with few proven weapons. The Browns had no vision and no real plan going forward. Cleveland went through quarterbacks like an athlete goes through tube socks; they were disposable and treated in similar fashion.

As a rookie in 2005, Charlie played in seven games and threw for 1,002 yards while completing 60 percent of his passes with 4 TDs and 5 INTs. In 2006, Charlie's first pass of the year, against the New Orleans Saints, went for a 74-yard touchdown to receiver Braylon Edwards. Naturally, it was called back for a holding penalty. It was emblematic of his career with the Browns. After the team's 1-5 start, Offensive Coordinator Maurice Carthon resigned. In week thirteen, Charlie was hurt in the first half of a game with the Kansas City Chiefs. He was out with a deep bone bruise in his wrist until the final game of the season, a loss to the Houston Texans that finished a 4-12 campaign.

Charlie finished that 2006 season playing in 13 games, going 252 of 393 passing with 10 touchdowns, 17 interceptions, and a 72.0 quarterback rating. Still, the Browns were already looking for another signal caller. In the 2007 draft, they selected Notre Dame quarterback Brady Quinn with the twenty-second pick of the first round.

In the 2007 preseason, Quinn was slotted as a third teamer. Charlie won the quarterback job in a preseason competition with Derek Anderson, yet he was benched at halftime of the season opener, a 34-7 loss to Pittsburgh. Incredibly, just two days later, Frye was traded to the Seattle Seahawks for a sixth-round draft pick.

The NFL just rolled its eyes collectively at the Browns' bizarre move. It was unprecedented. According to the Elias Sports Bureau, Frye was the first quarterback since the NFL/AFL merger in 1970 to start his team's season opener and be traded before week two. That was the Cleveland Browns right there, in a nutshell.

Obviously, the NFL is no place for poor timid souls.

"What I didn't know until I got to Seattle is that they were shopping me and Derek [Anderson] all that week before the opener. Seattle told me that the trade was done on Thursday [before the opener]," Charlie said. "But really, that was probably the best thing that could've happened to me. I got to learn from Mike Holmgren, Jim Zorn, and Matt Hasselbeck. I just got to see the game differently, see how to play the position, soak up the West Coast offense. That really saved my career and embedded in me later how I teach—a lot of that is from what I learned in Seattle."

Charlie approached his new role as a backup quarterback with professionalism and toughness. Those are traits that keep a player in the NFL for years. He played in two games during the 2008 NFL season and three games for the Oakland Raiders in 2009. He started a game against the Denver Broncos that year but was injured in the fourth quarter. He played two more games in relief to finish the year.

Frye signed a one-year, $1.2 million deal in 2010 but suffered another wrist injury in training camp, which required surgery. That was the end of his playing career. In five years as an NFL quarterback, he appeared in 26 games, completing 419 of 677 passes (62 percent) for 4,154 yards, 17 touchdowns, and 29 interceptions. He was sacked 79 times and posted a 69.7 quarterback rating.

Although he was done as a player, that didn't end his career with the sport. Charlie had a wife, two sons, and a daughter to consider, and it was time to move into J-O-B mode.

Charlie decided to stay in a field he knew best, the football field. So he moved into the coaching ranks. In the summer of 2012, he took a high school coaching job in Orlando, Florida, as an offensive coordinator, and after two years at Jones High School, he moved on to a similar role at Wekiva High School in Apopka, Florida.

Transitioning from an NFL player to high school coach may seem unconventional, but it didn't bother Charlie. He had to learn what it was like to teach the sport from a new perspective. What better place to start than at the most fundamental level?

"The kids today don't have the black-and-white drawings of the plays in a playbook," Charlie said. "They're learning in a completely different way. They're on Twitter, Snapchat, Instagram, whatever. They look at pictures, quote lyrics, stuff like that. After the game, some of the kids rush to their lockers to pick up their cell phones to see what's being said about them on social media. I mean, who cares? You've got to block that stuff out. But that's the way they're growing up. I had to learn how these five-star, big-name, hotshot quarterbacks are wired. It kind of simplified my teaching to make it obtainable to them. Now if I put a play up there for them, there's always a picture underneath it to illustrate what we're trying to teach. It's amazing the retention that way. Starting in high school, that transition, instead of jumping into the league, I think it really helped me."

Prior to the 2018 season, I hired Charlie at Ashland to coach our wide receivers. His knowledge was off the charts, and with his NFL background, we were able to keep him for only one season. The next year, he became the offensive coordinator at Central Michigan. The transformation of the program was immediate. In 2018, the Chippewas had gone 1-11 under Head Coach John Bonamego. In Coach Jim McElwain's first season, the 2019 team with Frye at the helm led the Mid-American Conference in total offense with 6,070 yards, and the team posted an 8-6 record, a seven-game improvement. It was the best turnaround in Division I college football that year, and Charlie was named the assistant coach of the year in the Mid-American Conference.

Charlie was at Central Michigan for two years before landing the job as quarterbacks coach with the Miami Dolphins. After one season there, he went to work for James Franklin at Penn State as offensive analytics coordinator in 2022. Frye then took a job as offensive coordinator at Florida Atlantic in 2023.

"One day I would like to be able to lead a program," Charlie said. "That's a natural for me to be out front."

MAN IN THE ARENA

Of course it is, just like it is for anyone with courage and conviction. Just like Teddy Roosevelt said in "The Man in the Arena": "It is not the critic who counts; not the man who points out how the strong man stumbles, or where the doer of deeds could have done them better. The credit belongs to the man who is actually in the arena, whose face is marred by dust and sweat and blood; who strives valiantly; who errs, who comes up short again and again, because there is no effort without error and shortcoming; but who does actually strive to do the deeds; who knows the great enthusiasms, the great devotions; who spends himself in a worthy cause; who at the best knows in the end the triumph of high achievement, and who at the worst, if he fails, at least fails while daring greatly, so that his place shall never be with those cold and timid souls who neither know victory nor defeat."

Heart & Courage of Convictions

"If you don't stand for something you will fall for anything."
—Steve Bartkowski

Charlie said in the interview for this book that my belief in him as our quarterback empowered him to be successful. My belief in Charlie Frye extended far beyond his courage and ability at the quarterback position. My belief in Charlie Frye was in his heart and in his courage of convictions.

It takes courage of your convictions to follow a commitment to excellence—to dare to be different, dare to be great, to be unafraid to speak up and take a stand. Charlie can believe strongly enough in something that he wills it into reality. He believed he could play quarterback in the NFL, and he went out and proved it.

I've always admired players and coaches who have good, courageous hearts that are built for others. Charlie has always been dedicated to his family, his teammates, and his coaches. He never wanted to disappoint the important people in his life. I believe this has always been the intrinsic motivation that kept Charlie so laser focused.

Charlie Frye was a player who regardless of fame or fortune would never do anything to embarrass his family. He was the type of player who would not only take the heat for his teammates but also share his offensive MVP award with the team. And Charlie was the player on our Akron team who took my firing most personally. He told me once that he blamed himself for our staff being fired.

"If only I could have led our team to one more win," he said.

Before I left Akron, Charlie stopped by the house with a framed picture of us together on the sideline at the Rubber Bowl. He autographed the picture "Charlie Frye No. 5, Thanks for Everything, (7-5)."

I have always felt honored to have had the opportunity to coach Charlie Frye, and I have always valued our relationship. When Charlie was the starting quarterback for the Cleveland Browns, I asked him if he would lend his celebrity status to start a golf tournament in Ashland, Ohio. The event would raise money to support Mike Gottfried's Team Focus program for fatherless boys. To this day, Kip Matteson, Warren Jones, and Zane Gross continue this charity golf tournament.

My best Charlie Frye story has to do with a thirty-inch, ten-pound walleye I have mounted on my wall. Charlie and I have made lots of trips to Lake Erie since his playing days at Akron. Our trips to Lake Erie and boating to Put-in-Bay or Rattlesnake Island have always been fun and adventurous. There have been a lot of great fishing days, none more successful than one with Captain Pat on his Irish C charter boat. But my favorite fishing trip was in my boat, Sea Eagle, over Gull Reef, casting for walleye in the shallow rocks.

I had just made a cast, but I needed to net a fish for one of the other guys, so I handed my rod and reel to Charlie. By the time I was able to get back to Charlie, my rod was still in his hand, but it was bent in half. Charlie didn't want to give me the rod and reel back. He continued to battle for a few more minutes with the drag in full release, but eventually and reluctantly he gave up on the fish, concluding that the lure must be caught in the rocks.

The only place the lure was caught was in the mouth of this monster walleye. I told Charlie after he netted my trophy fish how much I appreciated him hooking it for me.

Courageous Competitors

"Number 1: Cash Is King. Number 2: Communicate. Number 3: Bury the Competition"–Jack Welch

Stocking your team with talent and creating an expectation of hard work and sacrifice are the first steps in the blueprint to building a winner. Just as important as talent and work ethic is recruiting competitors, courageous competitors—competitors who have courage and live on the edge. They are not afraid to break their comfort zones. They are not afraid to lose, to get hurt, or to be embarrassed. To them fear is an illusion.

It is the courage to take risks that separates teams and organizations in our culture of mediocrity. Anyone or any team can be ordinary, but it takes courage to excel. It was Virgil, the ancient Roman poet, who said, "Fortune favors the bold." The teams I coached often faced opponents with more talent, but it was unacceptable to ever face a team with more courage.

It takes courage to get out of the stands, off the sideline, and into the game. There may be several strikeouts before hitting a home run or a few three putts before making a birdie. Golfers are quick to learn that 100 percent of their putts that come up short don't go in the hole. There is no glory in a lag putt. One must remember: the greater the risk, the greater the reward.

RISKS
"To love is to risk not being loved in return, to live is to risk dying, to hope is to risk despair, to try is to risk failure, but risks must be taken, because the greatest hazard is to risk nothing. The person who risks nothing does nothing, has nothing, is nothing. Only a person who risks is free."–Author Unknown

I believe that in business, just like in athletics, life shrinks or expands in proportion to one's courage. Courage is a highly visible characteristic of great teams. They play to win. This is much different from playing not to lose.

Make Fear an Illusion
"I can accept failure. Everyone fails at something. But I can't accept not trying." –Michael Jordan

Courage is not the absence of fear; rather, it gives us the ability to compete through fear. Teams and organizations are often frozen by fear of failure.

DON'T BE AFRAID TO FAIL
"You've failed many times. You fell down the first time you tried to walk, you almost drowned the first time you tried to swim, you didn't hit the ball the first time you swung a bat. . . . R. H. Macy failed seven times before his store in New York caught on. English novelist John Creasey got 753 rejection slips before he published 564 books. Don't worry about failure; worry about what you will miss if you don't try."
—Author Unknown

My peers have questioned many decisions I've made throughout my career. Why would I take over a team with little or no job security? Why would I schedule a team knowing they may end up being a four- or five-touchdown favorite?

Unfortunately, there are times when the scheduling was not something I could control. I was always in favor of playing the most competitive schedule possible. I felt that playing great competition in the opener or early in the season gave me the chance to really motivate the team in the offseason to be prepared to be its best right out of the gate. I also felt it would be an opportunity to evaluate our squad and know exactly what we needed to do to improve and become a better team. Good competition always brings out the best in a team and exposes weaknesses.

Still, I was never in favor of playing teams before we were ready to compete at their level. I learned many lessons at Akron when faced with this challenge. One, nothing good ever results from losing. Two, regardless of the odds against your team winning, play hard and play to win.

In 1997 we opened the season against Nebraska, the eventual

national champions. We lost 59-14. At the time I was upset, but when Nebraska beat Oklahoma 69-7 and went on to an undefeated season, the blow softened. We played hard, and we were physical against the Cornhuskers. We rushed for over one hundred yards. This was a goal we had committed to going into the game. The media's pregame hype of players "being carried off the field on stretchers" was just that, hype.

When I took the head football position at Massillon High School, many in my Ohio high school coaching fraternity questioned my decision. I inherited a team that was on probation and banned from postseason play by the Ohio High School Athletic Association for alleged recruiting violations. The Tigers had lost four straight games to archrival Canton McKinley.

When I talked with the Massillon Board of Education about the position, I was asked by board member Ann Lightfoot, "Do you know what happens to the coach and his family in this town when he losses to McKinley?" I told her, "I'm not planning on losing to McKinley."

Anytime a team leader jumps into any situation or job opportunity, that individual must be thinking I'm going to be successful. When Woody Hayes interviewed for the Ohio State football job in 1951, an Ohio State Board of Trustees member asked him if he was concerned about job security. "I'm not here for security," Woody said shortly. "I'm here for the opportunity."

That mindset doesn't ponder failure. I believe to accomplish anything in life we must be aggressive and go for it. We must be positive, not passive; make fear an illusion and never allow it to become an obstacle.

There were times in my career that I found myself questioning my journey. I wondered if the challenges I was facing were insurmountable, if the setbacks I was experiencing may be fatal to my career. But then I realized that it was courage that had led me to that point in my journey, and it would take courage to continue that journey.

Leaving Ohio State to go to Akron was a very difficult decision. Coach John Cooper had just signed a new contract, and his best teams were on their way. There was a time when I nearly pulled out of the search process at Akron. It was during an informal meeting with Akron Athletic Director Mike Bobinski when we were close to my commitment to take the position. We were at the Sheraton Suites in Cuyahoga Falls, Ohio. I excused myself to return a call from Charles Woodson, out of Fremont, Ohio.

For those who don't know, Charles Woodson was Ohio's 1994 Mr. Football. He was a two-way prospect at defensive back and tailback who had just finished a spectacular career at Fremont Ross High School. Charles was a priority recruit, just as Orlando Pace had been the year before. Some players are considered difference makers, and Woodson was one of them. Ohio State wanted him desperately. Not only was Charles the best football player in the state, but his other leading contender was Michigan, our archrival. Losing him to the Wolverines could be catastrophic.

I had worked over a year building a relationship with this recruit and getting him scheduled on an official visit to Columbus. When Charles heard I was about to leave Ohio State, he called to cancel his visit. Damon Moore, a player I had recruited the year before from Fostoria and who had played against Charles in high school, was going to be Woodson's host. So I called Damon and asked him to call Charles. I also called Coach Cooper. He was really upset with me. He knew Charles Wodson was a special athlete. One of his college teammates called Charles "Superman," because his physical attributes seemed otherworldly. The fact that Charles ended up at Michigan, beat Ohio State three times, and won the Heisman Trophy while leading Michigan to the 1997 national championship didn't help me with the pain and anguish I felt for letting down Coach Cooper and the Buckeyes.

Still, once I made a career decision, or a team decision, my only focus was on being there and finding a way to win. There were going to be times no matter how calculated the risks or how competent the planning that a team's best just isn't good enough. Although I hate losing and loathed being fired, I always refused to look back with regret. My only regret would be not trying.

All teams are on a journey, and failure is always a part of any journey, hopefully only a small part of the journey. Along the way there will always be success and failure. Every journey, every season, is a totality of moments.

The weak and less aggressive teams stand back and allow these moments to define them. Winning teams look for and seize defining moments. This takes focus and courage—courage to compete and to not be overcome by the fear of a difficult situation. It takes courage to compete and enjoy the challenge, courage to act rather than to react.

COVID
"Life is a grindstone, and whether it grinds you down or polishes you up is for you and you alone to decide."–Seneca

In 1979, I was involved in a serious accident. An automobile was coming from the opposite direction and passing on a double yellow line at the crest of a hill. We collided at sixty miles per hour and rolled down an embankment. I regained consciousness as the jaws of life were cutting me free from my tangled-up Mustang with its engine in my lap.

My most serious injury was a shattered femur. To this day, I have a steel plate in my leg from my hip to my knee. It took nearly a year for me to get out of a wheelchair and off crutches. I thought that my rehab and coaching a season on crutches at Crestview was difficult. Later, after getting fired despite a winning season at Akron, that was about as much adversity as any coach might expect.

That was before COVID.

In the one-hundred-year history of Ashland University football, only twice was a football season canceled: once during World War II and one during COVID.

To say it was a difficult and challenging time is an understatement. In Ashland, Ohio, we dealt with the same masking, testing, vaccine, and daily changes in policy and procedure that confronted all Americans.

What added to the adversity we faced was COVID coincided with a dire fiscal situation at Ashland University. Our team lost coaches, our football budget was cut, and our entire staff was furloughed for three months. Wow. How to find the courage to face this challenge? How to find the courage to keep our team and what coaches we had left together?

I was convinced that how we approached the adversity of the COVID pandemic would define Ashland football for many years, if not decades. Below is one of the first of many letters I sent to coaches, players, staff, alumni, and boosters attempting to communicate and motivate during our extended "no-contact" time of the pandemic.

Journal Entry: Friday May 1, 2020

"I'm not sure when we will kick off our one-hundredth season of football, but I'm sure that we will, and when we can play again, we must be ready.

"As an old history teacher, I can tell you that our country has gone through much more difficult times than now. World Wars, Great Depression, Social and Racial unrest ... and guess what, we have always found a way to keep going and to grow even stronger.

"We have an amazing country with remarkable people. Smart, talented, passionate, tireless leaders who will continue to relentlessly find a way to beat this virus. I'm going to be ready for when we get our game back. I challenge you to do the same thing.

"Our country needs football to recover. Next to serving in the military, football does more to prepare the next generation of leaders than anything else in our country. We can't afford the next generation of leaders in America to miss the opportunity to play this great game. I read somewhere that the next generation in our country will be defined by the corona virus. I believe the next generation of leaders in America will have been made stronger by the adversity of COVID.

"Many of you have had your hearts ripped out and your lives turned upside down during this pandemic, but you stayed the course. Stayed together, stayed strong. I challenge the leaders on our team to continue to lead. It takes courage to lead in a time of crises!

"There is nothing about this virus that is fair. But what in life is ever fair? A football team is made up of different races, different religions, and different socioeconomic groups. But we are all drawn together by our love for the game. By our love for our teammates. By our love for the grind. Football has always been there for us and will continue to be there. Football gives us all hope. As we continue to face the day-to-day challenges in the world today, it is football that has made us courageous and football that teaches us to persevere and 'never surrender.'

"Finish strong with your off-campus academics. Stay in shape. Stay together, support one another. Continue to believe in our country, our university, and most importantly, our team. When we come back together our common cause will be to win the GMAC Championship in our 100th year of football."

Because of the commitment of the players, coaches, staff, alumni, and boosters, the Ashland Eagle football team finished 10-2 and won the Great Midwest Athletic Conference Championship in 2022. The Eagles continue to win championships today under Head Coach Doug Geiser.

Moral Courage
"Courage, a virtue—a marker of moral excellence."–Aristotle

A team with moral courage can stand straight and not sway, no matter which way the wind blows. A gale force wind may cause a team leader to change strategy but never core beliefs.

Teams with moral courage can maintain their convictions and win without compromise, the compromise of a team's integrity or the compromise of a team's commitment to serve one another. Moral courage is at the core of a team's character and excellence.

Too often in team building we focus solely on the courage to overcome fear in difficult or painful situations. Courage is defined as being brave or fearless. In Joe Ehrmann's book *Inside Out Coaching*, he defines moral courage as, "doing what you believe is right, even if others disagree, doing what is morally right even in the face of criticism, ridicule, rejection, or retaliation."

A team's moral courage will be tested every day. Every day there will be pressures that cloud a team's moral courage. A team that achieves excellence lives each day with the courage to do what is right rather than what is convenient or easy. When under the stadium lights or in the dark of night, a team that achieves excellence chooses to do what is right.

Moral courage is defined as making good decisions all the time.

There are always eyes on you that are watching and impacted by your actions.

LITTLE EYES UPON YOU

There are little eyes upon you
And they're watching night and day.
There are little ears that quickly
Take in every word you say.
There are little hands all eager
To do anything you do;
And a little boy who's dreaming
Of the day he'll be like you

You're the little fellow's idol,
You're the wisest of the wise.
In his little mind about you
No suspicions ever rise.
He believes in you devoutly,
Holds all that you say and do;
He will say and do, in your way,
When he's grown up like you.

Here's a wide-eyed little fellow
Who believes you're always right;
And his eyes are always opened,
And he watched day and night.
You are setting an example
Every day in all you do,
For the little boy who's waiting
To grow up to be like you.
-Author Unknown

Key Points for Poor Timid Souls

1. It takes the courage of your convictions to follow your commitment to excellence.
2. Great players and coaches have good, courageous hearts that are built for others.
3. Fill your team with competitors who have the courage to live on the edge and to break comfort zones.
4. Make fear an illusion.
5. The greater the risk, the greater the reward.
6. Teams are often frozen by the fear of failure.
7. Regardless of the odds, play hard and play to win.
8. Whenever starting a new position, a team leader must expect success. A team leader must come to work every day with the same enthusiasm as the first day.
9. Never regret a decision; only regret not making one.
10. Moral courage is at the core of a team's character and excellence.

–CHAPTER FOUR–
ONE HEARTBEAT

T.E.A.M.—Together Everyone Achieves More

Photo of Luke Fickell courtesy of Wisconsin Athletics

Bio Box: Luke Fickell—Head Football Coach, Wisconsin Badgers

Background: The oldest of three children born to Pat and Sharon Fickell.

Athletic Achievement: Three-time state champion high school wrestler started fifty games as a defensive lineman at Ohio State.

Scholastic Achievement: Columbus DeSales graduate, honor student. Ohio State University graduate with a degree in exercise science. Academic All-Big Ten.

Professional Achievement: Interim head football coach at Ohio State (2011). Head football coach at the University of Cincinnati with a 57-18 record from 2017 to 2022. His 2021 Bearcats were the first team outside the Power 5 conferences to make the college football playoffs. Head football coach at the University of Wisconsin beginning in 2023 with an 8-6 record. He had a 76-38 record in nine years as a head coach heading into the 2025 season.

Accolades: Luke was selected as the consensus National Coach of the Year in 2021. He was the co-defensive coordinator on Ohio State's 2014 national championship team. Cincinnati has posted five eleven-win seasons in school history, Fickell recorded three of them.

Personal: Luke and his wife, Amy, have six children: Landon, Luca, twin sons Aydon and Ashton, and twin sons, Laykon and Lucian.

Discovering talent, intelligence and drive all in one individual is the jackpot of recruiting to any position of value. I was fortunate to know just such an individual in Luke Fickell. His story is unusual in that Luke's yearning to be part of a team trumped even the God-given ability he possessed to reach for the highest individual athletic achievement in all of sports: an Olympic gold medal.

My first encounter with Luke was while I was an offensive line coach at Ohio State. He was a wildly talented wrestling prospect who had already begun to make what some viewed as a perplexing decision: college football was the path he wanted to pursue.

That choice raised more than a few eyebrows within the state, simply because Luke was considered then, and even to this day by some, the greatest heavyweight wrestler ever seen at the Ohio high school level. That's a bold statement considering Ohio has produced past Olympic and NCAA champions, like Tommy Rowlands, Dustin Fox, Greg Wojciechowski, Bill Kerslake, and George Bollas (The Zebra Kid in pro wrestling circles).

Yet the esteemed Pat Galbincea, who covered high school wrestling for thirty-eight years at the Cleveland Plain Dealer, famously said, "To borrow a phrase from the late pro wrestler Wild Red Berry, 'even the most stupidest dolt' could see Fickell was earmarked for greatness."

Luke was undefeated at 106-0 on the mat his final three years at Columbus DeSales High School. As a 189-pound sophomore, he pinned four of his five foes, all in less than ninety-five seconds, at the state meet.

His junior and senior years were even more dominating, and intimidating, despite moving up to the heavyweight division. Some wrestlers simply forfeited rather than face Luke as he racked up two more unbeaten seasons and a couple of state championships.

Whispers were everywhere that this was not only an Olympian, but a budding gold medal winner embodied in a six-foot-four, 235-pound package that was simply stronger and quicker than anyone else on the mats at a similar age.

"[The Olympics] was my go-to dream from the time I was young," Fickell said. "It was all wrestling. That's what I wanted to do. I was going to go to college, I wanted to wrestle and do all of those things.

But then the football thing happened, and I really liked football too."

Luke's uncle was a wrestling coach; his dad was an assistant wrestling coach. So why play college football?

That he did may take a bit of analysis. Luke grew up the oldest of three children in a Catholic family influenced by the shadows of Ohio Stadium just a few miles away. His peewee football coach was a man named John Hicks. Woody Hayes considered Hicks and Jim Parker his greatest offensive linemen. Hicks finished second to John Cappelletti in the 1973 Heisman Trophy balloting, still the highest finish ever for an offensive lineman. At a very impressionable age, Luke learned football at the knee of a living legend.

"He was the largest man I'd ever seen," Luke said of Hicks. "Like my dad, Mr. Hicks was very similar, a no-nonsense guy, very to the point."

When Luke was eleven years old, Hicks told Pat Fickell his son was destined to play major college football, even before his prodigious wrestling talent had emerged. In the end, Hicks was right. While Luke was dominating on the wrestling mat, his high school baseball coach, Phil Callaghan, thought he had major league ability as a first baseman. In football, Luke was a two-time all-Ohioan for a state title contender at Columbus DeSales.

After his junior year in high school, scholarship offers poured in from football and wrestling coaches around the country. But as any Columbus resident can attest, the call of Ohio State football is nearly impossible to ignore.

It wasn't just that. Luke found something in the sport that spoke to him—the experience of being around a team.

"It probably wasn't until after my junior year of football that there was a little bit of a shift. We went pretty far in the playoffs that year, and I just remember a big shift in the enjoyment of it. I just really enjoyed being a part of a team. It's not that you're not part of a team in wrestling, but that is obviously much more of an individual sport."

"I just think that was the gist of it, being part of a team."

That concept of being part of a team would influence Luke well beyond school. As a college freshman, he was hurt and redshirted during the 1992 season at Ohio State. He started a school-record fifty games after that.

When I was coaching the offensive line at OSU, my players hated going up against Luke in practice. Even if it was a half-speed pass rush or double-team drill, he would find a way to win. There was no practice speed for Luke; he knew only full speed. This made us better.

He was also part of a very tight-knit group of teammates. Luke lived with defensive ends Mike Vrabel and Matt Finkes. They made up the core of Ohio State's defensive line from 1994 through 1996. Any Ohio State football fan can tell you these were high times.

In 1994, Head Coach John Cooper had yet to beat Michigan (0-5-1), and new Athletic Director Andy Geiger was under heavy pressure to make a move if the Buckeyes couldn't turn the tide that season against their hated rivals.

I was part of the coaching staff in an uneven season. We lost three games but were ranked number twenty-two when the fifteenth-ranked Wolverines came to town. This Ohio State-Michigan game was my third opportunity to coach in this great rivalry. Up to this point I had experienced a traumatic loss and a disappointing tie to the team up North. I couldn't wait to feel the emotion of an Ohio State win over Michigan.

As the team took the field for The Game, they ran through a tunnel of Ohio State greats. Rex Kern, quarterback of the 1968 national championship team, said they wanted to show the players they were behind them. Jim Stillwagon, a former all-American middle guard, said he wanted to look in the players' eyes and make sure they were fired up.

Our defense played well early, and we led 12-3 at halftime. But the usually mild-mannered Coop thought it should've been more. He went on a tirade at the half that ended with him punching a dent in the blackboard. It was completely out of character—and fired up the team even more. Offensive tackle Korey Stringer said, "It was a bad day for the blackboard."

Midway through the fourth quarter, we were leading 15-6 when Michigan quarterback Todd Collins dropped back to pass. Luke was rushing the passer and got a paw up that batted the ball into the air. He hauled it in and was tackled at the Wolverines' twenty-two.

Five plays later, we scored the clinching touchdown for a 22-6 victory, the first win over Michigan since Earle Bruce's last game in 1987.

"It's a good thing if you don't watch the rest of that game because the rest of that game was not real good [for me]," Luke said with a chuckle. "I think that might have been my second career interception, and with exactly zero yards return, as usual. But that was the only time of my playing career that we won that game."

As the final seconds ran off the clock, the fans stormed the field. Coach Cooper was carried off the field after leading the celebration. He got his new contract.

The adrenaline rush and the euphoria from the game lasted for hours. Several of the coaches and their wives went out to celebrate with the fans. Late into the night, we realized Coach Cooper had gone home, not out to celebrate. So we traveled to Upper Arlington to bring the celebration to him.

That was also the last season I was on the staff at Ohio State. I took the Akron head coaching job prior to the 1995 season, but Luke had two more big years with the Buckeyes. The 1995 squad was 11-0 and ranked number two before falling at Michigan, followed by a loss to Peyton Manning and Tennessee in the Citrus Bowl.

In Luke's senior season, Ohio State had to replace Heisman Trophy winner Eddie George, Biletnikoff winner Terry Glenn, all-Big Ten quarterback Bob Hoying, and first-round NFL draft pick Rickey Dudley at tight end. Yet the 1996 Buckeyes were even better than the 1995 squad, thanks to Luke and a stifling defense.

Ohio State finished as Big Ten cochamps but stumbled again versus Michigan in a costly 13-9 upset in Columbus. That defeat was the only blemish in a season that concluded with a number two ranking in the final polls.

Luke teamed with Vrabel and Finkes to form an imposing defensive line that was the soul of that squad.

"You had a group of guys that played a lot of ball together," Luke said. "We all lived together and hung out together and spent a lot of time together for those years. You're playing for each other as much as anything."

"I look back at my college career and without the guys that were around me . . . I wasn't great or anything but the guys who were around me were damn good. Mike Vrabel had fourteen sacks, and he says I helped make him better. But to be honest with you, his ass helped make me [better]."

Just a couple of days before the Rose Bowl game against undefeated and second-ranked Arizona State, Luke tore his pectoral muscle. Such an injury can make it difficult to raise your arm, let alone play football. Luke wouldn't think of sitting out the final game of his career with teammates who had become like brothers. He played the entire Rose Bowl in tremendous pain.

Deep in the fourth quarter, Arizona State quarterback Jake "The Snake" Plummer eluded a fierce pass rush that included Luke and squirted free for an 11-yard TD dash that gave the Sun Devils a 17–14 edge with 1:40 to play. The TV cameras captured the utter frustration on Luke's face just after Plummer scored.

"First of all, we had just lost to Michigan in a game we should have never lost in a million years," Luke said. "Then in the Rose Bowl, to play like we had defensively and then feel like you're going to lose it at the end. . . . You just think about those guys you've shed the blood, sweat, and tears with all those years, and the focus was finally on us, and that's how it ends up? In that moment, it was tough."

When Joe Germaine tossed a short touchdown pass to David Boston with nineteen seconds remaining to give Ohio State the win, it capped one of the most thrilling Rose Bowl games ever and provided a more palatable ending to Luke's Buckeye career.

"It's okay to talk about it now," Luke said. "I was definitely hurt, but it was worth it."

Luke signed as an undrafted free agent with the New Orleans Saints, but an ACL tear ended his football career, and he returned to Ohio State as a graduate assistant in 1999.

After I became the head coach at the University of Akron, I was looking for a defensive line coach. I remember talking to Dave Kennedy, the strength coach at Ohio State at that time, about hiring Luke. I told Dave I was concerned that Luke had very little coaching experience.

"Are you crazy?" Kennedy said in the blunt fashion he was known for, and in far more colorful language than I can share here. "If you have a chance to hire Luke Fickell, make that happen right now."

Of course Dave was right. Luke immediately became one of our best recruiters. He signed Domenik Hixon out of Columbus. Dominic ended up being one of the best players ever at the University of Akron and went on to a Super Bowl career with the New York Giants.

"Now that I'm in a position where I am today, and looking back on it, I'm like, 'Why in the hell would you have hired me?'" Luke asked me. "You're looking for guys that have experience. You had to take a leap of faith to put someone so young in a role like that, where you trust in the people dealing with young men.

"I say all the time that the best thing that ever happened to me was that I went to Akron for two years because all I knew was where I played in the Big Ten and being at Ohio State. You don't recognize how spoiled you might be, whether it's the resources, whether it's the attention, all those different things are shaping you.

"I mean, when I got to Akron, it was 'You mean our guys don't have their own lot? They must drive over to the field from campus?' Just stuff that you took for granted before."

While it was a different world for Luke at Akron, the experience stayed with him as he developed that mantra of "one heartbeat" and the capacity to overcome challenging circumstances from a disadvantaged standpoint in terms of talent, resources, etc.

"It was definitely a baptism by fire," Luke said. "But I probably accelerated through a lot of learning through that adversity, figuring out who you are, the leadership angle, different things like that."

The players Luke coached at Akron started to play at a higher level, and Coach Fickell demanded that they bring that same edge to practice every day—as he did at OSU.

On a personal level, I witnessed the fierce competitor that Luke Fickell has always been, both on the racquetball court with his fellow coach and former NFL offensive lineman Keith Uecker and on the golf course with his former teammate and later NFL Head Coach Mike Vrabel.

As far as toughness, my friend Mike Zucker tells a story of Luke ripping a treble hook out of the bridge of his nose on a bass fishing trip. A couple of other coaching friends tell a story about Luke wrestling a wild boar on a night hunt in Texas.

I once took him deer hunting on some property in southeast Ohio owned by my friend Rollie Layfield. Luke had never hunted deer before, but before the day was over, he had kicked up and shot at more deer than anyone else in the hunting party. If he was going to fail, it wouldn't be from lack of trying. Luke was always willing to jump in and try to win at anything.

After two years on my staff, Luke interviewed with Jim Tressel at Ohio State and was hired as the special team's coordinator before the 2002 season. It was a magical season that ended in a national championship for the Buckeyes, in no small part due to special teams. In punter Andy Groom and place kicker Mike Nugent, Ohio State had the best special teams combination in the country. No one knew better how to take advantage of a special team's edge than Jim Tressel, who once famously said, "The punt is the most important play in football."

Tressel also had a huge influence on Luke and further entrenched the teamwork benchmark into his DNA.

"When I interviewed with Jim Tressel, we talked for two hours, and not one thing was said about football," Luke said. "I'm thinking, This is not exactly what I expected. But then you recognize that if somebody is going to hire you, what he wants to talk about is what it's going to be about if you end up there."

In 2004, Luke became the linebackers coach and in 2005 added the title of co-defensive coordinator at Ohio State. In 2010, he was chosen the Assistant Coach of the Year by the American Football Coaches Association.

When OSU parted ways with Jim Tressel just before Memorial Day in 2011, the school administration asked Luke to step in as the interim coach. It was an impossible situation. The Buckeyes were facing NCAA penalties that included probation and recruiting limitations and eventually, following the 2012 season, were slapped with a bowl ban. It was late in the football calendar; spring practice had already concluded, and summer camp was barely two months away. The powers that be asked Luke to step in and guide the program through the 2012 season.

To make things even more difficult, true freshman Braxton Miller proved to be the most talented quarterback on the team. That would be a rugged scenario for any head coach, let alone an interim head coach, not to mention someone who had never been a head coach before at any level.

Luke took it all in stride. He sought advice where he could and patched together a 6-6 season that resulted in a bowl berth.

When Ohio State hired Urban Meyer as the full-time head coach in November 2011, he was encouraged to retain Luke on his 2012 staff. Meyer could have been uneasy about that scenario, but after a meeting between the two men and their wives, the offer was extended to keep the Buckeye alum in Columbus.

Luke had chances to leave to head up his own program, to be a coordinator at another school. Yet again, he took the unorthodox path.

"The reality is what is tough, those are the situations that make you better, make you grow," Luke said. "Everybody should want to be challenged. Comfort isn't the greatest thing in the world."

Meyer appreciated the continuity Luke provided for the returning staff and players.

"He was in a very interesting situation before I got here, and he had no real reason to be as loyal to me as he has been," Meyer said at that time. "He's an Ohio guy. He's a Buckeye. I knew him from afar. I watched closely how he handled this situation. I thought, He's a man's man. Obviously, he's everything you hope for Ohio State."

In December 2016, Luke took the head coaching job at the University of Cincinnati. He succeeded Tommy Tuberville, who had gone 4-8 that season, including 1-7 in the American Athletic Conference.

Now he was in a situation where his experience at Akron probably helped him. The mantra of one heartbeat was never needed more than at this point. The Bearcats were going to have to play better as a team than perhaps their talent level might indicate.

Luke's first team, in 2017, was also 4-8, but his second year the program experienced a tremendous turnaround, going 11-2, including a Military Bowl win over Virginia Tech. Luke was chosen the AAC Coach of the Year, and the Bearcats were suddenly a force in the conference.

Cincinnati finished 11-3 in 2019 and again won the American Athletic Conference. In the 2020 COVID season, UC went 9-1, 6-0 in the AAC, and ranked number eight in the final national polls. That campaign shot expectations through the roof for 2021, and the Bearcats were ready for them.

Fickell's team started the year ranked number eight in the polls and won at Indiana and at number nine Notre Dame as part of a 4-0 start. Suddenly, Luke had a top five squad on his hands, and they soon advanced to number two after wins over Temple, Central Florida, and Navy.

Then came a noon game at Tulane, a club that had won only two games that year. Cincinnati played its worst half of the season and managed just a 14-12 halftime lead. Yet this is where Luke saw his team go to another level.

"It was a bad game, where nothing was going well," Luke remembered. "The first half was just awful, and it was a humbling experience for the entire team. But to be honest, it was almost like a weight was lifted off the group after that, where we kind of recognized the joy of playing together and quit worrying about where this thing is going to lead to in the very end. Let's enjoy the things that we're doing and continue to grow from this point. We were different after that. It was almost like a turning point for us."

UC pulled away for a 31-12 win and convincingly handled the remainder of its schedule. Cincinnati finished 13-0, ranked number four, and qualified for the College Football Playoffs. It was the first and only time as of this writing that a team outside the Power 5 conference qualified for the four-team playoffs.

Losing 27-6 to number-one-ranked Alabama in the national semifinals became a footnote to all that team accomplished under Luke's leadership.

"You've got to have people that have the same belief systems," Luke said. "You're going to make some gut decisions on some people, but you never really know until you've been in adverse situations with them, go through some battles, go through some fires, what do you really know? You hope they grow a helluva lot."

He stayed at UC for one more autumn, a 9-4 season, before accepting the head coaching job at Wisconsin prior to the 2023 season.

Luke took his mantra of "TEAM" (Together Everyone Achieves More) and began to instill it into the Badgers' program too.

It was a big change for Luke and his wife, Amy, and their six kids, who were lifelong Ohioans. But just as his family provided the grounded support he enjoyed growing up, his family ties provide a similar foundation now—one that he draws from at home and at work. It's one heartbeat.

"It's the example that we set, the things we do every single day, that I think is a helluva lot more important than the rah-rah speeches and all the other things that people see on Saturdays," Luke said. "I learned that kind of thing from my father at a young age. He's just a guy that worked on a railroad, but he was one of those guys that what you say you're going to do, you do. I mean, if you don't set that example yourself, if you're not living it, if you aren't that example for the people around you, how do you really expect that from them?"

Team Culture

It's important to have courage and skill and be a tireless worker. But there is no "I" in team excellence. In business and in athletics the thing that counts the most is teamwork.

Edgar Albert Guest noted the philosophy in his poem:

TEAMWORK
It's all very well to have courage and skill
And it's fine to be counted a star,
But the single deed with its touch of thrill
Doesn't tell the man you are;
For there's no lone hand in the game we play,
We must work to a bigger scheme,
And the thing that counts in the world to-day Is,
How do you pull with the team?

They may sound your praise and call you great,
They may single you out for fame,
But you must work with your running mate
Or you'll never win the game;
Oh, never the work of life is done
By the man with a selfish dream,
For the battle is lost or the battle is won
By the spirit of the team.
You may think it fine to be praised for skill,
But a greater thing to do Is to set your mind and set your will
On the goal that's just in view;
It's helping your fellowman to score
When his chances hopeless seem;
It's forgetting self till the game is over
And fighting for the team.

No one, no matter how talented, can do it on their own!

Building team culture begins in the first team meeting. Never minimize the importance of this meeting. There is only one opportunity to make a positive first impression. Give as many people as possible the opportunity for an introduction at this first meeting. Have the team take out their phones and add your cell number to their contacts.

Begin the meeting with an acknowledgment that leadership change can be unsettling to a team. Challenge the team to understand that change is a constant in life and that winners in life see change as an opportunity.

Assure the team that you will lead them with a sense of urgency and work every day to earn their trust. Make sure you have the full attention of the team and that there are no misunderstandings. Tell the team they will be winners. Tell the team you will help them reach excellence in all areas of their life.

At the end of the meeting, schedule as many personal meetings with as many team members as possible. In these meetings give them the opportunity to commit to you as their new leader. Make it clear the number one thing you want is loyalty, and the number one thing they will get from you is respect.

I recall my individual meeting with Jason Taylor at the University of Akron after our first team meeting.

Jason not only accepted the change in leadership; he committed to a plan that would lead him to becoming a third-round NFL draft pick for the Miami Dolphins and an eventual member of the Pro Football Hall of Fame.

The capacity to be loyal and respect others is a great foundation for team excellence. To be loyal is to care about people.

Mother Teresa said, *"There are two types of people—people who need help and people who help people who need help."*

This is at the core of a team or a family. Helping others unconditionally *is* "Team Brotherhood," or love. Teams with this culture have teammates who care about one another. They are selfless. They share one heartbeat.

Great team culture is inclusive and belonging. The Latin for community is *communitas*, which means "shared by many." *Communitas* derives from "com," which means "together," and "munus," which means "gift to one another."

The definition of a true team is knowing that as individuals we belong to each other, we need each other, we affect each other. Those traits make us a team. The culture of a team must be built around the belief that the collective sum of a team is greater than its individual parts. "We makes me stronger." The secret of the team's strength is its ability to work together. Two is better than one if you are as one. Just imagine an entire team acting as one.

Team culture allows common people to achieve uncommon results. A team mentality and a group identity are easy concepts to understand but difficult to achieve.

There is a selfish beast in every one of us that makes it difficult to totally commit to a group effort. We all live within the framework of some type of team.

Vince Lombardi said, "Individual commitment to a group effort—that's what makes a team work, a company work, a society work, a civilization work."

Studies have shown that when people feel their thoughts are valued, they are more productive. Specific, well-defined jobs and roles on a team forge a culture of personal value as well as respect for the value of others on the team. This in turn also has a positive impact on the morale and motivation of a team.

Trust and integrity may be the two most important characteristics of team culture. Trust is not only the basic glue that holds a team together, but it also provides an enduring bond for great teams. Trust is the truth—face-to-face—no memos. Conflict is good and should not be avoided with a team built on trust. Attack the truth head on and the team will never be jeopardized. Never assume that there is trust on a team. Earn it!

Every few seasons I would do an anonymous survey with the teams I coached. I would ask the players:

Do you trust the competence of your leaders?

Do you trust the character of your leaders?

Do you trust your teammates, offense, defense, special teams, offseason program?

Have you ever been in a situation on this team that caused you to lose trust?

What can the leaders on this team do to build trust?

The results of these surveys always provided helpful insights for team culture building. Trust and integrity have a set of basic rules: Do the right thing. Be genuine. Be yourself. Be accountable. Be honest. Be humble. Be respectful. Honor your commitments.

"Take pride in being an individual of integrity. . . . People will gravitate to you, seek your counsel, and cherish your friendship."–Lou Holtz

Team Leadership

"A team leader doesn't get his platoon to go by getting up and shouting, 'I am smarter, I am bigger, I am stronger, I am the leader." He gets men to go along with him because they want to do it for him and they believe in him."–Dwight D. Eisenhower

Team culture reflects leadership. Leaders on the team have the courage to be a servant to the purpose or the mission of the team. Leaders understand their responsibilities come in the following order: to the overall organization, to the team, and then to the individuals on the team. Leaders and their own interest and comfort must come last.

Coach Jim Tressel and I spoke on leadership at the spring 2024 Major Issues Lecture Series, sponsored by the Ashbrook Center at Ashland University. Jim, a national championship coach at Ohio State, identified the "ability to serve" as the most important characteristic of leadership.

When I was asked to define leadership, I quoted John Maxwell's *The 21 Irrefutable Laws of Leadership*: "the ability to influence, as simple as that." Good or True, leadership is the ability to influence or move a team or an individual on the team in a positive direction. Poor or False, leadership is just the opposite. Poor or False leaders can tear teams apart and drive them to failure or at best mediocrity. Good or True leaders strive to reach excellence.

There are many ways to facilitate leadership. I would always have the team elect fifteen accountability captains, with each captain representing 10 percent of the team. A leadership team within the team. The captains would be trained in leadership. Accountability captains would meet together and also with their teams. Accountability teams would spend time together in camp, compete together in the off season, and plan team activities and community service together.

Most importantly, accountability captains handled team discipline by taking responsibility for the actions of the members of their team.

One season a group of accountability captains developed a team leadership code by researching and reading the most compelling books they could find on leadership. Many of the books selected by the accountability captains were either written by military leaders or to train future military leaders. I have always felt that next to serving in the military, participating on a team in a competitive sport is the best preparation for young people in life—and for future leadership opportunities.

One of the books selected was the *Ranger Handbook*. My oldest son was a graduate of the United States Military Academy at West Point and was an Army Ranger. I remember visiting him after he returned from leading an Army infantry unit in Iraq. His staff meeting room was not very different from the room where I met with my staff back at the school.

There was one very significant difference. In my facility were pictures of all-Americans and championship teams. If I did a poor job as a leader, there would be fewer pictures, and I might get fired. In his staff room were pictures of the eighteen-, nineteen-, and twenty-year-old young men who didn't make it home to their mother or wife or children.

Ben seldom talks about his time in Iraq. But after reading an account of his experience in Ramadi, Iraq, I know why he was awarded the Bronze Star. It took a great leader to be able to complete the mission and get everyone of his men back to their families.

Poor leadership in the military has the most tragic consequences. I believe this is why the military has the best trained leaders and their books on leadership are the best written.

Below is the leadership code adopted by the Accountability Captains.

- I will be a servant to our cause.
- I will put the team first and take responsibility for the young players.
- I will not make or accept excuses.
- I will have the courage to confront.
- I will make it clear where I stand and what I believe.
- I will maintain my integrity in what I say and what I do.
- I will be self-motivated at all times.
- I will be relentless in my preparation and play with confidence.
- I will compete against perfection.
- I will lead from the front.

There are many types of leaders. There are quiet leaders who are great role models. There are vocal leaders who are enthusiastic. There are leaders who have earned their position, and there are leaders who have been crowned because of their standing. There are also uncrowned leaders who have no position, status, or title. They are not a captain or a senior or a four-year starter. I always look for these uncrowned leaders.

I remember a young man on one of my teams who was a true freshman. His name was Justin Hood. He went on to become a great captain and team leader on one of our championship teams. Today he has become a leader in the NFL as the defensive back coach for the Atlanta Falcons.

As a true freshman, he was the leader of the best scout team in America. No one asked him to take this position. There was no position for a scout team leader. But there was a need, there was a void, and Justin has spent his entire life looking for opportunities to lead.

The recent survey results of executives in business and sport on the characteristics of team leaders listed competence atop all other traits. Along with competence comes credibility and confidence. This is why in sport your best leaders are often your best players, and in business your best leaders are often the most productive in their jobs.

The survey identified additional "most important" characteristics of leaders: honest, selfless, inspiring, hardworking, accountable, and courageous. When I coach leadership, I also teach the truth and fundamentals of team leadership.

In 2012, I was asked to speak to the graduates of Leadership Ashland. The class signed and presented me with the book *The Truth About Leadership* by James Kouzes and Barry Posner. In this book, the authors identify ten truths that became my fundamentals of leadership:

1. Believe you can make a difference. Words and actions can inspire.
2. Credibility is the foundation. Confidence is a characteristic of strong leaders.
3. Values drive commitment. Communicate team priorities that reflect personal and team values.
4. Focus on the future. Turn the page and stay focused on the next play, the next game.
5. You can't do it alone. Cultivate a bond on the team to a common cause.
6. Trust rules. Commit to actions that earn trust and eliminate actions that destroy trust.
7. No challenge, no greatness. Have the courage to confront risk and the uncertainty of change.

8. Lead by example. Lead from the front and walk the talk.
9. Leaders are learners. Be a better leader tomorrow than today.
10. Lead from the heart. Be passionate and love the team.

Team Communication
"Effective teamwork begins and ends with communication,"
–Mike Krzyzewski

Great team leaders are master communicators. Team culture is supported and nourished through open, honest, and clear communication. When a leader fails it is often because of poor communication. Too often today our communication skills are compromised because of the impersonal aspect of our phones and other technology.

Text messages and emails have replaced our ability to personally communicate. For effective team leadership, communication skills are just as important as technical skills.

The best-selling book *Successful Coaching* by Ranier Martens identifies three dimensions of communication: sending-receiving, verbal-nonverbal, and content-emotion. Strong leaders are typically better at the sending, verbal, and content sides of these dimensions.

When a leader makes a commitment to becoming a better communicator, it traditionally involves becoming a better listener or learning to be more consistent with their emotional and nonverbal communication. Including a small digital image, an emoji, with a text message does not cover the emotional and nonverbal dimension requirements of being an effective communicator.

Committed listening, or "receiving," is the foundation of communication. Being a committed listener often means suspending judgment. There are many listening strategies for effective communication in leading a team. I learned to use empathetic questions to draw out insights. We want to ask questions to help recreate events. Ask for specific examples and test assumptions as you listen. All these strategies will improve a team leader's ability to communicate.

Author Roy Bennett said this about listening, "Listen with curiosity. Speak honestly. Act with integrity. The greatest problem with communication is we don't listen to understand. We listen to reply. When we listen with curiosity, we don't listen with the intent to reply. We listen for what's behind the words."

If you ask a member of your team how their family is, how their grades are, or how they feel, the answer will always be the same: okay. If you ask a member of your team what games their parents have attended, what classes they are taking this semester and which they like or dislike most, or what they're doing to treat that shoulder injury, you may learn something about the person.

The team feeds off the team leader's communication, verbal and nonverbal. After losing a game, you will have a difficult time getting your team back up if you walk around all week with your head down.

It is also important that the team leader's message be consistent. After a loss is not the best time to communicate. Emotions run high, and it is easy to say something to the team that you can't get back.

After turning the corner at the University of Akron, we lost to a team that we should have beaten. I was upset and ripped into the team after the game. The next day, senior captain and all-league kicker Zac Derr stopped in my office. He told me the team was hurting and my personal insults after the loss were not consistent with how they thought I felt about them.

I apologized. I appreciated his honesty. I learned a valuable lesson in team communication. Furthermore, if a team member takes the time, and finds the courage, to look you up with a question, put your phone down and listen.

Blake Dickson was a senior captain on our offensive line early in our Ashland tenure. He stopped in the office one day, but it took me about six questions before I discovered why. He finally admitted his teammates were upset with him. He told me he had really gotten after them on the bench early in the game Saturday. He started to apologize. I told him no need. He was trying to win games, not friends. He had earned the right to get after the other players, and nothing is stronger than a teammate holding other teammates accountable. With the leadership of players like Blake Dickson, we won nine games that year.

To enhance your ability to communicate, there are four accountability questions that can be used as a teacher, as a coach, and as a team leader. These questions will add to the team leader's ability to teach without lecturing or judging. They will also add to a leader's ability to give ownership to the members of the team.

The four accountability questions are as follows:
1. What did you do?
2. Was it right or wrong?
3. What could you have done?
4. What will you do next time?

A team leader's communication serves any or all of four purposes: to instruct, encourage, praise, or criticize. Too often there is too much criticism and too little instruction. Another way to improve communication is to make sure the praise and the criticism are as timely and specific as possible.

Effective communication is critical for team culture. To be an effective team leader one needs to provide meaningful feedback on a regular basis. To make the feedback meaningful, always speak with the intent to link the feedback to what the team cares about.

Feedback should not be linked to fear (fear is a short-term motivator). Make feedback an opportunity, not a threat, and focus on what is missing, not what is wrong.

Leading a team is engaging the team in communication. For this to happen there must be an agreement from the team that they want to be supported and challenged. Not everyone on a team will accept this challenge, and simply put, no matter how well you communicate, "you can't coach hostages."

Know the difference between people who are just on the team and those who are committed to the team. Just being on a team benefits personal ambition and involves blaming others, making excuses, and asking, "What's in it for me?"

Being committed to the team benefits team ambition and involves accepting responsibility and asking, "What's in it for us?" Engage in communication with those committed to the team, and a great team culture will become a reality.

The Law of the Chain
"A chain is no stronger than its weakest link, and life is after all a chain."—William James

As a competitor, I would always be more creative in my motivation of the team in rivalry games like Massillon-McKinley, Ohio State-Michigan, Akron-Kent State, or Ashland-Findlay. At Ashland, we were 12-4 versus our rival Findlay. At Massillon, we were 3-1 versus our rival McKinley. At Akron, we were 7-2 versus our rival Kent State. I have always credited our team culture for our success in rivalry games.

Before one Akron-Kent State game, I stopped at the hardware store on my way to the Sunday team meeting. I purchased a bundle of thin boards. I asked different players at the meeting to stand in front of the room to break the single boards over their knees. They had no problem.

Then I stacked eight boards together and asked if anyone would be able to break the boards now. No one tried.

Each of the boards represented a position group on our team, and the eight boards stacked together represented the team. I glued the boards together and painted these words on the front of the board:

"Oh, never the work of life is done by the man with a selfish dream, the battle is lost, or the battle is won by the spirit of the team."—Edgar A Guest.

I also purchased a long chain with which to hang the board. I promised all the seniors that with a win, they would get a link of chain as a token of their team commitment. I added these words to the board: "and a team is only as strong as its weakest link."

It is the law of the chain. The strength of the team will always be impacted by its weakest link. The team is not for everyone. Not everyone will take the journey, or should take the journey, or can take the journey. Some just don't want to go. Some won't change or grow. Some have a different agenda or other plans. Some are just not capable; the issue is ability. Thank these people for their past contributions, wish them well, and move on.

Many times, a team leader will choose to serve, to save, or to train the weak links to become stronger.

Several things will happen when a weak link remains on the team. The team will identify the weak links. The stronger members of the team will either ignore the person and allow the team to suffer or help the person attempt to make the team successful. If they are good teammates, they will help.

Regardless of what they do, there will always be resentment. No one likes to lose, and a team is only as strong as its weakest link. Eventually the stronger members of the team become less effective and begin to question the team leader's ability and courage to make difficult decisions for the good of the team.

Team leadership will never be easy, and team culture will always reflect team leadership. A team can't win or be successful without leadership. Team excellence will never be achieved without a leader who is willing to fight for the team!

"Forgetting self 'til the game is over and fighting for the team."–Edgar A Guest

PARADOXICAL COMMANDMENTS OF LEADERSHIP

1. *People are illogical, unreasonable, and self-centered. Love them anyway.*
2. *If you do good, people will accuse you of selfish ulterior motives. Do good anyway.*
3. *If you are successful, you win false friends and true enemies. Succeed anyway.*
4. *The good you do today will be forgotten tomorrow. Do good anyway.*
5. *Honesty and frankness make you vulnerable. Be honest and frank anyway.*
6. *The biggest men with the biggest ideas can be shot down by the smallest men with the smallest minds. Think big anyway,*
7. *People favor underdogs but follow only top dogs. Fight for a few underdogs anyway.*
8. *What you spend years building may be destroyed overnight. Build anyway.*
9. *People really need help but may attack you if you do help them. Help them anyway.*

10. Give the world the best you have, and you'll get kicked in the teeth. Give the world the best you have anyway.

Dr. Kent M. Keith, Author of Paradoxical Commandments

Key Points for One Heartbeat

1. Building team culture begins at the first team meeting.
2. Loyalty and respect are at the core of team building.
3. Trust and integrity are the most important characteristics of team culture.
4. Team culture reflects leadership.
5. Good or True leadership is the ability to influence or move a team or a player on the team in a positive direction.
6. Anyone can lead. Find a need and believe you can make a positive difference.
7. Great team leaders are master communicators.
8. Leaders most often fail because of poor communication.
9. The strength of the team will always be impacted by the weakest link.
10. Team excellence will never be achieved without a leader who is willing to fight for the team.

PART TWO:
FOCUS ON THE PROCESS

The process for building a winner begins with hope. Hope is dreaming dreams and setting goals. Goals are milestones in the pursuit of our dreams, and they provide a team with direction. The world makes room for teams that know where they are going. Goal setting also creates a team's cause. There is nothing stronger on a team than a common cause, one that everyone on the team believes in and is willing to fight for.

Winning teams state what they want to accomplish and how they plan to do it. They follow the plan, plan the work, and work the plan. The plan is the climb. Winning teams climb until their dreams come true. A goal without a plan is worthless, and a plan without belief will fail. Regardless of how good the plan is, if the team is not all in, it will not work. Sell the plan. Build confidence in the plan. Believe in yourself. Believe in the team. Believe in the cause.

–CHAPTER FIVE–
DARE TO DREAM

"Every great dream begins with a dreamer. Always remember, you have the strength, the patience, and the passion to reach for the stars to change the world."—Harriet Tubman

Photo of Steve Clinkscale

Bio Box: Steve Clinkscale, NFL assistant coach: Los Angeles Chargers

Background: Steve was born September 21, 1977. He is the oldest of four children. Steve's father, John Arthur Clinkscale Jr., was a Navy veteran and a Youngstown police officer for nearly twenty years. His mother, Yvonne, worked with troubled juveniles. Her places of employment included Belmont Pines, a residential treatment facility for those suffering acute behavioral issues.

Athletic Achievement: A standout in football and track at Youngstown Chaney High School, Steve was recruited to Ashland University. At AU he was a four-year starter at defensive back and team captain. He was selected to play in the NCAA Division II All-Star game, the 2000 Snow Bowl, following the 1999 season. Clink was part of the Eagles' 1997 Midwest Intercollegiate Football Conference championship squad, which earned an NCAA Division II postseason berth.

Scholastic Achievement: Clinkscale graduated from Division II Ashland University in 2000 with a degree in sports science and a focus on therapeutic recreation.

Professional Achievement: Steve was co-defensive coordinator for the 2023 national champion Michigan Wolverines. He was also the defensive coordinator at the University of Cincinnati. His coaching career began in 2001 at Ashland University and included stops at Western Carolina, Toledo, Illinois, Cincinnati, Kentucky, and Michigan before his move to the Los Angeles Chargers as their defensive backs coach in 2024.

Personal: Steven and his wife, Elaine, have six children: Brandon, Isaiah, Elijah, Zion, Zivon, and Carlo.

Steve Clinkscale can reflect on his career in wonder. It started in the tough streets of Youngstown, Ohio, and as of this writing has reached an NFL coaching box. It began with a sudden change in occupation just after he earned his college degree. The journey included several stops on the coaching carousel, featured a national championship as a co-defensive coordinator at the University of Michigan, and reached the highest level as an assistant coach with the Los Angeles Chargers.

Still, Steve rarely Dared to Dream of such a climb, even as a youngster. In fact, unlike several people who draw a paycheck in professional sports, he wasn't groomed in athletics. He was simply too busy focusing on whatever was on his plate at the time.

"I liked catching critters, going fishing, playing two-square, football, and running sprints, stuff like that," Steve said of his upbringing. "That really occupied my mind, I never even watched too many sporting events on TV because my parents kept us busy on the weekends. They were strict at home about chores and homework."

Hence, Steve didn't grow up with athletic heroes. He looked to his youth coaches for athletic inspiration, a role he would fill for others as an adult.

Clink's family lived on the east side of Youngstown, a rugged, gritty area bordering on metropolitan status but teetering on decay from decades of neglect. When Steve was still an elementary school student, his family moved to the Brier Hill section on the north side. That is where he first found his athletic aptitude, playing youth football for the South Side Braves in the Volney Rogers league.

"It was an entirely different side of town for me," Clink said. "I learned toughness and grit and learned how to play the game at a higher level because I didn't know much of anything at that point."

In junior high, he attended St. Anthony's, and although he was a year younger than his peers, he proved to be one of the football team's better players.

At this point, Steve already had full scope of some of the troubles that plagued his hometown. Violence was a fact of life in a city decimated by the closure of the steel mills—and frequently referred to as the belt buckle of the Rust Belt. Youngstown State University

President Jim Tressel, a legendary football coach at YSU and Ohio State, noted the community's despondence after losing nearly fifty thousand jobs in a five-year period ending in the early 1980s.

Steve and his parents were determined his future would not be dictated by such surroundings.

"My motivation was really survival," Steve said. "I thought the best way to survive Youngstown was to get in a position where I can go to college and not have to worry about the environment."

When he left junior high school, Steve was able to choose which public high school he would attend by filling out something called a racial balance form. He selected Chaney, which he considered the city's best public high school for its combination of athletics and academics.

Chaney famously produced 1942 Heisman Trophy winner Frank Sinkwich, who was a star for Coach Wally Butts at Georgia. Sinkwich went on to become an All-Pro for the NFL's Detroit Lions and was voted the NFL MVP in 1944. When asked how he had become such a great athlete, Sinkwich noted Youngstown played a role.

"I learned early in neighborhood pickup games that I had the desire to compete," Sinkwich said. "When people ask why I succeeded in athletics, I always say, 'I didn't want to get beat.'"

Steve knew well that chip on his shoulder that Sinkwich carried. It was something so many Youngstown-area athletes have in common to this day. A number of them Dare to Dream.

"It's not just talent that gets you where you need to be. I'm still trying to prove everybody wrong, that somebody, a young man from Youngstown, can succeed," Clink said. "You must work hard and have that desire to achieve what others believe you're not able to do. That's how a lot of kids from Youngstown are wired, and I'm Youngstown through and through."

At Chaney, Steve thrived under the tutelage of Head Coach Ron Berdis. In twenty years with the Cowboys, Berdis had thirteen winning seasons, compiled a 128-77 record, won fourteen City Series titles, and qualified for the Ohio High School Athletic Association playoffs eight times. His best team was the 1997 squad, which finished as state runner-up not long after Clink graduated. Berdis was inducted into the Ohio High School Football Coaches Association Hall of Fame in

2024.

Berdis was immediately impressed with Clinkscale. Steve started on special teams as a sophomore and was a standout his junior and senior year as a fullback and outside linebacker. A bit undersized at five foot eleven and 170 pounds, he found a collegiate fit at Division II Ashland.

"Ashland had some success in the past, and it was unique at the time," Steve said. "It was the only Division II school in the state of Ohio. I thought it would be competitive, and I was just excited about it. Not being in the city anymore, being in a little safer environment, it was appealing to me."

Steve earned playing time as a red-shirt freshman for Head Coach Gary Keller. The Eagles' best season was Clink's sophomore campaign, when they won the 1997 Midwest Intercollegiate Football Conference championship. Four of that team's last five wins were by a TD or less, including a stirring 27-20 homecoming victory over Saginaw Valley State. AU qualified for the NCAA Division II playoffs to conclude that season.

In 1999, Steve was a team captain and selected to compete in the Division II national all-star game, known as the Snow Bowl at that time. An NFL career wasn't in the cards, but Steve was a strong student, and his mother was a big influence guiding him toward a potential career in nursing.

With a degree in sports science and a focus on therapeutic recreation, Steve figured football was simply a vehicle—his Dare to Dream—in a quest to rise above the challenging streets of Youngstown. He moved to Maryland to begin his professional career and was there for just under a year when he took an internship opportunity that led to a full-time job back in Ohio. He accepted the position at a hospital and had been just a couple of months into that new job when his former coach called about a coaching opening on the Ashland University football staff.

"Coach Keller called me maybe three days before camp started and said one of his coaches, Doug DeVito, was going to take a step back and wondered if I was interested," Clink said. "He just said, 'The way you carry yourself as a player, the way you've always been a guy who speaks his mind at the right time, I need men like that around me.'

"I was like, 'What the hell?' So I went down there, and I didn't know anything about coaching, and I thought I was going to be like a player, where you do these two-a-days and you break in between.

"It wasn't like that at all. You think of the players being exhausted because of all the running and everything; the coaches are working in between those meetings and when the players are sleeping. I was more exhausted and tired as a coach. I was just learning this new profession, and now I'm going to start learning this one, but it just kind of took off from there. I knew I had found my niche."

Steve was a bit concerned he may have been disappointing his parents by changing his career path, but his mother reassured him.

"She said, 'You've always been a coach, a leader, and a person who's always been a go-getter," Steve told the *Warren Tribune Chronicle*. "You've always been able to communicate, boss people around. She felt that I always had those qualities to be a coach, and now it's gotten to where it's taken off for me."

A couple of years after his hiring, the entire AU coaching staff was dismissed.

"That was a pretty big setback, because I was coaching with the staff that I played for," Steve said. "That was a big hurdle to overcome."

The athletic director who hired me, Bill Goldring, strongly recommended I interview Steve. Bill always had a good feel for people and hiring people who fit at Ashland. Steve fit. He was an alumnus. He was an outstanding student and football player at AU.

"When I first took the [coaching job] under Coach Keller, my number one concern was the African American students not finishing school there when I was a player," Steve said. "My first year there [as a player], we would get a lot of talented young men, and we had a study table. But after that, we didn't have it. I watched guys come in and out, and one of them was Delano Smith, a good friend of mine. He played as a true freshman and then failed out of school. Then he went back and took care of his business while he was living in Toledo and came back and finished his career, and he had a great career.

"But he was really the only success story that was able to do that. Most of them would fail out and you'd never see them again. It wasn't just the African American student, but that's how I felt, like those were the guys that weren't having success, the retention that we needed. So when I took the job, I asked to oversee academics. That was my major concern. It wasn't even about football. I just wanted to make sure those guys would graduate. That was really the only reason why I wanted to take the job, to be honest with you. I ran the study table on my own, helped the guys get tutors—that was really my focus."

I met Steve for the first time at the Wendy's on US 250 just outside of Ashland. He was well prepared for this unofficial interview, and he made a great first impression. I was most impressed with his passion and commitment to AU football and to the academics of the AU football players, including the study tables he had set up for the team.

It didn't take long to validate my initial thoughts about Coach Clinkscale. He had a strong feel for the players on the team. Who were the leaders? Who were the best players? He was also an excellent recruiter and evaluator of talent. He had recruited many of the really good players we had inherited and continued to recruit great players every season.

Most importantly, Steve convinced me we could win with this team. They were talented and gritty and would compete. They just needed some tough love. They needed to know we believed in them, and we asked them to recommit to us like they were being recruited for the first time all over again.

In the two years prior to me being hired to coach the Eagles, they had posted two consecutive two-win seasons. In our first year, we improved the program to 5-6. The second season, we won nine games. It was because of Coach Clinkscale's insights that we committed to winning with the team that Coach Keller had recruited. Too often with coaching changes the new coach wants all his own players and ends up continuing to lose with his team of new young players.

On a personal level, Steve was excited to start a family. I was sure he would make a fantastic father. He was a father figure and excellent role model to many of the young men on our team.

I wrote a letter of recommendation for Steve to help him adopt his son Isaiah.

"I remember you would let everybody come to practice and would get in your golf cart and go over to the families and visit," Steve told me. "You would just leave practice, go play with the kids, I mean, be on the ground, playing with the kids. And that changed my entire perception of what coaching was about.

"When I started to move on and work for different people, some did the same, some didn't. Some talked about it. Most talk, but most don't live it. So when I decided who I wanted to work for or work with, that became a big part of it.

"Jim Harbaugh is a big family man. He's got seven kids. Our families are invited anywhere. His family, the players' families, your family can come to practice every day if you want to."

One day the local car dealer Scott Harris stopped in my office to ask, "How is Stevie doing?" He told me he had become a mentor to Steve when he first came to Ashland. I could tell he cared a great deal for Steve. Scott told me in his own way that as soon as he met Steve, he knew he was special and destined for greatness. Since that meeting with Scott Harris, I can't count the number of people who have shared with me a similar feeling about Steve Clinkscale.

Steve and I both love to fish. When the bite was slow, we had lots of time to talk. Mostly about where we had been, and where we hoped to go. Not once did Steve ever talk about coaching in the NFL or being the co-defensive coordinator for the national champions. Steve often talked about making a difference and becoming his best self. To that end, I encouraged Steve to network a bit. I was pushing him to Dare to Dream.

On a recruiting trip one evening, I suggested to Steve that he go down to Columbus and hang out with Ohio State's coaches as much as he can, get out of his bubble, and bring back one or two things that can help our program.

"I started linking up with the Ohio State staff at the time, the Mel Tuckers of the world," Steve said. "Mel really gave me the big push to understand football, defensive back play, a little bit."

Steve was never that coach always on the phone looking for his next job. He was always focused on the task at hand. I told him once it was okay to dream about other opportunities in the game of football, but it was important to make where you coach the biggest, the best, and most important job in America. You must coach like you are going to be there your entire career. If you do that, you will get lots of opportunities to move on in coaching, and Coach Clinkscale has had lots of opportunities.

We added the title of linebackers coach to Steve's job description in his final season for us, and he was already serving as secondary coach as well as academic liaison. He was a demanding coach. He could love them up, but he wasn't afraid to rip his players either. That's not an easy balance to maintain, and in Steve's case, he was very close in age to our players when he was on staff. He continued to learn and grow.

In 2007, Steve's last year on our staff, Ashland made the Division II college football playoffs. After seven seasons at Ashland, Steve interviewed for and accepted a job at Western Carolina. He was Daring to Dream.

"It was hard because not only did I coach at Ashland for seven seasons, but I was also there as a player for five," Steve said. "At that point in my life, about a third of my life had been spent in Ashland. I had that comfort, and the fans and my family. I could be home in less than two hours, all that stuff. And suddenly, the next job opportunity was in North Carolina.

"I talked to a couple of my mentors about it, and they were all supportive. They told me at my age, I just had to take this opportunity, explore it and learn from it, the good and the bad. So I took a leap of faith."

Steve was defensive backs coach at Western Carolina for a year when he was offered a job as special teams coordinator and cornerbacks coach at Toledo under new Coach Tim Beckman. It was a rebuilding job, but Clink and Company were part of a renaissance in Rockets' football. Toledo posted three consecutive winning seasons, racked up a 21-18 record with two bowl appearances and a Mid-American Conference West Division cochampionship. The 2011 team earned a bid to the Military Bowl. When Beckman was offered the job at the University of Illinois, he took Steve with him as cornerbacks coach. That meant coaching in the Big Ten, a much higher profile. Daring to Dream was starting to bloom for Coach Clinkscale.

After a year with the Illini, Steve was hired by Tommy Tuberville in 2013 at the University of Cincinnati. Today Tommy Tuberville is a U.S. senator from Alabama. But at that time, he had just left Auburn shortly after leading them to a 13-0 record, the SEC title, and a Sugar Bowl championship in 2004. He remains the only coach in Auburn history to beat in-state rival Alabama six consecutive times. Steve worked under Coach Tuberville as the Bearcats played in three consecutive bowl games. Clink was the defensive coordinator during the 2015 season, which triggered his next opportunity.

Coach Mark Stoops, another Youngstown native, came calling in 2015 from the University of Kentucky. Vince Marrow, Steve's cousin and another Youngstown son, was already on the Wildcats' staff and advocated for Clink. It was also a chance to coach in the Southeastern Conference, the toughest league in Division I college football.

"Mark Stoops did a lot for me and helped me understand more about DB play and just all around what it takes to be a factor in these young men's lives," Steve said.

At this stop, Clink earned a reputation as a strong recruiter, a rugged chore in the SEC. His knack for connecting with talented young men as a recruiter of elite talent was paying dividends.

"I'm just myself," Steve told Jon Jansen during a podcast for Wolverines Wire, a University of Michigan fans website. "I like to fish, so if I can recruit a kid in the western part of Michigan that likes fishing, or if he's on a farm, I've worked on a farm, or a young man in Detroit, I grew up in the inner city of Youngstown. I went to a private college [Ashland]. Michigan recruits know how important academics are. That's a thread we have in common—it's just being well-rounded. I've been blessed to have a lot of different experiences, but to also remember that I can't sell something other than myself. I'm just myself with those people and just try to build relationships more than recruit."

Steve was at Kentucky for five years and added the title of defensive passing game coordinator in 2019. UK led the SEC in pass defense in 2019 and again in 2020. His 2020 secondary topped the conference with sixteen interceptions, which ranked third nationally in the COVID campaign.

That performance drew the attention of Jim Harbaugh at Michigan.

The last conversation I had with Steve about his coaching career was when he was trying to decide if he should leave Kentucky and go to Michigan. It was not easy. Kentucky was trending up in the SEC under Coach Stoops. Steve really liked Coach Stoops and was just given a promotion and a raise.

Also, one must understand the landscape in Ann Arbor, Michigan, at that moment to understand the risk Steve was taking in entertaining his next job offer. In 2020, it was not an easy time for Harbaugh. He was 0-5 against Ohio State. The 2020 team went 2-4 in the COVID-shortened campaign, and the wolves were barking in the athletic administration.

I remember we talked for quite a while. Steve shared with me all the positives of both positions. At the end of the conversation, I do remember telling Steve just one thing: "It's Michigan." He would be in position to win a national championship at one of the Blue Blood college football programs in the country. Steve knew the challenge the Wolverines were facing, but it didn't faze him. He took another leap while continuing to Dare to Dream.

"They had a change," Steve said. "One of their coaches left, and they were interested in someone coaching the safeties, which was really appealing to me because the corners coach at the time was Mike Zordich, who played high school ball at my alma mater, Chaney, and then at Penn State. Very similar to Ashland, I got there right before camp began, and Mike Macdonald is the new defensive coordinator, and we're running the Baltimore Ravens' defense [where Jim's brother John is the head coach and where Macdonald served as a defensive assistant for seven years]. So now I'm working in a pro defense, and that was very appealing to me too."

Steve was hired as the defensive backs coach and as the defensive passing game coordinator. Michigan's fortunes changed that ensuing fall. The Wolverines went 12-1 in the regular season, finally beat Ohio State, and won the Big Ten championship before falling to Georgia in the national semifinals.

In 2022, with Jesse Minter as the new defensive coordinator, Michigan finished 13-1 and again won the Big Ten crown and thumped the Buckeyes before losing to TCU in the national semifinals.

In 2023, it all came together. Michigan went 15-0, knocked off Ohio State for a third straight season, won a third consecutive Big Ten title, and captured the national championship for the first time since 1997. When the season concluded, Jim Harbaugh was offered the head coaching job with the Los Angeles Chargers. Steve Clinckscale was one of the coaches he took with him to the NFL.

"Talking to Coach Harbaugh before I took the job [at Michigan], I felt like people were always questioning me," Steve said. "I felt like it's time to prove people wrong. I want to come there, and I want to beat Ohio State. And he was like, 'Well, let's do it together.' Jim loves people. He wants them to be themselves, and he doesn't try to make you be something that you're not. We had a young, vibrant staff, and he really fed off our energy. He treats us like we're a family.

"There was one time my wife went out of town a couple of years ago, and we were playing Rutgers. I had nobody to watch my stepson Carlo, and Jim said, 'You can bring him on the trip.' So we put him on the plane, and he came with us.' He sees us as a family."

Steve has really done a good job of staying in touch with me and AU as he's climbed the coaching ladder. He has always been appreciative of our time together. He would send us recruits to sign when he couldn't get them signed at whatever Division I school he was coaching. They were always good players.

Several years ago, Steve told one of his cousins, Gei'vonni Washington, that he wanted him to play at Ashland. Gei'vonni had bigger plans. With prodding from Steve and me, he became an Eagle. Geo rushed for more than twelve hundred yards in his first season at Ashland and was the conference freshman of the year. Gei'vonni went on to a four-year, all-conference, and all-American career at Ashland.

Every season Steve would call and ask how his nephew was doing. He was excited to hear of his success on the field but was most interested in his work academically.

That's the core that Steve has always kept in mind. If you're going to Dare to Dream, you must put in the work that can help make your dream a reality.

"My wife, Elaine, with her understanding and devotedness has taught me to see the truth in my calling," Steve said. "Elaine has helped me reflect and grow as a human being; I want to give her a special thank you for bringing out the best in me. And my parents instilled in me a 'never surrender' mentality. Also, the families with the church homes I've had in Mansfield and Toledo and everywhere I've coached, they've all helped me mold my personality and my craft. I'm always working and trying to change things, and I never take a step back and kind of just look at life and go, 'Man, I'm superproud of my life.' I hope that the legacy that I left affects somebody. That's really all I want."

Steve will always carry an intense passion for Youngstown. One of his proudest accomplishments, even while coaching in the NFL, is that he was able to recruit a couple of players from his hometown, Jason Hewlett and D. J. Waller, to be part of Michigan's national championship run. Both were freshmen, and Waller in particular had a fine campaign. He played in eleven games, made twelve tackles, and was Freshman Defensive Player of the Week several times as selected by the Wolverines' coaching staff.

"If there's a moment in my life that I don't talk about very often, it's the moment that I was able to convince two families from Youngstown to let their two young men come play for me at Michigan," Steve said. "They both went to Chaney High School as well, my alma mater, and they actually won a national title too. So you've got three people right there from Youngstown that were part of that. Youngstown can still be a pretty violent place. But we can all go back now and show the young kids that 'Hey, these guys you may know, look what they did.' It can give them hope that maybe they can take the same path too and not go on the streets that take over their lives. To me, that's awesome."

Goals Are Milestones in the Pursuit of Our Dreams

"Step by step I can see no other way of accomplishing anything. I always had the ultimate goal of being the best, but I approached it step by step." –Michael Jordan

All teams dream of daring to do mighty things. All teams reach a place in time when "good" no longer becomes "good enough." The world needs dreamers. More importantly, the world needs dreamers who pursue their dreams with all their heart.

Unfortunately, all but a few teams each season allow their dreams to die. Teams that were once bold and courageous fall into comfort zones where once again "good enough" is acceptable.

Teams that quit dreaming of glorious victories will never find excellence, only mediocrity. Without dreams there will always be regrets of what could have been or what should have been. Fortunately, it is never too late to start dreaming again.

All winning teams have the courage to dream big. Dreams give teams hope for the future. Goals represent possibility and keep dreams from drowning. Hope is dreaming dreams. Goals become specific to the dream. Dreams are out there someplace and somewhere. Goals are a team's day-to-day, week-to-week, season-to-season specific destinations. Winning teams keep their eyes focused on their goals. This is the top priority in the process of motivating a winning team. Having a team mission, a team cause, and well-defined team goals is recognized as the strongest force for all team motivation—and the most important part of a team's journey.

Goals motivate and inspire team commitment. There is no greater team goal than a commitment to excellence.

Obstacles become excuses when teams take their eyes off their common goal. A team is lost and wonders aimlessly without goals. There is no destination. Goals give teams objectives, purpose, and tracks to follow. A team without goals is like a ship without a rudder, floundering in no direction. With goals a team knows exactly where it's going and exactly what it is working toward every day. Team goals provide incentives and create such a power that they literally propel a team toward excellence. The most amazing thing about goals is they keep a team on course when obstacles make progress slow and difficult. With that, goals become the milestones to our dreams.

Goals should never be confused with daydreaming or wishful thinking. Goals are dreams, but dreams that are being acted upon. All great teams are obsessed with clearly defined goals. All great teams achieve excellence as they strive toward accomplishing their goals and then commit to even greater goals.

The world makes room for teams that know where they are going.

The clearer the team's goals are communicated and visualized, the more desire, determination, and effort will be given to reach these goals. Furthermore, the more ownership the entire team takes in setting goals, the more desire, determination, and effort will be given to reach these goals.

S.M.A.R.T.E.R. Goal Setting
"A man's reach should exceed his grasp, or what is a heaven for?"
—Robert Browning

After spending a couple of years at Ohio State as an assistant coach under John Cooper, I took time to review my personal and professional goals. I wrote down on an OSU notecard eight goals that I believed reflected my life priorities of God, family, and football. On my list of goals, number eight was to become a Division IA head football coach by the year 2000. I was hired by the University of Akron in 1995. I have always tried to set challenging goals within realistic time frames for myself and for my teams.

I'm reminded of a day about five years prior to my coaching at Ohio State. I interrupted a family trip with a stop in Columbus to see the new Ohio State indoor facility. I remember telling my two boys that day as we walked around the new Woody Hayes facility that someday their dad would be an Ohio State football coach. Dare to Dream.

Dare to Dream and then set S.M.A.R.T.E.R. goals. You'll need them every step of the way to succeed. Set S.M.A.R.T.E.R. goals that are Specific. These goals should be clear and detailed. Set S.M.A.R.T.E.R. goals that are Measurable. Measurable goals are motivating. Set S.M.A.R.T.E.R. goals that are Attainable. Only you can hold yourself back from accomplishing these goals. Set S.M.A.R.T.E.R. goals that are Realistic. Goals should be based on your awareness of your strengths and weaknesses. Set S.M.A.R.T.E.R. goals that are Timely. These goals are set day-to-day, week-to-week, season-to-season. Set S.M.A.R.T.E.R. goals that are Exciting. Goals should reflect your passions in life. Set S.M.A.R.T.E.R. goals and "Ready, set, go." No excuses.

"The world is moving so fast these days that the man who says it can't be done is generally interrupted by someone doing it," said editor/writer Elbert Hubbart, and he died in 1915.

One season I had Archie Griffin, the only two-time Heisman Trophy winner, talk to my team on goal setting. Archie told the team that his six brothers and one sister were blessed with great parents who loved them and set a great example for them. Archie said his mother was a tough lady who was a disciplinarian and made sure they were doing the things that needed to be done. She had just three goals for her children, and they didn't include the Heisman Trophy or the NFL. The three goals concerned church, college, and athletics. Archie said the goals were written on a three-by-five index card and tacked to the headboard of their beds. Archie beamed with pride when he listed all the accomplishments of his siblings.

Team goal setting must reflect the values of a team. To set team goals, evaluate the priorities of the team, the strengths of a team, and the weaknesses of a team. Goals should be written to accentuate the positives of the team and to eliminate the negatives of the team.

Often in team building it takes "reach up" goals to achieve excellence. The 1999 campaign was our first winning season at the University of Akron. We decided to win, and we did. For the 2000 season we realized that we must "reach up" and go higher than the 1999 goal of a winning season to the goal of winning our first league championship—a goal we accomplished.

What is the importance of reach-up goals? First, these goals increase commitment. Second, they create a need for new knowledge, additional resources, and a new way of thinking. Third, no team ever stays the same. It either improves or declines, but it never stays the same. Reach-up goals keep a team moving in the right direction.

To meet the higher demands of achieving reach-up goals, teams must think differently. They must learn to solve new problems and deal with higher expectations.

There are four questions that assist a team in setting reach-up goals. What is our team's desire—where do we want to be? What is our team's leverage—how do we apply our resources to make the biggest difference? What is our team's connection—what can we create together? What is our team's focus—what are our most important goals?

The biggest challenge in setting team reach-up goals is underachievers. Team underachievers must be constantly reminded that "okay" is not a goal. Just like everyone else, underachievers want to win, but they may be inattentive or lack self-discipline, become easily distracted, procrastinate, or use excessive excuses. In that case, their goals must be prioritized daily with constant accountability, encouragement, and focus. Often underachievers have an intense fear of failure and must be convinced there is no failure when one commits to a team goal!

Professional golfer Raymond Floyd said this about his life and goal setting: *"Set goals in life; set them high and persist until they are achieved. Once they are achieved, set higher and higher goals. You will find your life will become happier and more purposeful by working toward positive goals."*

"CLIMB 'TIL YOUR DREAM COMES TRUE"
Often your tasks will be many,
And more than you think you can do.
Often the road will be rugged
And the hills insurmountable, too.
But always remember, the hills ahead
Are never as steep as they seem,
And with Faith in your heart start upward
And climb 'Til you reach your dream.
For nothing in life that is worthy
Is never too hard to achieve
If you have the courage to try it
And you have the Faith to believe.
For Faith is a force that is greater
Than knowledge or power or skill
And many defeats turn to triumph
If you trust in God's wisdom and will.
For Faith is a mover of mountains.
There's nothing that God cannot do,

*So start out today with Faith in your heart
And 'Climb 'Til Your Dream Comes True'!*
—Helen Steiner Rice

Key Points for Dare to Dream

1. If one dream dies, it's never too late to start dreaming again. Dreams give teams hope.
2. Obstacles become insurmountable when teams take their eyes off the prize.
3. Keeping a team focused on its goals is the chief building block in the process of achieving team excellence.
4. Having a team mission, a team cause, and clearly defined team goals is the most important part of a team's journey.
5. Goals give a team objectives, purpose, and tracks to follow.
6. The more ownership the entire team takes in setting and communicating goals, the more desire, determination, and effort will be given by the team to reach its goals.
7. There is no greater team goal than a commitment to excellence.
8. Dare to dream and set S.M.A.R.T.E.R. goals: Specific, Measurable, Attainable, Realistic, Timely, Exciting, and "Ready, set, go!"
9. Set reach-up goals with teams to build commitment, keep teams growing, and keep teams moving in the right direction.
10. Team underachievers must have their goals prioritized daily with constant accountability, encouragement, and focus.

–CHAPTER SIX–
HAVE A PLAN

"Have a plan to build better. Have a plan to build faster."
—Dwight Schar

Photo of Dwight Schar

Bio Box: Dwight Schar- Founder NVR

Background: Dwight Schar was born on February 8, 1942, in Virginia. He was one of six children. His mother, Mary, came north to Ohio after separating from her husband and raised her children in a four-room home with an outhouse.

Athletic Achievement: Dwight played football and baseball and ran track at Norwayne High School. When Dwight was a senior running back and linebacker, his Bobcats played but lost in the Wayne County championship game. Schar played one season of football under Hall of Fame Coach Fred Martinelli at Ashland College (as Ashland University was known until May 12, 1989). But with limited game action, Dwight had to leave the team to work his way through school. He describes his collegiate athletic career as "uneventful."

Scholastic Achievement: Schar graduated from Ashland College in 1964 with degrees in business and education. Due to his many philanthropic endeavors for the school, a statue of him was created just outside the gates of the Ashland University football stadium.

Professional Achievement: After a brief stint as a teacher, Dwight worked at Ryan Homes. He eventually left to start his own business, NV Homes, which eventually absorbed Ryan Homes. He overcame a Chapter 11 bankruptcy filing in 1992 to lead NV Homes (later NVR Inc., which also functions as a business in the mortgage-banking sector) to become the largest home builder in the United States. Schar was the executive chairman and CEO of the company. In 2022, at age 80, he retired. On June 6, 2020, Dwight was inducted into the National Association of Homebuilders (NAHB) National Housing Hall of Fame during a ceremony held at the National Housing Center in Washington, D.C. In 1993, Dwight became a minority owner of the Washington Redskins. He sold his share of the franchise in 2021. Schar became active in politics too and served as the national finance chair of the Republican National Committee at one point. His net worth at the time of this writing is $2.72 billion.

THE SPIRIT OF A TEAM

There were approximately one thousand billionaires in the United States as of 2025. Few if any were born into more humble circumstances than Dwight Schar. An understanding of his upbringing only leads to further admiration of what Dwight has accomplished in his life. It's truly stunning.

Dwight was born on February 8, 1942, in Virginia. He was one of six children. Dwight's mother, Mary, came north to Ohio with her brood after separating from her husband. Her plan was to raise the youngsters in a better home environment and support them while working as a cook in a nursing home. They landed in rural Northeast Ohio near Mary's family, in a four-room house. Indoor plumbing was a luxury they could not afford. An outhouse had to suffice.

By the time Dwight reached his teens, he was working on his uncle's farm, and he stayed there when his uncle got sick. As a seventh grader, Dwight was enrolled in the Norwayne school district, and he started playing football as a freshman. There were only four hundred students in the entire school system, K-12, so youngsters with an athletic inclination were encouraged to participate in multiple sports. Schar was one of those athletes who competed in football, baseball, and track. In football he was initially a running back and defensive back but eventually moved to linebacker. The Bobcats were decent, playing for (and losing) the Wayne County championship his senior year. But it was what was happening off the field that was shaping him. Dwight was particularly focused in the classroom, and he began taking courses that today would be considered college prep.

"I remember my mother saying to me, 'Why are you taking these courses? You know we can't afford for you to go to college.' But as Confucius said, 'The trip of one thousand miles begins with one step.' For me, that was my first step. I didn't know how I was going to get there. But it seemed like at that particular time, the only way to be successful was to have a college education."

Schar's plan began in high school, when he was already accustomed to working on the farm in summer and during after-school hours. Before attending college, he added time as a painter to his sweat résumé. At Ashland College, he worked nights at a factory and washed dishes at a downtown restaurant to make ends meet. He couldn't afford to live in a dormitory, so he stayed in a shack dubbed the Haunted Huts for thirty-five dollars per month. At another point he sublet a place from his cousin that cost him ten dollars a week.

Schar also dabbled with football as a sophomore at Ashland under Hall of Fame Coach Fred Martinelli. But limited action and the need to find cash to subsidize his education soon ended his athletic career.

Toward the end of his days as a student, Schar didn't have enough cash to pay tuition and finish his required course work. So he went to the Ashland Savings Bank and explained the situation to the bank manager. In the spirit of a different time, the bank manager told Dwight to write out a check to Ashland College for his tuition; the bank would make it good. The bank manager then told Dwight to come see him when he had the cash to pay off the debt—which is precisely what he did.

"You know, the interesting part about planning is when you set an objective for yourself, you might not know how you're really going to get there," Schar said. "But if you harness your mind that this is what you want to achieve and you live it every day, every day will create an opportunity for you that you can take the initial step in that direction."

"I was a poor kid who kind of worked my way through high school, worked my way through college, but Ashland gave me the opportunity. It was almost like the town worked with me. I just believe that a college degree was a foundation that allowed me to think bigger. When I graduated college, it was one of the happiest days of my life. That gave me a lot of confidence, really. I had just put so much into it."

A few years later, when Schar was better established, he had the opportunity to pay it forward. He stepped in on behalf of two brothers-in-law who had dropped out of school and were living in Chicago.

"I went to the Dean of the school and told him about both of them and asked if they could get back in school," Schar remembered. "I was able to talk to that dean, and he let both back in the school. Both graduated from Ashland, and they both had successful careers as a result. I was really a nobody. I was just a kid going in and talking to them about two people that at different points in time really needed to get back into school. That's a case where Ashland let them in, and I really think it changed their lives for the better."

When Schar left Ashland in 1964, he had two job offers from Ohio public schools. One was from Crestline to be a teacher, assistant football, and head track coach for $5,000. The other was from Stow, where he would be teaching only junior high school science for $4,900. He chose the latter, located near Kent State University. Dwight thought maybe he would get his master's degree, but he soon found his head turned in a new direction.

He started looking around the area to buy a house and opened a conversation with the home builder. In turn, Schar was asked if he would be interested in a part-time job selling homes after school and on weekends. Real estate would be a side job to enhance his income beyond a teacher's salary.

Dwight immediately discovered he had a knack for the field. After just one semester, he quit his teaching position to devote attention full time to the home-construction business. By the age of twenty-six, he was overseeing the Dayton division of an Ohio home building company.

"They were having trouble selling homes when I took over the service department and a number of other things," Dwight recalled. "They put me in charge of running the largest operation they had, the one losing the most money. I was lucky enough to turn that around, and I was selling lots to Ryan Homes, which was headquartered in Pittsburgh."

That connection led to another step as his plan evolved. Dwight realized he was making more money selling lots than he was in building homes on his own. So he called Ryan Homes and asked for a job. That's how his business journey really blossomed.

He started in Pittsburgh in one of four divisions at Ryan Homes. Schar advanced to running two of the four divisions, then moved into the Mid-Atlantic area surrounding Washington, DC. The region was exploding and quickly became the largest operation across the company's holdings.

Schar was bristling to go off on his own, but contractual obligations prevented him from starting his own business. Finally free of those constraints in 1980, he had $50,000 to live on and start his own operation. The company he formed was North Virginia Homes Inc. (NVHomes). The company's growth was astonishing.

North Virginia Homes Inc. was the earliest iteration of the modern-day company NVR. A mortgage service was added in 1984, and Dwight took the company public in 1986. In 1987 NVR purchased his old employer, Ryan Homes, in a $312 million deal that made his company the largest home builder in the United States at the time.

Still, Schar had to absorb some setbacks along the way. A huge downturn in the housing market was one of them. Another obstacle was created by the early-1990s recession. Worse, a change emerged in the banking laws that impacted how loans were structured from short-term to long-term debt in the real estate industry. It all conspired to force Schar's company to file bankruptcy in April 1992.

"We looked at a number of different alternatives, but this is the one with all the circumstances that we have to work with—with the bondholders, with our banks, with the market," Schar told the *Washington Post* in 1992. "We felt this was our best alternative."

In essence, NVR had bought too much land, then found itself holding the bag when interest rates turned, land values sagged, and construction slowed in the early 1990s, according to a March 20, 2005, story in *U.S. News & World Report*. The company had borrowed heavily to buy out the bigger rival, Ryan Homes. That purchase created a vulnerable financial position made worse by the events of the time.

Dwight was devastated personally. The company's stock price collapsed to thirty-one cents per share. But Schar said learning from his mistakes and acting quickly to correct them are paramount to having a plan to take the next step.

"Really what happened was I was flying high and doing well, and what caused the bankruptcy was in 1989 they changed the banking laws that changed the borrowing limits they had to borrowers. In the real estate industry, you really needed long-term debt. I, and most other builders, were working off short-term debt. So I went to my bankers and said you need a long-term deal, and they said, 'No, no, everything's fine. You're good. We can give you more attractive rates short term.' Well, when that happened with the banking laws, it changed, so the banks could no longer lend me money. So what happened is that all my one-year extensions got eliminated because they weren't permitted by the federal government to provide loans for me. So what happened is they were calling all the loans.

"I had about effectively a billion dollars' worth of debt. I went from a $200 million net worth to minus fifty-four dollars because it foreclosed on all those things. So in the end I guess one of the things that it taught me about life a little bit is that you really must understand all the risks that you're taking.

"I never thought one of the risks I would have to take is a political risk, like when the federal government changed the banking laws. It was when George Bush was president, and I went to Washington and was talking to the head of the Treasury. This was his department, and I remember telling him this new law coming in was going to create bankruptcies. I just didn't realize at the time that I was going to be one of them."

Dwight said he had always viewed bankruptcy as a stigma. Yet he had no choice. NVHomes filed for Chapter 11 bankruptcy. The company restructured its debt primarily by issuing $160 million in new junk bonds to pay off bank creditors and distributed most of its stock to former bondholders. That effectively gave it ownership of the reorganized company. It also allowed NVHomes to continue operations while significantly reducing its debt burden.

Individually, it allowed Schar to gain some perspective too.

"I remember having a guy call me up one time, and he asked how I was doing," Schar said. "How was I dealing with this? I remember telling him about a biblical story of the guy who complained he had no shoes until he met a man with no feet. You just must deal with it."

Dwight said he leaned on his personal relationships and his professional reputation to climb out of the hole and salvage his company. He sent out letters to subcontractors and asked them to extend credit. Several folks just told him to pay them when he could. They had faith in Schar. Some developers let him build on their lots and pay when a purchase was completed. He was also able to use customer deposits, and the operation grew from there.

"The perspective of the company is that it had a financial problem, and not an operating problem," spokesman Douglas Poretz told the *Baltimore Sun*.

The company emerged from bankruptcy just fifteen months later, in September 1993. NVR again went public, and Dwight took on the role of executive chairman of the board. The following month, NVR's stock price stood at $10.25. By 2005, it had risen to nearly eight hundred dollars on the American Stock Exchange, up 77 percent, or 44 percent annually. The comeback was described by *U.S. News & World Report* as "dazzling."

"The wonderful thing about it was that because we've always been good to other people and we had a good reputation, people were good to me," Dwight said. "That's how we really survived. It was the goodness of other people that helped us, and we had a good team. There is no I in team, but there are two i's in idiot."

In 2012, NVR acquired Heartland Homes, and in 2019 it was added to the S&P stock market index. Dwight retained his role atop NVR until 2005. He remained as executive chairman of the board until he retired in 2022 at the age of eighty. Today, NVR includes the brands of NVHomes, NVR Mortgage, Ryan Homes, Heartland Homes, Rymark Homes, and Fox Ridge Homes. As of November 24, 2023, the company boasted a market capitalization of $19.69 billion and a closing stock price of $6,195.06. According to Forbes, that made NVR the second most expensive stock in the United States, behind only Warren Buffet's Berkshire Hathaway Inc.

The company issued a glowing press release when Dwight retired.

Schar's leadership and strategic guidance through many business cycles, including the global financial crisis, have led to the long-term success of NVR.

"Schar has been instrumental in transforming NVR into the third-largest homebuilder in terms of market capitalization, as well as achieving industry leading financial returns," the company stated.

Dwight's personal wealth obviously ballooned as his company grew. As a result, his philanthropic and personal investments are vast and varied. One of the most interesting investments was in 2003 when he became part owner of a minority share of the Washington Redskins, along with Robert Rothman and Frederick W. Smith, for $200 million. Eventually, Schar owned 15 percent of the team for $112 million. In 2021, he sold his share for approximately $320 million after a court battle with majority owner Daniel Snyder.

"I got to know Joe Gibbs, and we used to go to training camp," Schar said. "Joe is a wonderful human being. It was great for my boys. They got to go to training camp and catch footballs from the quarterback. My one son worked with the guy that did the salary cap stuff. So he learned that. He got to work at the games. I mean, it was just a great experience for him to be around that kind of environment.

"On Sundays, you pull in underneath the stadium, you park the car, go to the elevator, and walk out onto the field. You go to the locker room, whatever. It was fantastic."

Schar again made headlines when he was involved in one of the largest home sales ever. In 2004, Dwight bought the Palm Beach oceanfront mansion Casa Apava for $70 million from Cosmetics mogul Ron Perelman and his wife, actress Ellen Barkin. The 33,000-square-foot property included an ocean view and a lake view, a movie theater, an oversized outdoor pool, a pool house, multiple guest houses, a gym, spa, a boat deck, a walk-in humidor, and millions in furnishings. The location of the estate was dubbed Billionaire's Row, with Dwight's neighbors including Netscape founder Jim Clark, Tampa Bay Buccaneers owner Malcolm Glazer, clothing magnate Sidney Kimmel, and Sotheby's owner A. Alfred Taubman.

"It's a major wow property with Old World elegance and a lot of presence," said Paulette Koch of the Corcoran Group's Palm Beach office in a story for the *New York Post*.

"He's bought a fabulous property—it's a classic Mediterranean-style house that had an open-checkbook renovation," said John Pinson, head of the local realtors association. "There's really not another house like that."

Obviously, Dwight had become a man of rare means and one with a myriad of philanthropic pursuits. This is how I got to know him. Schar has made numerous charitable donations through the years, including $50 million to the Inova Health System to build a cancer center in Fairfax, Virginia, and $75 million to support Inova Health System's heart and vascular programs. There was another $10 million given to the George Mason Schar School of Policy and Government. In 2014, $12 million was contributed to Elon University, the single-largest donation in that school's history. He also sent $200,000 to his old school district so that Norwayne students could have up-to-date technology at their fingertips.

At his alma mater, it is estimated that Dwight and Martha Schar have given nearly $40 million. Their gifts have led to a new education building, a nursing school, restoration and beautification projects on campus, and the Dwight Schar Athletic Complex.

I will never forget the excitement I felt on the day I received "the call" from our college president, Dr. Fred Finks. Finks, along with Jack Miller, our athletic facility campaign chair had been working with Dwight Schar for quite some time to secure the lead gift to build a new athletic facility at Ashland University. Just before my call from Finks and Miller, Dwight committed to the largest gift (at that time) in the history of our university. I knew at that moment the positive impact this facility would have on our total athletic program, our university, and our community.

Dwight liked and trusted Dr. Finks, and he believed in the leadership of Jack Miller. Dwight Schar's legacy at Ashland University will be forever tied to this gift. The spirit of our campus was enhanced forever.

When we first dedicated the Dwight Schar Athletic Facility, we met with Dwight and his family for a quick lunch at the convocation center. To his surprise, when we started the walk across the parking lot and street back to the athletic facility (thanks to Athletic Director Bill Goldring) more than five hundred student athletes formed a tunnel and cheered Dwight all the way. We stopped in front of the Troop Center for the unveiling of Dwight's statue.

The following football season was the first to be played in the new stadium. I found out during pregame of our homecoming game that Dwight was in attendance, and he was invited into the locker room to address the team before the kickoff versus Wayne State. Wayne State had played for a national championship the year prior, led by my good friend Paul Winters. Paul was my offensive coordinator for nine years at Akron, and we have always been close. Our games were always competitive because we knew each other so well. But this game was even more significant. Wayne State was the fourth-ranked team in the country and a big favorite. A win versus Wayne State would put us in a tie for first place in the conference.

I felt the pit in my stomach grow as Dwight walked into the locker room. The first thing he did was admire the massive, brand-new locker room that his generosity had helped build for us. He told the team that it was quite a bit nicer than the one his Redskins' franchise had used when he was a minority owner. Next, he challenged our young men to play to the final play and prophetically predicted there would be a player on our team who would have to make a play at the end to win the game.

After a hard-fought game, with forty-four seconds left and the score tied 17-17, Eric Schwieterman had his second interception. Then, with twelve seconds left, tailback Anthony Taylor rushed for thirty yards to the Wayne State twenty-six-yard line. There were four seconds left in regulation when kicker Greg Berkshire attempted a 43-yard field goal into a gusting wind. He split the uprights on the final play of the game for the win, 20-17.

I could feel the meaning of the moment and the significance of what Dwight Schar had meant to our football program transform into pure joy.

Creating a Strategic Plan

"Every minute you spend in planning saves 10 minutes in execution; this gives you a 1,000-percent return on energy."
—Brian Tracy, Author/Speaker

Winning teams visualize their success; what do they want to achieve? What is the mission? What is the cause? What is the vision of what is possible? I had several teams design their championship ring prior to winning the championship. Then I would have an artist's rendering of the ring painted on the wall outside the locker room. Each day as they walked past the artwork of this championship ring they were given a visual reminder of the team goal.

Once a team knows the specific, tangible, intended destination, its objectives have been established. Now the team must determine what it will take to accomplish these goals. What steps must it take? How long will it take? What is the plan of attack? What is the game plan?

The value of effective team planning is vital. "Fail to plan, plan to fail." An effective team plan is like the preparation needed to take a team on a journey. Most everyone has traveled with their family and realizes all the planning and preparation necessary to make a trip. Imagine a football team with a travel party of 150 and the planning it takes to travel: food, rooms, buses, planes, and equipment needed just to go on one road trip?

Every team is constantly on a journey. The journey of multiple years is a team's strategic plan. Each team shares a season journey together with a defined beginning and end. This is most often the yearly plan. Of course, there is always a weekly plan and a plan for the events of each day.

My strategic plan was best in five-year intervals. This was because of recruiting cycles. The mission of this plan and the vision of this plan were always the same: to win championships by recruiting, developing, and retaining the right people. To be winners both on and off the field.

This plan always required as much information as possible and an analysis of all the teams' situations. Assessments, assumptions, and beliefs were researched, studied, and questioned. Internal and external strengths and weaknesses were listed, and the threats or opportunities they presented were considered.

My strategic plans always included three sections: 1. Recruiting, Academics, Player Development, and Roster Management; 2. Fundraising, Marketing, and Facilities; 3. Strategies and Winning.

Each section listed goals and strategies, a timeline, the person responsible, and the resources required.

I always shared the goals, strategies, and action plans listed in this document with all the stakeholders in our program. More importantly, I worked hard to sell this document to everyone in our program.

In my last strategic plan, 2017-2022, year five in the facility section listed "Build a Field House." The Niss Athletic Center was dedicated on January 28, 2022. Our strategic plan was essential to this facility becoming a reality.

My yearly plan was broken down in one notebook with sections for the offseason, spring season, summer preseason, and in-season. My yearly plan always included a calendar with all 365 days scheduled.

I would always pass out the weekly plan to the staff and players at our Thursday team meeting, and we would always post our daily plan or schedule in the locker room.

Completing all these plans takes a significant amount of time. This is not a waste of time; it's time gained by organization and the elimination of wasted time.

For example, a daily practice plan was really an eight-hour plan. It would take four hours to prepare the plan, two hours to execute the practice plan, and two hours to evaluate the practice plan.

Once these plans are completed, they must be constantly evaluated. There must be criteria established to evaluate all planning. I asked these questions when evaluating our daily practice plan: 1. Are the athletes given the opportunity to practice in game like conditions? 2. Are we using our time efficiently? 3. Are the facilities and equipment being used in optimal ways? 4. Are the athletes being challenged to compete at a high-energy level and experience a reasonable amount of success?

When evaluating a plan, it's important to track the progress of the plan. Only then can milestones reached be rewarded and the team motivated to keep working.

Furthermore, all plans must be flexible. After the practice week ended and the game plan was finished, I often reminded the team that not once in my career of leading teams on the field well over four hundred times did the game go as planned. So the plan was always flexible, with a reminder to everyone on the team, "Always keep your knees bent, your head on a swivel, and be ready to handle the chaos."

Adam Shaheen—Attack the Plan
"Plans are of little importance, but planning is essential."
—Winston Churchill

Once the plan has been established, the team must actively attack the plan. "Plan the Attack. Attack the Plan." When a team puts a plan into action, it breathes life into the team. Every team plan is a journey—a journey in pursuit of excellence. Dwight Schar often quotes the Chinese proverb "A journey of a thousand miles starts with a single step." By living out and taking every step of the journey as one, focused and determined, one step at a time, the team is on the path to excellence.

Teams motivated to achieve excellence finish the plan. They take the vision of the original dream and turn fantasy into reality. No matter how long it takes, no matter how hard it becomes, no matter how difficult it seems, the team finishes the job. Individually and collectively a team will do whatever is needed to bring the dream to life.

When Adam Shaheen became a football player for the Ashland Eagles, he attacked his plan. Adam played football and basketball while in high school at Big Walnut near Columbus, Ohio. Adam loved football but was offered a scholarship to play basketball at Division II Pitt-Johnstown. Even though Adam contributed to the basketball team at Pitt-Johnstown his freshman year, he never lost his love for football.

When Adam came to visit us concerning his transfer to Ashland University, I told him we had two tight ends on scholarship and that he would have to earn the first available scholarship for a tight end. This didn't matter to Adam because he had a plan. Adam believed in his plan; he was committed to his plan. Sitting there in my office that day with his father and assistant coach Doug Geiser, Adam shared his plan.

He said he knew he needed to get bigger, faster, and stronger. He started to share with me the specific training regimen he had put together. He had a plan that included diet, lifting, and running. He had researched all the NFL combine numbers for a tight end. He had put a three-year timeline together to be able to reach these NFL measurables.

He also knew he needed to master tight end skills, techniques, and fundamentals to reach the NFL. Adam said he had researched our offense and liked tight end coach Reggie Gamble.

I assured Adam that day that our football program would give him the opportunity to attack this very ambitious plan.

So Adam committed to playing for Ashland University in 2014. In his first season as an Eagle, he was our third tight end on varsity and played on the JV team. It was a pleasure to watch Adam play and witness his dedication, and he earned a scholarship after that first semester at Ashland University.

The 2015 campaign was a breakout season for Adam Shaheen. He caught seventy passes, good for the highest total of any tight end at any NCAA level. Adam continued his dominance at the position in 2016 and earned first-team all American honors.

Most importantly, Adams's plan was a success. He had reached all his physical marks. He was a solid six foot six, 270-pound tight end who could run like a receiver and block like an offensive tackle. Adam was drafted in the second round in the 2017 NFL draft. Adam Shaheen was the highest- drafted Division II player since Walter Payton in 1975. He played five seasons for the Chicago Bears and the Miami Dolphins.

Individualized Planning
"We cannot drive people; we must direct their development."
—Henry Gantt, Project Manager

Like with Adam Shaheen, the process of an individual team member planning is vital to the team achieving excellence.

Every week during the football season there will be a new game plan for special teams, offense, and defense. Equally important, I asked everyone on the team to complete this weekly player plan (be specific as possible):

What will you do this week on the field, in the weight room, or with your treatment to physically become a better football player?

What will you do this week on the field, in film study, or during football meetings to become a better prepared football player?

What will you do this week on the field, in the community, or on campus to become a more complete team football player?

I would then remind the team that positive results (touchdowns, takeaways, wins, and championships) would be there when they eliminated all the distractions and noise and focus on the process of getting better each week. That process includes having a plan and making a commitment to that plan. It includes believing in yourself, your teammates, and your coaches, and in the process—"This Week"—one week at a time.

There are four easy steps I would use when helping a player or directing the team when planning:

Visualize: See what is possible for you to do or to become. Know what you want, your intended destination.

Conceptualize: Create a plan and then prepare every step of that plan with a strong and determined sense of purpose.

Actualize: Put the plan into action. Breathe life into your mission. Take what you planned to do and actually do it.

Realize: Finish the plan. See it through. No matter how long it takes. No matter how hard it gets. Finish the job.

Planning for Opportunity

"Spectacular achievement is always preceded by unspectacular preparation."–Hall of Fame quarterback Roger Staubach

Preparation is most often credited to hard work. Often, we hear that when the two equal teams compete, the best prepared team wins. We know hard work takes sacrifice, discipline, and desire. These are all intangibles critical to working hard and being prepared.

In this book, I have gone so far as to include hard work as one of the foundations to achieve excellence. But I do believe that with a good plan, teams work smarter and more efficiently. With a good plan, teams will be better prepared.

The Roman philosopher Seneca is credited with the quote "Luck is where preparation meets opportunity."

The quote is most often interpreted as meaning that people can put themselves in the best position to take advantage of opportunities by being the best prepared. My contention is that planning well is critical to being best prepared.

Being prepared for opportunities in life has always driven my plan in life. Maybe this is why I've always felt that my teams were lucky. If luck is ultimately the result of good planning, then I strongly agree with the quote "I would rather be lucky than good, any day."

There are many opportunities that your team may never get. But if you keep your eyes open and plan well, there may be opportunities a team can obtain that otherwise would have been missed. A missed opportunity can have tragic consequences.

To achieve excellence, a team must plan and prepare to make the most of every opportunity given.

OPPORTUNITY

"Opportunity comes to everyone. Some people accept it; some do not. Only those who do [accept opportunity] find fulfillment in life. Whether you accept opportunity is not a matter of chance, but of choice. When opportunity comes, choose to accept, for it is on the wings of opportunity that your desires will be carried to success."–Winnerscope 1989

Key Points for Having a Plan

1. Once a team focuses on the specific, tangible, intended destination, its objectives have been met.
2. An effective team plan is the preparation needed to take a team on a journey.
3. It takes significant time for a team to complete a strategic plan, a yearly, a weekly, and a daily plan. This is time well spent.
4. Team plans should be flexible. When evaluating team plans, it is important to track their progress.
5. The team's strategic plan is the program's compass and must be shared with all the stakeholders.
6. Teams that are motivated to achieve excellence attack and finish the plan.
7. It is important for individual team members to buy into the process of having a plan and committing to the plan.
8. There are four steps to planning; Visualize, Conceptualize, Actualize, and Realize.
9. Teams with good plans work smarter and more efficiently.
10. A team that plans for opportunity is a team that is well prepared.

–CHAPTER SEVEN–
YOU'VE GOTTA BELIEVE

"Before you can win , you have to believe you are worthy."–Mike Ditka

Photo of Nate Moore courtesy of Scott H. Shook

Bio Box: Nate Moore—Head Football Coach, Massillon High School

Background: Nate was born February 1, 1981, and grew up in Cincinnati. He later moved to a nearby suburb, Mason, Ohio. His father, Jerry, was a teacher, librarian, assistant principal, and principal before finishing his education career in state testing. Nate's mother, Debra, frequently worked as a school secretary but was largely a homemaker.

Athletic Achievement: Nate started as a senior on the offensive line at Mason High School in 1998. He went on to play college football at the University of Dayton, where he was a first-team all-American in 2002 and 2003 at right tackle.

Scholastic Achievement: Nate graduated from Dayton in 2003 with a degree in education.

Professional Achievement: Nate was the Division VI Coach of the Year at Minster in 2011. In 2014, Moore led Cincinnati LaSalle to the Division II state championship, was chosen Ohio's Division II Coach of the Year and the Cincinnati Bengals Coach of the Year, and earned the Paul Brown Award for Excellence and Leadership. He became the head coach at Massillon and led the Tigers to three consecutive state runner-up finishes before capturing the 2023 Division II state championship, the first on-field title in school history. Nate was voted Ohio's Division II Co-Coach of the Year and the MaxPreps.com National Coach of the Year. Nate is the only football coach in Ohio to win the state championship at a private and public school.

Personal: Nate is married to Becca Moore. They have three children: Terrence, Eli, and Ella.

My interaction with Nate Moore was triggered by my unsuccessful recruitment of one of his players at Cincinnati LaSalle High School, Avery Larkin. That detail didn't work out, but he left an impression on me that certainly did. Nate's journey from late-blooming high school football player to National High School Coach of the Year has an unlikely beginning and multiple stops along the way.

Nate was born in Cincinnati, and when he was entering junior high his family moved to Mason, a suburb northeast of the city, best known for being the site of Kings Island. Nate's Dad, Jerry, was a teacher, and his mom, Debra, frequently worked as a secretary in the school system. But mostly she was a homemaker for Nate and his brothers. He was the middle of three sons, flanked by Zachary (the oldest) and Aaron (the youngest). Nate's interest in football was fostered by his maternal grandfather, Thomas Plummer, who had Ohio State season tickets. Nate's grandfather took him to a few games at Ohio Stadium, and the adventures left a mesmerizing impression.

"That whole experience was just unbelievable," Nate reflected. "When I was in English class at the Cincinnati School for Creative and Performing Arts, I had to write a letter to somebody and send it. So I wrote a letter to John Cooper and signed it 'Go Bucks!' He sent me a box of programs from that season, a hat he autographed, and a towel. That made a Buckeye fan out of me."

Neither of Nate's parents were interested in athletics, but his grandfather would toss the football with him in their backyard on Alwil Drive in Reading, Ohio. By seventh grade, Moore was in Mason's junior high pipeline, and after an aborted attempt to play quarterback, he was slotted as a lineman.

"I think I was a quarterback for about three practices, and I tried to execute a three-step drop and it fell about twelve yards short. The coach kind of puts his arm around me and says, 'Nate, we're going to need you to play a different position.' I choked back the tears a little bit and said, 'Yes, Coach,' and I was a lineman from then on."

Nate didn't see any action as a seventh grader and very little as an eighth grader. But he liked being on the team and stuck with it. "You've Got to Believe" is the title of this chapter, and what Moore believed in was his passion for football. He liked working out in the weight room. He liked his friends on the football team. He liked being part of the squad. His lack of playing time and individual success didn't curb the excitement he was deriving from the sport. Even as a junior in high school, he was still playing on the junior varsity team at Mason High School. Few kids stay with a team in such a scenario, as there seems little chance at varsity playing time even as a senior.

"The coach was Tim Lichtenberg, his brother Tom was the head coach at Ohio University. Tim moved me to center. My sophomore year I was finally starting to play consistently on the JV team, and I loved it. It was tons of fun. My junior year I was like six two, maybe 195, and they really wanted me to win the varsity job at center. The coaches were transitioning Mason into a two-platoon program, and they really wanted our defensive end to just play on defense and me to take over as the starting center. Well, we scrimmaged Roger Bacon, and their nose tackle just dominated me, so our defensive end had to play both ways that year, and I played JV again. I played center and defensive end, started both ways on JV. Most people would probably look at that as a giant negative after getting demoted like that. But I had so much fun playing, it really didn't bother me. I just wanted to play."

By the time of his senior season, Nate had developed into a six-foot-four, 250-pound specimen who was the unquestioned starting center for the Comets. He turned in a fine season, and drew recruiting attention from Miami, Bowling Green, Dayton, and the University of Findlay. He rejected the preferred walk-on offers at Miami and Bowling Green and accepted a partial scholarship package at Dayton.

"All of a sudden, I was a good football player," Nate said. "Dayton was a completely different experience from high school. I knew by the second practice I was the best freshman offensive lineman. I traveled my freshman year, and my sophomore year they moved me to left tackle."

Nate was primed for his first collegiate starting role when a knee injury, a tear of both the ACL and MCL, wiped out his sophomore season completely. But he hung in there and thrived under Dayton Coach Mike Kelly. The Flyers went on to win back-to-back Pioneer

Football League championships in 2001 and 2002 while compiling a 21-2 mark over those two campaigns. Nate was a stalwart on the offensive line and earned all-American honors in 2002 and 2003.

"My last day I'm walking out of the locker room, and only the emergency lights were on, and I'm thinking, I don't know that I'm ready for football to be done. So I got hooked up with a semipro team out of the Cincinnati area, and I probably did ten practices with them in the preseason. I went back to Dayton and told one of the coaches about it, kind of bragging about it, and he just looked at me and said, 'What are you doing?' I was stunned by his response. But I thought about it, and he was right. Where was this going to lead me? Semipro football? Don't you have a job? That turned my mind towards coaching."

Moore took a job as a physical education teacher at City Day Community School in downtown Dayton and volunteered to coach for the legendary Jim Place at nearby Dayton Chaminade-Julienne. Place gave him $1,000 to become the assistant offensive line coach, a deal that was in place for three years. It was also while teaching at City Day that Nate met his future wife, Becca. They would become a formidable team.

"When Nate and I started dating, he was very upfront with me from the beginning," Becca said in her book, *Massillon Against the World*. "He sat me down and said, 'Look, I'm going to be a head coach someday, and that's going to take a lot of time and support. Do you think you can handle being alone and the pressure that comes with it?' I don't think I really knew what I was getting into. I just knew I was in love with him and was like, 'Whatever. I can adapt to anything. I mean really, how hard could it be to be a coach's wife? You go to the game on Friday nights, cheer, buy food from the concession stand, and celebrate wins. [It was a] piece of cake in my book. Wrong answer."

After Nate had been at Chaminade-Julienne a couple of years, Jim Place moved on to Hamilton. Moore hoped to follow him, but there were no openings on the teaching staff at C-J, so he stayed in Dayton for another year while on the job search. Finally, he was able to rejoin Coach Place at Hamilton in 2007 and was on staff there through the

2009-2010 school year. When Place retired, Moore knew he wasn't ready for a head coaching job as big as the one at Hamilton. He would have to start small, so he interviewed at two high schools, Minster and Waynesville. Nate chose Minster, but before he and Becca forged their new path, he went to see his old college coach, Mike Kelly.

"I got in a little bit of trouble a couple of times at Dayton, and he could have really hammered me," Moore said. "He showed me a lot of compassion and grace, and I don't think it was because I was a good player. I wasn't that good. We all knew the expectations, and I violated that, and I took my punishment. But he showed me some grace when I didn't expect it, and that meant a lot to me."

When Nate got the head coaching job at Minster, he felt like he needed to meet with Coach Kelly and apologize for those incidents before he could truly perform his duties as head coach.

"So I went back to meet with him. I went to his office and apologized for being a dickhead. He looked at me, and I'm sure he was thinking, I appreciate it, but I don't know why you're telling me these things. I just felt like I needed some sort of atonement for my sins as a player. How could I set a standard or hold anybody accountable if I didn't do that?"

Nate already had a belief in how he wanted to go about his business. He moved to Northwest Ohio in 2010 and jumped into the Midwest Athletic Conference, the toughest small-school league in Ohio—if not the nation. Moore was molded in the Greater Miami Conference, a strong big-school league. Yet he found the coaching in the MAC to be at a different level. It was an eye-opening experience.

"The level of coaching was just phenomenal," Nate said. "In the GMC, if you had good players, you were good. But in the MAC, all the kids are basically the same. Nobody has a roster of monsters. There isn't one school with a bunch of athletes that nobody else has. If you're going to win up there, you have to coach your ass off."

In the three seasons prior to Moore's arrival, Minster was 0-10, 5-5, and 1-9. The school had one of the smallest enrollments in the league. There was little confidence in the program. Morale was a significant problem. The voices outside the program could be distracting, but Nate thought the most disruptive voices could be found inside the school, and not intentionally. Parents, boosters, teachers, fellow students—some were inadvertently fostering a culture of coping, rationalizing. Those voices were unintentionally enabling a losing mentality.

Nate's first year at Minster, his first year as a head coach, was borderline miraculous. The Wildcats started 0-4, including a 41-6 loss to state powerhouse Marion Local and legendary coach Tim Goodwin. It looked like a repeat of Minster's 1-9 record from the previous season might be in the cards. Nate called Becca, who was living in Hamilton to be near her doctor while navigating a difficult pregnancy. He was wavering a bit mentally. Becca offered him a much needed pep talk.

"Maybe I'm not cut out for this," Nate said to Becca." Maybe I wasn't ready. I'm trying to be a head coach before I'm ready."

Becca put an end to that talk. She did believe in Nate.

"Nate, before I married you, you told me you were going to be a head coach. You didn't say it would be easy. You were made for this; you'll figure it out."

Nate said, "I'm sure you're right. But you know, if you lose too many games, you could get fired."

Becca chuckled. "Nate, you aren't going to get fired. I'll see you Friday, and we will win."

Nate remembers that blowout loss to Marion Local as a turning point for another reason.

"One of our kids was hurt, so I ran out onto the field to attend to him, and I peeked at their defense, expecting to see killers over there, and I wasn't seeing it," Nate said "I mean, they were killing us, but their kids weren't killers. They looked like my kids. They're just regular guys. That's when we finally got some things going, after that game."

Just like that, Minster ripped off an unexpected five-game winning streak and reached the playoffs. After a first-round postseason win, the Wildcats pulled off the biggest upset of the Ohio high school football season, stunning Marion Local 30-26. Nate now had a victory over Goodwin, something very few Ohio high school coaches can claim to this day. Minster fell the next week to Sidney Lehman in the regional finals, but the Wildcats posted a 7-6 record and a regional runner-up finish. Any self-doubts Moore had had dissipated for good.

Nate stayed at Minster for the 2011 (9-4) and 2012 (9-3) seasons, ending with playoff losses to Goodwin and Marion Local. Then the Moore family started looking for an opportunity at a bigger school. Nate found one near his family on the west side of Cincinnati at LaSalle High School. The Lancers had not been to the playoffs the previous two seasons, yet the school oozed with talented athletes while competing in the Greater Catholic League South Division.

"Minster was way different than LaSalle," Nate said. "Minster was like Mayberry. I mean it really is a phenomenal place. I still have friends there. At LaSalle, they have a little bit of everything. There are families that struggle financially to send their kids there or receive scholarships. There are some incredibly wealthy families and everything in-between."

LaSalle is also a private school, and the marketing of the institution is geared toward student admissions and enrollment through recruitment. Yet the football program had issues that were also very different from those at Minster. At LaSalle, individual athletes generated social media voices virtually on their own. Recruiting LaSalle players to college programs was a feeding frenzy. Team goals took a backseat to the athletes' plans after high school. In Nate's first season, 2013, the Lancers had one receiver who went to Alabama and another to Eastern Michigan.

Yet getting those individual pieces to think, to believe, as a team would take more than a season. Moore's first year started the opposite of his first year at Minster. LaSalle pounded Oak Hills 42-14 at the University of Cincinnati in the season opener and followed up with two more victories. But then it all came apart. A seven-game losing streak finished the season.

"We had some good players on that team," Moore said. "It was a bad 3-7. We got embarrassed at home by [Columbus] DeSales. We still could have made the playoffs. In week ten, we were leading Elder by a touchdown at the half, and we just gave that game away in the second half. I was just thinking, We've got to get this straightened out right now, or I could get fired."

Nate went about fixing the weight room and setting up

accountability checkpoints. He took a trip to an Ohio State practice conducted by Urban Meyer and noted an address by former Navy SEAL Marcus Luttrell, whose story in Afghanistan was the basis for the film Lone Survivor. Moore began studying warrior cultures and their preparations for going into battle. At Michigan State, he picked up on a mantra of each position group developing a crest, something that position group decided was an identity for its room.

"When I first started, I was pretty much a carbon copy of Jim Place, both on purpose and by accident," Moore said. "I coached for Jim for five years, and that was about all I knew as an assistant. Then I started picking and choosing things that I had learned, what I liked, what fit for what we were trying to accomplish. Then it was about accountability and developing proper leadership."

To that end, Nate took his team on a retreat at Camp Higher Ground in Indiana. The goal was to become the tightest-knit team in the country. It was one hundred hours without social media, character-building bonding. Nate felt his team grow together through that experience. He was soon proven correct.

In 2014, LaSalle met Colerain in the season opener. It was a rivalry game, and Colerain was coming off back-to-back regional final appearances. It was no contest, as the Lancers rolled 41-20. The roll continued with four more victories before LaSalle went into a midseason matchup with two-time defending Division I state champion Cincinnati Moeller. The Crusaders had a nineteen-game in-state winning streak but were no match for LaSalle, who dealt them a 34-9 beating. The only blemish came the following week in a tough, 24-21 loss to Cincinnati St. Xavier, a Division I powerhouse. Still, the Lancers earned a piece of the Greater Catholic League title.

Next came the postseason, where LaSalle had never earned a playoff victory. That box was checked in the first outing, a 48-28 pounding of Glen Este. The victory triggered a remarkable run of running-clock affairs that dotted the Lancers' postseason odyssey. In Ohio high school football, once a team opens a thirty-point lead in the second half, the clock stops only on change of possessions, injuries, or scoring plays. The goal is to speed up the game dramatically between two mismatched teams and avoid injury for overmatched players. For

LaSalle, every game for the rest of this season would be played under these rules, as they overwhelmed every remaining foe, including Harrison (56-24), undefeated Mount Healthy (38-6), unbeaten Olentangy (48-13), and undefeated Nordonia (55-20).

Riding the exploits of running back Jeremy Larkin, who would become a finalist for Ohio's Mr. Football Award (eventually won by future Heisman Trophy winner Joe Burrow), the Lancers rolled into the state semifinals to meet Olentangy. That's when the Northwestern recruit really put on a show. Larkin returned the opening kickoff ninety-eight yards for a touchdown, and the rout began. He finished the night with 239 yards rushing and 6 TDs.

In the state title game at Ohio Stadium, Larkin had another 104 yards rushing and two touchdowns, while Avery Larkin added a pick-six in a 55-20 ambush of Nordonia.

"We were just so focused and dialed in," Moore told the Cincinnati Enquirer. "I don't think there was anything that could've distracted us. It was a beautiful moment. We had incredible leadership on that team. It was a special group of guys."

Chief among them was the star running back Jeremy Larkin. He had clearly bought into the team concept Moore was trying to establish after a tough first season.

"In the postseason, I loved the aspect of winning," Larkin told the Cincinnati Enquirer in a story commemorating the tenth anniversary of that team. "At the end of the day, I'd rather have a team championship than a Mr. Football award."

At this juncture, I became directly involved with Nate Moore. I touched base with him while trying to recruit Avery Larkin. I failed to land that player, but I wasn't done recruiting at LaSalle. It was hard not to be impressed with Nate. LaSalle's run in the Ohio high school football playoffs was the talk of the state in football coaching circles.

I was driving back from a coach's convention in Nashville shortly after the season ended, and the people at Massillon called me. I was the head coach at Massillon from 1988 through 1991 before leaving to take an assistant coaching job at Ohio State under John Cooper. Although this was nearly twenty-five years later, I remained a Massillon Tigers fan and maintained a strong relationship with the school and its administrators. The Tigers had just completed a 7-4 season, but it ended with a thud, a 56-7 loss to Perrysburg, the worst loss the program had absorbed since 1931. That result prompted a coaching change.

With Massillon in the market for a new head football coach, they asked for my thoughts. I quickly focused on Nate Moore and asked him if he'd have any interest in the position. On the surface, moving from one Division II high school to another within the same state may seem a lateral move. But Massillon is no ordinary program. The godfather of the sport, Paul Brown, established a daunting program there when his coaching career began in 1932. The Tigers have produced twenty-three NFL players and won mythic national titles and twenty-four state poll titles (although none on the field at that point, a sore spot with all Massillon fans). Home games are played at Paul Brown Tiger Stadium, which seats approximately twenty thousand fans and is the envy of some college facilities.

Massillon is known nationally by all American high school football fans. For years fathers there presented every baby boy born in Massillon with a football before he left the hospital. Columnist Ron Maly once noted the reach of Massillon High School's football brand in the *Des Moines Register*:

> *"In the beginning, when the Great Creator was drawing plans for this world of ours, he decided there should be something for everyone. He gave us mountains that reach to the sky, deep blue seas, green forests, dry deserts, gorgeous flowers, and gigantic trees. Then he decided there should be football, so he gave us Massillon. He created only one Massillon. He knew that would be enough."*

With that kind of background, the pressure to win at Massillon is immense. Losing a game frequently leads some to post "For Sale" signs in the coach's front yard. Multiple documentaries have been produced about the community and its relationship to the sport. Such a setting is not for the weak-minded.

So Nate and Becca met with me and my wife, Dianne, and Jeff David. Jeff is a longtime friend and an influential person in the community. Nate's curiosity was aroused when he sought a raise at LaSalle, a figure the Lancers were unwilling to meet. That financial figure did not concern Massillon.

"I asked a couple of college coaches that I really liked and respected to look at our roster at LaSalle and Massillon's roster," Nate remembered. "Every one of them said, 'You'd be crazy to go to Massillon.' To be honest, that had the opposite effect on me. It was almost like I was challenged. I can remember my grandpa talking about Massillon a little bit. I just thought one day, on my deathbed, I don't have many regrets, but if I get offered the Massillon job and I don't take it, that's one I'm going to look back on and kick myself for passing up that opportunity."

I told Nate if he didn't take the job, they would never ask him again. I had been in that situation at Lancaster. They offered me the Massillon job, and I was hesitant. Jeff David's father, Paul, asked me to meet him at one of his stores in Columbus, Ohio. Paul was the founder of Camelot Music, a retail chain of over four hundred stores across the United States. Paul David was friends with Paul Brown and loved Massillon Tiger football. Paul told me that night that the Massillon offer was a one-shot deal. There would be no next time. That was the button they pushed on me twenty-five years earlier.

I think the challenge of finally bringing a state championship in the playoff era to Massillon was the clincher for Nate. The Tigers had a lock on the poll titles that were voted on by the media before 1972. But they had never won a crown in the playoff era. Detractors claimed Massillon was a paper tiger. It drove the town nuts to hear it, and winning a state championship had proved incredibly elusive ever since. Coach Gerry Faust at Cincinnati Moeller had proven to be a roadblock in the 1980s. Coach Chuck Kyle at Cleveland St. Ignatius proved nearly impossible to overcome in the 1990s. There were several years the Tigers reached the state finals, including a team featuring Chris Spielman, but Massillon simply could not close the deal.

That's the cauldron Nate Moore stepped into in 2015. On top of everything else, the Tigers were in a tough spot from a talent perspective. As the college coaches warned Moore, the LaSalle roster was far superior. While the Lancers won another state championship in

2015, the Tigers staggered to a 4-6 campaign while facing nine playoff teams. The cardinal sin was losing to archrival Canton McKinley in the regular-season finale. Rebooting one of the most storied programs in the country required an adjustment in priorities.

"To me, one of the things we had to get across is that the same things that make a great student or a great musician or a great choir member are the same things that make a great football player," Nate said. "We had to convince our kids that these characteristics weren't mutually exclusive. If you want to be a great football player, be a great student first. If you're getting A's and B's in your class, then I guarantee you if you care about football you're going to maximize whatever your ability is. You're going to be as good as you can be because you've learned to work hard in other aspects of your life. You already know this is the kind of dedication it takes to excel in the classroom, so you're going to know that's the level you must go to be a great football player. It was a process of convincing the players to believe that things besides the game of football are important for your development as a football player; anything less than that is putting the cart before the horse. Be a better student because you want to be a better football player."

The message resonated, and Massillon's football team GPA steadily improved. It was at 2.8 when he took over and moved above 3.2. Under Moore, the Tigers routinely have one of the top football team GPAs in Ohio, reaching 3.55 one year. The product on the field began to improve too.

In 2016, Massillon improved to 8-3 with a 21-19 win over Canton McKinley but lost its playoff opener to Dublin Scioto. The 2017 team improved again, fashioning a 10-4 record with a regional championship and a Final Four berth. By 2018, Moore had his program where it needed to be. This squad achieved its preseason goal of playing in 15 games, going 14-1 and reaching the state finals before falling 42-28 to Akron Hoban in the Division II state championship game.

That group set a precedent. Massillon was now knocking on the door to exorcise those ghosts that had haunted the program since the playoff era began in 1972. In 2019, it was a repeat performance, 14-0, before falling to Cincinnati LaSalle 34-17 in the Division II state championship game. The abbreviated 2020 season was impacted by COVID, but the Tigers still qualified for their third consecutive state finals, this time falling 35-6 to Akron Hoban. Crossing the Rubicon was proving tricky, even for Nate Moore. Yet he still believed he was the person who could get the program where it dreamed of being.

In 2023, finally, that dream was realized. The Tigers finished 16-0 and beat Division I state champion Lakewood St. Edward 15-13 along the way. Massillon finished it off by edging Akron Hoban 7-2 in the Division II state championship game at Canton's Tom Benson Hall of Fame Stadium. Nate was Ohio's Co-Coach of the Year and the MaxPreps National High School Coach of the Year. Those accolades came on the heels of a thrilling title tilt. The state championship game was a defensive struggle that wasn't clinched until an Akron Hoban pass bounced off the chest of an open receiver in the end zone with just 1:22 remaining.

I was standing on the sidelines on that last drive, that last play, when the Hoban quarterback saw a kid in the corner of the end zone and the ball cut loose to him. Nate talks about "the poison," and here's where I start to drink some of that poison. The ball is in the air and floating through the air, and I'm thinking not again. No, no, not again. I shouldn't be thinking that. I should be at a point where I know he's not going to catch the pass. We're going to win the game. But we as a community, we had not really gotten to that point. We were snakebit. But you've Gotta Believe, and I was as guilty as anybody when I saw that ball in the air.

When I shared my reaction to that ball in the air at the end of the game Coach Moore confidently responded, "It would make me really proud if this was true, that everyone in the stands thought that kid was going to catch that ball and all of our players and coaches on the sidelines believed that was going to be an incomplete pass."

The victory lifted a cloud that had stubbornly hovered over the community for decades. The state championship was cathartic for the players, coaches, fans, and the entire city.

"Notre Dame counts their championships before the BCS [Bowl Championship Series] era; Ohio State counts their national championships before the BCS era—and so do the Massillon Tigers,"

Nate told the statewide TV broadcast crew after the game. "I don't feel like we needed this to validate our program. Maybe to some people we did, and now it's done. It's now accomplished. The Massillon Tigers have won a state championship in the playoff era. This 2023 Massillon Tiger team is immortal. They're going to live forever. Nobody's going to forget these guys."

The following year, the 2024 squad finished 11-3 and was regional runner-up while playing a national schedule. Meanwhile, Nate has compiled a 110-25 record in his ten years at Massillon, shattering Paul Brown's coaching record of eighty victories at the school. Becoming the winningest coach in Tigers' history was an elusive achievement for everyone who followed Brown—except for Nate Moore, seventy-five years after Brown left for Ohio State. Some pondered that the school would rather fire a coach before reaching that milestone than allow anyone to eclipse Brown's mark.

But Nate wasn't among them. He brushed off those concerns, just as he had brushed off the expectations others placed on his program.

"Every team is different, but you really must block out the outside noise. Every team has different strengths and weaknesses. [In 2024] we had plenty of talent, but what we lacked was leadership. That was my failure. I couldn't find a way to properly develop it. We had good kids, kids that anyone would enjoy being around."

Obviously, Nate believes in his players, his team, and his program. He learned a long time ago You've Gotta Believe.

The Massillon-McKinley Game
"I'm not exaggerating when I say the game to me was as big as the Ohio State-Michigan game or an NFL Championship game."
–Chris Spielman

Coach Moore is 9-1 versus rival Canton McKinley. This is the best record and the most wins by any Massillon coach in this ancient rivalry game. A must read is the Massillon Tigers "History of the Rivalry"; only then can one begin to understand the extraordinary tradition of Massillon versus Canton.

My first season as the head coach at Massillon, Earle Bruce, a former

Massillon and Ohio State head coach, called me the week before the Canton game and reminded me that I was hired for only one reason at Massillon: to beat McKinley.

McKinley had beaten the Tigers the past four years under the leadership of the legendary Coach Thom McDaniels. Coach McDaniels had compiled an 11-7 record versus the Tigers, and he was leading a "Drive for Five," hoping to win five consecutive games versus Massillon.

I'd spent the entire season preparing our team for this one-game season. At the same time, our school superintendent, Alexander Paris, was leading a campaign to pass a bond issue to build a new high school. Similar bond issues had failed on the previous six attempts. Al asked me to write a column in support of this bond issue.

I wrote the following, "We realize our goal is to be a State Football Championship Team and to continue our tradition of football excellence. A new high school will not only help us to accomplish this goal but more importantly enable us to become a school district with a tradition of academic excellence."

The game kicked off in Massillon at 2:00 p.m. on November 5, 1988.

I arrived early at the stadium and happened to pick up one of the game programs the boosters planned to sell to the fans as they entered the game. The picture on the cover of the program was an artist rendering of the new high school with a set of hands holding the students. Above the drawing in bold letters these words were printed: "Their Future is in Your Hands." I'm sure this message was directed at the citizens of Massillon, but I took it personally.

It was a rainy day, and the turf at Paul Brown Tiger Stadium was muddy. This game ended up being the last game ever played on grass inside this temple of a high school stadium.

Our only score that day was a halfback pass to the tight end. Jamie Slutz, one of our backup quarterbacks, was inserted into the halfback position in the Power I formation on the goal line. Jamie was left-handed, so we faked the sweep with him to the left side, and he delivered a perfect touchdown pass. As of this writing, Jamie Slutz serves as the mayor of Massillon.

With just seconds left in regulation, the score was tied 7-7 when our quarterback/kicker Lee Hurst missed a FG attempt wide to the right. The game was going into overtime, the first for this storied rivalry.

Canton McKinley took the ball first in overtime but failed to score after a pass in the end zone went through the hands of their tight end.

Once again, we needed a field goal to win. This time the snap was low and short, but our holder, Todd Porter, was able to get the ball set and, Lee Hurst split the uprights. After the win, the fans stormed the field. Then, on the following Tuesday, the citizens of Massillon stormed the ballot box. Issue 12 passed by a comfortable 1,785-vote margin, and the new $21 million Massillon Washington High School was built.

"You've Got to Believe"

Massillon football stars like Lin Houston and Chris Spielman were groomed in the culture of the Massillon-McKinley game. McKinley fostered elite players in this game too, from a trailblazer like Hall of Famer Marion Motley (one of the famed first four Black men to break pro football's color barrier) to three-time all-American Mike Doss.

McKinley also has produced superb coaches, including Don Nehlen (West Virginia) and Ben Schwartzwalder (Syracuse), who, like Paul Brown, always respected this great rivalry.

Paul Brown is the godfather of Ohio football coaches, reaching the pinnacle at every level. A culture of excellence followed him at each stop, from Massillon to Ohio State to the Cleveland Browns. The year Paul Brown was honored as a Distinguished Citizen in Massillon he stopped at my football office at the old Washington High School. He had sent me several messages wishing me good luck after I was hired, but this was our first meeting. He sat in the office for well over an hour that day and lectured me on the history of his hometown and Massillon Tiger football.

Before he left, he invited me to his box at Paul Brown Stadium for an early preseason Bengals game. I couldn't believe as a young high school football coach I was really going to have an opportunity like this. I will never forget the experience. I basically watched and listened as Paul Brown, then team president, evaluated every aspect of the game. He nearly filled a yellow legal pad with notes and assured me that he would personally deliver them to Coach Sam Wyche after the game. Coach Wyche did end up leading the Bengals to the 1990 Central Division title that year. Coach Brown passed away the next year and is buried in Massillon.

Believe in Yourself
"The future belongs to those who believe in the beauty of their dreams. With a heart full of faith, mountains can be moved."–Eleanor Roosevelt

All team leaders set goals and plan how to accomplish the goals. However, from what I have experienced, some miss the most important step in the process. They don't spend enough time selling the plan and building confidence in the team's ability to accomplish the plan.

Most teams that lose just don't believe. They don't believe in either their dreams, the plan, or the value of the journey. And no matter how awesome their dreams are or how well thought out their plans, they have no chance if they don't believe. The single most important determination of a team's success is what the team believes.

Belief is just believing, believing in things yet unseen. There are three parts to belief in a team, all equally important. First is the self-esteem of everyone on the team. Second is the belief in your teammates and the team leaders. Finally, there is the belief in the team journey, or the team cause.

Self-esteem and self-worth are the most important things in everything we do. We were all created in God's image with unique talents and abilities. Our talents are a gift from God; what we do with our talents is our gift to God.

Edward Everett Hale said, "I am only one, but I am one, I can't do all things, but I can do some things, and those things I can do by God's grace I will do." The difference between a successful journey and a failed journey is our belief. We must have a belief that we are destined for greatness and our best is yet to come. I was always certain the next team I coached would be my best team.

If we ever quit believing in ourselves, we are destined to become average and ordinary and willing to accept mediocrity.

President John F. Kennedy said, "We have faith in our future only if we have faith in ourselves."

Positive Attitude and Confidence
"Men die of fright and live of confidence."–Henry David Thoreau

To maintain high self-esteem, one needs a positive attitude and an abundance of self-confidence. Self-esteem is most important in all that we do. I believe most everyone begins life feeling pretty good about themselves; they have high self-esteem. And yet as we grow older, our self-esteem gradually erodes because of negative feedback. Negative barriers can create self-imposed limitations. Athletes and teams with great attitudes learn how to break down these barriers.

Attitude is the way we face life. It's not what happens to the team; it's how the team reacts to it. A season is 10 percent what happens to the team and 90 percent how the team responds to it. The remarkable thing is that every team has a choice regarding the attitude they embrace. Just like every individual on the team, the team itself is in charge of its attitude.

Ability determines potential, but attitude determines performance. And there is an old coaching adage that reminds us *"potential will get you fired."*

To have a positive mental attitude is a matter of choice. The moment you make that choice is the moment it becomes much easier to believe in yourself. Attitude is determined by the greatest computer you will ever own; we call it the human brain. Program the brain with positive data and you will have a positive attitude.

Every great team possesses a mental attitude of confidence. Confidence is not complacency, but it is that quality that stirs within a team the feeling that your team is superior to your opponent's and that with a commitment to your team game plan your team will win. Confidence just does not happen; it must be earned. It is the product of being prepared. It is the product of rigid training and conditioning, long hours of practice, prior success, and an embrace of the everyday standards of excellence.

Allow confidence to replace doubt.

"Valor grows by daring, fear by holding back."–Publilius Syrus

In the end, the teams that most often fail are the teams that lack confidence and the courage to try.

Michael Jordan said, "I can handle failure. Everyone fails, but I can't stand not trying. In the end the only people who fail are those who do not try."

Orlando Pace—I Believe in You

"Our chief want is someone who will inspire us to be what we know we could be."–Ralph Waldo Emerson

For a team to achieve excellence, the members of that team must believe in one another. The most powerful and encouraging words are "You can do it" and "I believe in you."

When my coach or teacher or teammate came up to me, put their hand on my shoulder, and said these words, it stirred me; it motivated me. During my forty-five-year coaching career, these words were my most powerful motivator.

There was one season I remember at Ashland University when we started out 0-2, and we had not yet played our toughest opponents. We should have won both games, and I was as low as I could be as a coach. I was standing outside the locker room after the game, and one of the last players to leave was our wide receiver Nick Bellanco. Nick was a great player as well as a great student. Today he is Dr. Bellanco. Nick said to me as he left that evening, "Coach, I believe in you, and I believe in this team, and we are not going to lose another game!" I was fired up. We won our next nine games and advanced farther than any team in our history at that time. It helps to know that your team believes in you.

A strong argument can be made that Orlando Pace may have been the best left tackle to ever play football. From Sandusky, Ohio, Orlando was the most highly recruited high school football player in the country as a senior in the 1993-94 school year.

During the offseason at Ohio State, I was given just two assignments. First, sign Orlando Pace. Second, get him ready to start at left tackle as a true freshman. This was an opportunity to end up being both the recruiting coach and the position coach for the top high school recruit in the country.

Thanks to our all-American right tackle Korey Stringer, I was able to accomplish both assignments. Orlando was impressed with Korey, wanted to play with him and learn from him. For over a year I did all I could to build my relationship with Orlando. I even set up a walleye fishing trip with Coach Cooper and Orlando's high school head coach, Larry Cook.

I worked with an outstanding Ohio State "committee man" who was a dentist in Huron, Ohio. Committee men were Ohio State alums who were our eyes and ears in the communities of our top recruits.

The closest I came to losing Orlando Pace was during his trip from Sandusky, Ohio, to Columbus for his official visit. As an Ohio State Coach and recruiter, I had access to the "Buckeye Air Force." My pilot was an alum who was an attorney from Dayton. He had a Cessna 172 Skyhawk, a four-seat single- engine aircraft.

We took off out of a private hangar in Rickenbacker Airport, heading toward a small airport in Sandusky. The airport had a short runway right beside Lake Erie. I told Orlando we would pick him up after his basketball game Friday night. After an interesting landing with the wind blowing hard off the lake, we met Orlando and his mother at the airport.

Even as a senior in high school, Orlando was six foot seven and over 300 pounds. I needed to copilot, so we stuffed Orlando into the small back seats. Orlando had never flown on a plane before, and our pilot started to joke with him while backing the wheels off the end of the runway, saying he had never flown with this much weight before and wasn't sure he had enough runway to get up over the lake.

On Sunday morning, I had breakfast with Orlando. He said it was a good visit, but he had one serious question. Could I please cancel his private flight home and make the two-hour drive with him back to Sandusky?

Orlando was everything we hoped for at Ohio State and had really played well as a freshman through the first five games. In the sixth game, Illinois came to Columbus with the number one defense in the country.

Their outside linebacker was Simeon Rice. He was six foot five, 245 pounds, quick and athletic, and leading the Big Ten with ten sacks. He would play the entire game over Orlando, and Illinois Head Coach Lou Tepper planned to cut him loose on third down.

In the locker room just before the players took the field, I routinely checked on the athletes I coached, looked them in the eye, shook their hands, and wished them good luck.

Orlando seemed a little different before this 3:30 p.m. kickoff in Ohio Stadium. I remember telling him during pregame that he was prepared and that he had the ability to block Rice. I told him I believed that someday he would be recognized as one of the best offensive linemen to ever play for the Buckeyes. I also told him that to be the best, he had to block the best and that he had that opportunity in the game we were about to play.

We led that game at halftime before falling short to a second-half Illinois rally. But Orlando played well. Simeon Rice had zero sacks.

Orlando went on to become the Freshman of the Year in the Big 10, a Lombardi Award winner, a Heisman finalist, the number one pick in the 1996 NFL Draft, an All-Pro, and eventually a Pro Football Hall of Famer. As I stood on the field in Canton, Ohio, with Orlando wearing his Gold Jacket, I was reminded that even great players like Orlando Pace need coaches and teammates who believe in them.

With high self-esteem and belief in your teammates and the leaders on your team, it becomes much easier to believe in the team. As a coach, I can have a great game plan for third downs, but when the plays are sent in to the eleven players on the field, if there is not 100 percent belief, we have no chance of making a first down. Every day, at every opportunity, remind the team of their goals and sell the team on the plan. Most importantly, coach belief every day. Belief is a state of mind. "You've Got to Believe."

STATE OF MIND
If you think you are beaten, you are,
If you think you dare not, you don't.
If you like to win but think that you can't, it's almost a cinch you won't.

If you think you'll lose, you've lost.
For out in the world, we find success begins with a fellow's will.
It's all in the state of mind.'
Life's battles don't always go to the stronger or faster man.
But sooner or later the man who wins is the one who thinks he can.
It's all in a state of mind.
—Walter D. Wintle

Key Points for You've Gotta Believe

1. The most often missed step in team building is also the most important step. The team leader must sell the plan to the team and build the team's confidence in their ability to accomplish the plan.
2. There are three parts to belief in team building: self-esteem, belief in teammates, and belief in the team.
3. Self-esteem is the product of a positive attitude and self-confidence.
4. Ability determines potential, but attitude determines performance.
5. Every team has a choice of attitude they will embrace.
6. Confidence is built by earned success and conforming to everyday standards of excellence.
7. The most powerful words of a team leader are "You can do it" and "I believe in you."
8. Even great players and coaches need the team to believe in them.
9. With high self-esteem and belief in your teammates, it becomes much easier to believe in the team.
10. Team leaders must coach belief every day. If there is not 100 percent belief in the team plan, it won't work.

PART THREE:
THE PURSUIT OF EXCELLENCE

The pursuit of the team's success is most dependent on the passion and the commitment of the team. Passion for a football player or coach comes from their love of the game. They love football. The best players and coaches on the team are the ones with the most passion, the most enthusiasm.

The Greek derivative for enthusiasm is enthos, translated to English as "God within." After passion is commitment. Team commitment is persistence, the will to keep going and never quit. Team commitment is the perseverance of triumph over odds.

Ultimately, team commitment is a "Commitment to Excellence," as outlined in this famous essay by coaching icon Vince Lombardi: "... *each Sunday, after the battle, one group savors victory, another group lives in the bitterness of defeat. The many hurts seem a small price to have paid for having won, and there is no reason at all that is adequate for having lost. To the winner is 100% elation, 100% laughter, 100% fun; and to the loser the only thing left for him is 100% resolution, 100% determination. And it's a game, a great deal like life in that it demands a man's personal commitment toward excellence and toward victory, even though the ultimate victory can never be completely won.* "Yet it must be *pursued with all one's might. And each week there's a new encounter, each year a new challenge. But all of the rings and all of the money and all of the color and all of the display, they linger only in memory. The spirit, the will to win, the will to excel, these are the things that endure, and these are the qualities that are so much more important than any of the events that occasion them. And I would like to say that the quality of man's life has got to be a full measure of that man's personal commitment to excellence and to victory, regardless of what field he may be in."*

THE SPIRIT OF A TEAM

–CHAPTER EIGHT–
YOU'VE GOTTA LOVE IT

"A great leader's courage to fulfill his visions comes from passion, not position."–John C. Maxwell

Photo of Matt LaFleur

Bio Box: Matt LaFleur – Head Coach Green Bay Packers
Background: Matt is the older of two brothers; sibling Mike LaFleur, seven years younger, is the offensive coordinator for the Los Angeles Rams heading into the 2025 season. Both boys were born to Denny and Kristi LaFleur. Denny was a longtime defensive assistant coach at Central Michigan University. Kristi was a Michigan state champion competitive cheer coach at Mount Pleasant High School.
Athletic Achievement: Matt was a standout in basketball and football while earning allstate honors as a quarterback at Mount Pleasant High School. He went on to Western Michigan but transferred to Saginaw Valley State. At SVSU, he led the Cardinals to three consecutive Division II playoff appearances. LaFleur set school records for passing yards (7,699) and touchdowns (67). He was inducted into the SVSU Cardinal Athletic Hall of Fame in 2021.
Scholastic Achievement: Bachelor's degree with teaching certificate from Saginaw Valley State. Masters of Science in Admin Central Michigan.
Professional Achievement: Best first three-year start of any head coach in NFL history, 39-10, with three NFC North championships at the helm of the Green Bay Packers. Heading into the 2024 season, he fashioned a 67-33 regular-season record, for a .67 winning percentage.
Accolades: LaFleur was the quarterback coach for Robert Griffin III's rookie of the year season in 2012 at Washington. He also was the position coach for Matt Ryan when the Falcons' QB won the NFL MVP award in 2016. The Falcons reached the Super Bowl before falling to the Patriots. In his first head-coaching season, Matt led the Packers to the 2019 NFC championship game.
Personal: Matt and his wife, BreAnne (Maak), have two sons: Luke and Ty.

Any NFL fan will immediately recognize the name Matt LaFleur. He is one of the top head coaches in the NFL and is off to a historic start to his coaching career. Matt won more games in his first three seasons than any other coach in NFL history.

I get a tremendous sense of pride playing a part in Matt's career. He coached for me at Ashland University and ranks as one of the most passionate people I ever hired. He had little choice in the matter. Matt is deeply rooted in the family business—coaching football.

He is a third-generation football coach. Indeed, his father, Denny, was a linebacker for Central Michigan's 1974 Division II national championship team. Denny set the school career tackles record with 324 stops. Matt's mom, Kristi (Barringer), was a cheerleader for the Chippewas. Their first date was a match made on the gridiron. Kristi is the daughter of "Bullet" Bob Barringer, who was the head football coach at Kalamazoo Loy Norrix in the 1960s and 1970s.

"My first date with Kristi, I was breaking down 16mm game film with her dad," Denny LaFleur told the Tennessean.

Denny LaFleur went on to become a defensive assistant coach at Central Michigan University for twenty-two years, and the couple had two sons, both of whom were destined to coach in the NFL. Matt and his younger brother, Mike, both experienced a typical coach's son's upbringing. Matt held phones on the sidelines during Central Michigan games.

"My mom, in order for me to be around my dad, she would drive me to their practices all the time," Matt said. "I remember being little and sometimes going to the 6:00 a.m. workouts. Being around the game so much, it just kind of fell into my lap. It's what I grew up with. It's what I knew. It's what I liked. I guess I was a product of my environment. They tell me my grandpa started coaching for $1,500 a year in the late 1940s. I just don't think there was any doubt where my brother and I were going to end up."

Summers were filled with football camps and players as babysitters. One of them was John Bonamego, a Central Michigan player cutting his teeth as a junior varsity coach at Mount Pleasant High School. Is there any wonder a passion to compete was part of the package from the start?

"[Matt's] dad actually recruited me," Bonamego told the Detroit News. "So when he was little, I babysat him and his brother. We'd play H-O-R-S-E. I had to keep the score close because [Matt would] get pretty pissed off. . . . I'd let him win."

When things didn't go Matt's way as a youngster, he wanted to analyze the reason. He still does. This trait came to the fore as early as junior high school. Luke Epple was Matt's eighth grade science teacher and junior high basketball coach. He remembers a game where Matt missed a potential game-winning three-pointer that rattled in and out.

Afterward, Matt reached out to Epple in the locker room: "He said, 'Coach, why didn't that go in?'" Epple told PackerNews.com. "I said, 'Well, you know what the shooting percentage of an eighth grader behind the arc is? It's not very high.' But he wanted to know that. He says, 'Why didn't it?' . . . because he was going to make it the next time.

"There were times where he'd ask, 'How do I get these guys to care?' Of course, I'd been at it for a little while, and I said, 'Well, you've got to remember they're eighth graders.' He was an eighth grader, but I could tell him that because he was beyond that as far as how he thought and approached the game. He had a rough time handling that."

Matt played three sports at Mount Pleasant High School: football, basketball and track. He was an excellent basketball player and an allstate pick as a two-year starting quarterback. Originally, he planned to follow his parents to Central Michigan, but when Denny was fired as part of a staff purge in 1997, Matt walked on at Western Michigan.

"[My Dad's firing] was a pretty traumatic thing for our family," Matt said. "I was all Central Michigan before that. When that happened, I didn't want anything to do with them."

Instead, he attended Western Michigan for two years, switched to receiver, and couldn't break through for playing time. So he transferred to Saginaw Valley State, where coach Randy Awrey was building a program—and where fate intervened.

In the 2000 season opener, Cardinals starting quarterback Garrett Small suffered a career-ending head injury. That put Matt in the starter's role for game two against powerhouse Grand Valley State.

Two touchdown passes later, SVSU had a 28-21 victory, and a star was born. Matt immediately led his team to the Division II playoffs and established a reputation for his competitive streak.

"I don't know that I ever really had a moment that clinched it for me," Matt said. "I just always felt like I could play, tried to always prepare myself to be ready to play, even if I wasn't starting."

As a junior in the school's first home playoff game, Matt rallied his team from a 32-7 halftime deficit against Indiana University of Pennsylvania. He promptly tossed 3 TD passes, and his touchdown dash finally pushed Saginaw to 33-32 with 1:27 remaining. Awrey sent in the two-point conversion play, but Matt stumbled and fumbled while trying to hand off on a jet sweep. An Indiana lineman scooped up the ball and headed for the other end zone. Yet LaFleur sprinted to catch up to the defender and fought off a pair of blockers along the way. The lineman saw he was about to be caught, so he tried to lateral the ball. Matt jumped on the defender with possession of the pigskin and hauled him down to preserve a breathtaking win—instead of what could have been a devastating defeat.

"I just hung on for dear life," Matt said. "I just bear-hugged him. That's something I'll definitely never forget."

Another play made a lasting memory on one of his college teammates. Receiver Glenn Martinez, who went on to play in the NFL, remembers the Cardinals playing against an all-American linebacker when LaFleur took off on a bootleg. Martinez decleated the linebacker with a devastating crackback block that resulted in a ten-yard run but not a first down. Still, the block ignited the crowd.

"You'd have thought we'd won the Super Bowl," said Martinez, who turned to celebrate with LaFleur. "Matt's pissed because we didn't get the first down. . . . I'm like, 'Shoot, I just knocked this dude out.' And Matt was like, 'No, we didn't get the first down. Get on the bench.' Matt was that type of leader." LaFleur still ranks in the top three in Saginaw Valley State's record book in pass attempts, pass completions, passing yards, and passing TDs. He had the ability, but at five foot eleven, 175 pounds, his stature worked against him going any further as a player.

"He didn't have the size to play in the NFL, but Matt had the ability," Awrey said.

Matt played briefly with the Omaha Beef and the Billings Outlaws in the National Indoor Football League, but his playing career was soon over. So he embarked on a career path that could keep him involved with his passion—football.

LaFleur earned his degree and began working as a student teacher in the Saginaw district. He also joined Awrey's staff as a graduate assistant tutoring quarterbacks and receivers. The next year he returned to Mount Pleasant to join Brian Kelly's staff as a graduate assistant at Central Michigan. LaFleur was there for two years and made connections with three people who would forever change his life.

The first was Kelly, whose passion and offensive coaching acumen fit Matt's drive to a T. The second was another graduate assistant, Robert Saleh, who would become Matt's best friend and roommate and a computer guru who made an impression on LaFleur with his high-tech wizardry. Saleh would also be in Matt's wedding, and he met the third and most important person of all, his future wife, BreAnne Maak.

Still, it wasn't exactly love at first sight. According to BreAnne, who was working as a student trainer at CMU, Matt did not make a good first impression. She was in the way while he was conducting a drill. He wanted her to move and did not ask politely, to say the least:

"There's no way I'm working with this guy again," BreAnne told PackerNews.com.

Matt doesn't remember it that way.

"She said I yelled at her the first time I talked to her because she was in the way of a drill, but I don't think that ever happened."

Regardless, it didn't deter Matt's pursuit of her, and he eventually won her over. It had to happen quickly, and permanently, because he wouldn't be in Mount Pleasant for long. His star was on the rise, and Matt made sure BreAnne was coming with him.

"I told her there are two kinds of wives: coaches' wives and ex-wives. Thank God I've got a coach's wife."

Matt's next stop was in Marquette, Michigan, where he was a full-time assistant at Northern Michigan coaching quarterbacks and wide receivers in 2006 under head coach Bernie Anderson in the Upper Peninsula.

This is where Matt first came to my attention. At Ashland, we beat Northern Michigan 27-10 in 2005, and frankly I wasn't impressed with their quarterback play. In 2006, Ashland had a sub-.500 team, but we still beat Northern Michigan 24-17 in a road victory. However, this was a very different game. I was thoroughly impressed by the improvement in their quarterback play. Buddy Rivera, a three-year starter, had an efficient senior season with 20 TD passes and just five interceptions. He left school with a record fifty-two career touchdown passes. As that game ended, I went across the field and sought out Matt to tell him what a fine job he had done with Buddy. I could see the improvement. It was stark. That stuck in my mind, or I should say Matt stuck in my mind.

In 2007 at Ashland University, we were fortunate to have one of the top-rated quarterbacks in Division II college football returning to our team. Billy Cundiff had an NFL arm and was a very tough and athletic player. In our postseason meeting, I made a commitment to Bill that I would use the offseason to hire the very best quarterback coach possible.

As I reviewed all the candidates who seemed to fit this position, I just couldn't stop thinking about that young coach from Northern Michigan. I knew Matt played quarterback at Saginaw Valley State for Randy Awrey, a coach I respected a great deal. When I talked about Matt with Coach Awrey, he shared with me the great competitor Matt was as a player and the passion he had for the game. It was the same passion he displayed as an assistant coach working for one of the most passionate head coaches in the country in Brian Kelly at Central Michigan. More homework revealed Matt was a coach's son, and I had always had a great deal of success hiring coaches who grew up on the football field. Most importantly, I had seen with my own eyes that Matt had taken a talented quarterback at Northern Michigan who had not been very productive and turned him into one of the best in our league.

After talking with Matt about the position—and hearing his depth of knowledge of the passing game patterned after Brian Kelly's high-flying offense—I knew I had to find a way to hire him. His vertical passing scheme was a change we really had to make in our program to emphasize Billy's strengths as a quarterback.

Matt wanted to be the offensive coordinator, and I agreed. So now all I needed to do was help Matt (and his now wife, BreAnne) make it work financially. The money isn't great at the Division II level, so we also helped BreAnne find a job near Ashland selling pharmaceuticals, and she was fantastic at it too. Now the pieces were in place.

I knew it would be hard to keep Matt. I asked him to give me a two-year commitment, and he agreed. That 2007 season we went 8-1 in the conference and reached the playoffs. Matt really transformed our offense. Billy was an all-American quarterback who threw for nearly four thousand yards and was a Harlon Hill finalist (the Division II equivalent of the Heisman Trophy).

"That was a fun year," Matt said. "We had some really good players. That was just a great opportunity for me. It was my first chance to be an offensive coordinator. I look back on it, and the tiny apartment, and living in Ashland, and you just think about the stops along the way that influence you. That was definitely one of them."

I loved Matt's aggressiveness. He always wanted to throw the football. If he had his way, we would throw on every down. In one game we were beating Mercyhurst and really pounding them on the ground. Over the headphones, Matt kept prodding me, "Coach, we can throw downfield all day on these guys. Coach, the downfield throw is open all day." I'm thinking to myself, *Matt, we're averaging nine yards a carry. Why the hell would I want to throw the ball?*

Matt was one of the smartest football guys I had ever interviewed. If his guys didn't get it, he'd rip their butt. He got that from his dad. He was demanding and intense and on top of everything and everyone on offense.

Yet what was most notable about Matt and his coaching style was his ability to be on fire and at the same time be a great teacher of the game. His football IQ was off the charts. His attention to detail and his ability to correct mistakes as they happened with an intensity and a clear challenge to do it right, to do it better, were impressive.

"Coaching is about holding people to standards," Matt said.

"Some guys you have to push on harder than others. Others are more receptive. You have to know your guys and let them know what you expect of them, what they're capable of."

I was looking forward to even greater things in 2008 with Billy returning for his final season and Matt molding him. Then, the strangest thing happened. I got a call from Gary Kubiak asking if he could hire Matt to coach for the Houston Texans. It was not the kind of call one gets every day at the Division II level.

But that connection Matt made with Robert Saleh during their days together as graduate assistants at Central Michigan took a dramatic turn at this point of his coaching journey. Saleh had a spot as a defensive intern on the Texans' staff, and when a similar spot opened on the offensive side of the ball, he recommended Matt for the job.

Matt struggled with the decision for a while. He would be taking a huge pay cut from more than $30,000 a year in Ashland to what they call a 20/20/20 guy, in his twenties, working twenty hours a day, making about $20,000 per year. In the NFL, these are called quality-control coaches, or draw boys. They are asked to constantly draw things up for coaches on the computer, on the dry-erase board, on cards. Matt wasn't even sure Saleh was serious.

"Honestly, I was like, 'Okay, sure,'" Matt said when reflecting on Saleh's call. "I didn't believe him." When Kubiak finally agreed to extend an offer, Matt wasn't sure what to do. He had made a commitment to me, BreAnne was soaring in her own career here, and the money was even worse than what I was paying him. Also, he would be uprooting himself and his newlywed wife for a different part of the country.

He conveyed those concerns to Saleh—who couldn't believe Matt didn't jump at the chance to advance to professional football.

"Matt! It's the N-F-L. Are you nuts? Have you lost your mind?" Saleh remembered in a story for the Tennessean. "You don't have a choice in this. You are coming. I'll make the family decision for you."

I sure didn't want to lose Matt LaFleur, and I know Matt felt bad because of the commitment he had made when I hired him just nine months earlier. But it was the NFL, and a great opportunity for this young quarterback coach, who was destined for greatness.

Matt left us, but with two presents. First, our offense had taken a huge step forward with the vertical passing concepts he installed. Second, Matt had recruited an all-Ohio quarterback from Ashland High School named Taylor Housewright who wanted to play for Coach LaFleur but stuck with his commitment to his hometown and became an all-American for us at Ashland University.

Matt worked for two years as an offensive quality-control assistant with the Texans, where he made an impression on Offensive Coordinator Kyle Shanahan.

"I was in awe of how much I didn't know," Matt said of working under Shanahan. "You're always pushing on each other. It definitely sparked a sense of urgency in me."

Then, at age thirty, Matt landed his first full-time NFL gig when Shanahan got the offensive coordinator's job in 2010 with the Washington Redskins. He immediately hired Matt as the quarterback coach. That was obviously the right move. LaFleur coached Robert Griffin III's rookie of the year 2012 season and then helped develop Kirk Cousins.

The staff was fired after the 2013 season, but LaFleur reconnected with Brian Kelly at Notre Dame. In 2014, He mentored Everett Golson, who threw for 3,445 yards and 29 TDs for the Fighting Irish.

That performance again caught the NFL's attention, and Matt's next gig grabbed everyone's attention. He reunited with Kyle Shanahan, now offensive coordinator of the Atlanta Falcons, and was tabbed as the quarterbacks coach, helping to shape Matt Ryan's MVP season in 2016. That campaign ended in the Super Bowl, albeit a heartbreaking 34-28 overtime loss to the Patriots.

In 2017, Matt reached the next rung on the coaching ladder as offensive coordinator for the Los Angeles Rams. The Rams finished the year 11-5 thanks to LaFleur's number one scoring offense, which registered 478 points.

In the offseason, he interviewed for a head coaching spot but didn't get it.

"Really, that was a break for me, because I wasn't ready for it yet," Matt remembers.

In 2018, he accepted the offensive coordinator role with the

Tennessee Titans under Mike Vrabel and added play-calling duties for the first time. An injury-plagued season to starting QB Marcus Mariota torpedoed the Titans offense, but it didn't hurt Matt's reputation.

On January 8, 2019, the Green Bay Packers hired him among ten candidates as their new head coach. He was all of thirty-nine and yet an instant success for one of the league's proudest franchises.

In 2019 the Packers went 13-3, won the NFC North, and reached the NFC championship game. Green Bay went 13-3 again in 2020 and 13-4 in 2021. The Packers are postseason regulars, and today, Matt is considered one of the top head coaches in the sport.

It's one of my proudest achievements to have played a small role in Matt's coaching career. Think about it: I get to claim Matt LaFleur on my coaching tree. That's quite an ornament!

Passion and Enthusiasm

"The successful man has enthusiasm. Good work is never done in cold blood; heat is needed to forge anything. Every great achievement is a story of a flaming heart."–Harry Truman

I had my first lesson on what it means to be passionate about something when I was a young high school football player. Keith Wakefield, my position coach and the Mansfield Madison Rams' defensive coordinator, was among the most passionate men on the planet. Coach Wakefield was one of those coaches who showed up every day wearing only shorts and a T-shirt, regardless of the weather. Late autumn in Ohio can be snowing and freezing cold, and on these occasions, while most of the team would be all layered up and shivering, he would show up in his shorts and T-shirt shouting his favorite words, "You've got to love it, men! You've got to love it!"

Although it was nearly fifty years ago, I can still remember one practice where Coach Wakefield was not happy with my execution of a forearm shiver, so he decided to demonstrate to me the correct way to do it. I'm sure Rod Schag, who was my best friend and defensive teammate, enjoyed watching this very effective coaching lesson.

Coach Wakefield was a man on a mission. He was always positive, and he fired me up. In a good way he seemed strangely unaware of anything around him but the mission.

His passion and love for the game were contagious. His energy and enthusiasm provided the spark the team needed to light its own fire.

As a high school senior, I was recruited to Bluffton College in Ohio. I still have an athletic newsletter they sent all the football prospects on their definition of enthusiasm:

ENTHUSIASM
"The keynote that makes us sing and makes men sing with us.
"The producer of confidence. It cries to all the world, 'I've got this, I've got what it takes'
"The inspiration that makes us wake up with a spring in our step, and love in our heart.
"It changes a pessimist into an optimist, a loafer into a producer.
"If you have it, your teammates get it, and your team loves it.
"If you haven't got it, then get down on your knees and pray for it."
"Enthusiasm is like passion, the love of your sport. If you don't have the love for your sport, you will never be able to work the long hours it takes to achieve excellence."

You can't fake enthusiasm. Maybe for a day or two you can fool yourself, but eventually the grind will be too hard, and you will walk away.

German philosopher Georg Wilhelm Friedrich Hegel said, "Nothing great in the world has ever been accomplished without passion."

This is why it is so important to find your passion, to do something you are driven to do. I had no idea I was going to be a coach, but I got there by following my heart. I had a real enthusiasm for athletics and the passion to compete. The secret to life is not what you like but what you like to do. Once you find something you like to do and that you are passionate about, make a commitment to it and you will achieve excellence.

The pursuit of a team's success is most dependent on passion and commitment to the team. Passion for a football player or coach comes from their love of the game. The best members of the team are the ones with the most passion, the most enthusiasm. The Greek derivative for enthusiasm is *entheos*, which translates to "the God within."

I hired coach Tim Rose as the defensive coordinator for our Ashland Eagles NCAA Division II football program. As he finished his sixth decade of coaching in 2024, Tim was as passionate as he was in his first year. After each season, Coach Rose would assure me he was still on fire. He would say that the flames weren't as high as they were thirty years ago, but they were still burning.

French General Ferdinand Roch said, "The most powerful weapon on earth is the human soul on fire."

Jeris Pendleton was a defensive tackle for Coach Rose and went on to play in the NFL. Here is what Jeris had to say about the inspiration Tim offered his players:

"Coach Rose's energy and passion for the game is unmatched. He will make you feel like you can run through a stone wall for him. You can hear the passion in his voice any time he is speaking. His pregame speeches will give you goosebumps. If you weren't prepared before hearing him talk, you definitely will be ready after his speech. I can't recall a day where he did not bring enthusiasm and passion to practice or to games. He's always fired up.

"So as a player, how could you not give your best effort? He inspires you to play with pride and passion, grit, and determination. Coach Rose is not only legendary, he is the G.O.A.T. I salute him and aspire to have the same impact on others he did on me."

Mission Statement

"Make your life a mission- not an intermission."- Arnold Glasgow

Team passion needs to be outlined in a team mission statement. I believe any team or organization could take the first few words of the beliefs outlined in one of my mission statements and write their own:
- To be a . . .
- To pursue excellence in . . .
- To secure a . . .
- To make a commitment to . . .
- To develop strong . . .
- To be part of a . . .

- To work within . . .
- To experience . . .
- To enjoy the . . .
- To compete with . . .
- To win . . .
- To bring honor to . . .

Not only would I challenge all team leaders to make a team mission statement, but I would also challenge them to make sure this document is printed, posted, and alive. It needs to be available to the team.

Each year I would include our Team Mission Statement in our staff handbook and review the document with the staff. I would also include it in our student handbook and review it with our team. Most importantly, I would always have it framed and hanging in my office as my guide and as a reference for many of the decisions I would make every day as a team leader.

Finally, I would challenge all team leaders to have everyone on the team write their own personal mission statement. A personal mission statement needs to be honest and reflect the instinctive possibility of what can be done. A statement that is simple, concrete, specific, and written down serves as a contract. This is your "why." It's from your soul what you were born to do. How can you make a difference?

It challenges the individual to answer these questions:
- What interests you the most?
- What do you dream of doing?
- What is your purpose?
- What are you most proud of doing?

It has been said that the secret to life is to love what you do. "Love what you do in life, and you will have a great life"— I've heard this, read this, lived this, and I believe this! This is passion.

> *By your own soul learn to live,*
> *and if men thwart you take no heed.*
> *If men hate you, have no care.*

Sing your song, dream your dream, hope your prayer."
—Unknown Author

I've been asked many times how I coached teams to play with such passion. The answer was always the same: I surrounded myself with people who seemed to have fun doing what they do. They loved the people they did it with, and they just enjoyed life or living in general. Positive, confident, and enthusiastic people make up the most passionate teams. Again, confidence, enthusiasm, and positive attitudes, like passion, are contagious.

The best members of any team will always be those with the most passion. How do you find passionate team leaders and members?

It begins during the recruiting or interview process with simple questions like "Why do you want to be here? How can you make a difference? What would you fight for? What makes you unique, and how do you express this part of yourself?"

Answers to these questions that reflect passion would include phrases like "I love this place. I love to compete. I love the people on this team." As Coach Wakefield said, "You've got to love it, men!"

Passion and Desire

"I use the word 'hungry' to describe what I mean when I talk about desire. Being hungry provides you with the physical and mental energies necessary for success."–Ara Parseghian

To excel as a team, the team must be hungry for success and hungry to simply become the best. This all starts with a dream and a plan. However, if the team is not inspired or has little desire, they will veer off course and never reach their goals. Without true love for what you do and the burning desire to be the best at what you do, you will never achieve excellence.

Once you find passion and desire, you will have the dedication and determination that is necessary to carry you to your dreams. Only the truly dedicated and most determined teams ever achieve excellence.

It's the intrinsic motivation of passion and desire that gives a team the strength to overcome obstacles, focus on goals, and outwork their competition. Passion and desire are where achievement begins.

Without desire, capable teams fail. Yet with desire, teams with average talent win. Strong desire gives a team a great sense of accomplishment. A team that has a burning desire to be great and acts upon that desire will achieve excellence.

Because of desire, all things being equal, the team that wants to win the most often wins. Strong desire is like a struggle or a fight for air as you are being held under water against your will.

Korey Stringer—He Played the Game He Loved

"I play football because I love the game. I love competitions, and I love to win. I make up my mind at the beginning of every game that I'm going to block the pressures out of my mind. I'm going to go out there and have some fun."–Dave Logan, NFL Receiver

"Let's get out there and have some fun." I can't begin to count the times I've challenged a team with these words as we left the locker room before a practice or a game. Earlier in this chapter, I explained that the reason my teams always seemed motivated was because I always surrounded myself with people who seemed to have fun doing what they do. They just enjoyed life.

Athletes generally start playing a sport because they enjoy it. It's fun for them. They enjoy making new friends. They enjoy learning new skills. They enjoy competing and improving and winning. It has always been true that an athlete must be learning, growing, and improving if they are going to win and enjoy the game.

Winning is fun. It improves your physical and psychological health. Winning boosts endorphins and decreases stress. The laughter and joy of winning releases serotonin, also good for your health. Having fun with the members of your team is essential to the culture, positive attitude, and energy of a team.

However, the number one reason athletes give for quitting a team is that the game stopped being fun. An athlete loses this joy for the game for one or two reasons. Either they have lost their connection with their teammates or they are not getting any better at the sport. They are not seeing results. They are not winning. Practice becomes harder and harder. Losing your love for the game means losing your passion.

If you don't love what you are doing, find another sport or another job or another passion. If you do love what you are doing, enjoy the grind, be a great teammate, and have some fun.

No one I ever coached had more passion and love for the game than Korey Stringer. Korey was a two-time all-American offensive tackle I coached at Ohio State. Korey played high school football for Warren Harding, where he was part of a state championship team. His first season at Ohio State, he was the freshman of the year in the Big Ten.

Korey loved the game. I believe Korey would have showed up to play the game with the same passion no matter if it was in front of ninety thousand fans at Ohio Stadium or in the parking lot of the local Walmart.

Korey was fun to coach. He was fun to be around. He always had a smile on his face and seemed to enjoy the game, enjoyed being around his teammates, enjoyed winning.

Kevin Seifert, a staff writer with ESPN, shared these comments about Korey from a couple of his NFL teammates. Todd Steussie was an offensive lineman who played with Korey when Korey was first with the Vikings:

"[Korey] was a guy who made you feel like his best friend," Steussie said.

Another offensive lineman for the Vikings. David Dixon, echoed Steussies' affection for Korey.

"He had a quiet sense of humor. He found humor in everyday things. Little things you would never notice, he would point out thinking they were so funny and joyous."

As much fun as Korey seemed to make the game, he was always all in. At times it seemed like he was having so much fun in meetings I wasn't sure that he was really paying attention. So I would quiz him about an assignment we covered in the meeting on the way to the field. Every single time he would have the right answer. So I would purposely change or add something to the assignment before we get to the field and then add or change it again on the sideline before his turn in the huddle. Again, 100 percent of the time he would get it right. The moral of the story is that it is possible to have fun and still be focused and intense and completely dialed in.

Korey is considered one of the greatest offensive linemen in Ohio State history. His great passion and genuine personality were instrumental in helping me successfully recruit Orlando Pace to the Buckeyes. Orlando was probably the nation's best high school football player in 1993 and absolutely our priority recruit out of Sandusky, Ohio. Recruiting him was my responsibility, but one of the big reasons Orlando signed with Ohio State was the influence of Korey Stringer.

When we started them both as bookend tackles on Ohio State's 1994 offensive line, I knew I was coaching the two best offensive tackles in all of college football. Against Michigan, we used an unbalanced offensive line look, lining them up side by side, helping us beat the Wolverines for the first time in seven years.

Korey had that kind of impact on the entire program. He was also a first-round draft pick, a Pro Bowler, and a second-team All-Pro for the Minnesota Vikings.

He Changed the Game
"Success comes to those who dedicate everything to their passion in life."–A.R. Rahman

Unfortunately, just as his career was hitting its peak, Korey died of heatstroke during the 2001 summer training camp in Minnesota. He was only twenty-seven. It was reported that Korey showed up to camp in excellent shape. At six foot five, 300 pounds, he was right at his college playing weight. But with the first two days of camp featuring temperatures above the 90 degree heat index, Korey showed signs of heatstroke and dehydration on both days.

When Korey collapsed, his core body temperature was reported to be above 108 degrees. We know now that trainers have only thirty minutes to get the core body temperature below 104 degrees.

Korey's tragic death was a national story. It shook everyone, and in fact changed the game of football. Soon afterward, the Korey Stringer Institute (KSI) was funded by the NFL. Deaths resulting from heatstroke immediately decreased. All levels of football across the country changed the way athletes trained in the heat. Most states enacted new laws protecting athletes. High school, college, and NFL teams changed their rules on when a team could practice, how often a team could practice, and how many days athletes needed for acclimation. Requirements for water and ice tubes on the field were enacted. Weight loss through dehydration was being monitored. The game was made safer.

I wish it hadn't taken Korey's death to alter the course of decades of erroneous thinking on the subject. But Korey's tremendous influence and impact on his sport resonated long after he departed the gridiron. That's the kind of influence his passion generated.

I will never forget attending the memorial service for Korey in his hometown of Warren, Ohio. His high school teammates and coaches from that state championship squad attended. They were joined by his Ohio State teammates and coaches from our 1993 Big Ten championship club. Coach Dennis Green, Chris Carter, and Randy Moss were just a few of the Minnesota Vikings in attendance too.

The entire community was there. The crowd was far too big for the auditorium, so speakers were placed in the parking lots for the overflow crowd. Korey was loved by his community. Korey also loved Warren. It was reported that on one occasion, he dropped off his entire Pro Bowl bonus check of $15,000 to the community center.

I will never forget the grief I witnessed that day from Korey's immediate and extended families. They were a close-knit group. They loved Korey and were so proud of him. As I sat there before the service began, I couldn't help but think about all the joy and laughter Korey had brought into the lives of so many people.

I count myself among them. I was a first-year college coach fresh off the high school fields and still finding my way when I first coached Korey. He could have big-timed me or tried to intimidate me. Instead, he made me feel like I was his all-time favorite coach.

At the end of the service, Korey's father spoke about his son. I can still remember hearing his father's final words and then reading them in the paper the next morning: *"Korey was a football player, he played the game he loved, and he loved the game he played."*

Key Points for You've Gotta Love It

1. The best team leaders have passion for what they do and are passionate about holding people to specific standards.
2. Passion and enthusiasm are contagious. Often they are the spark a team needs to light its own fire.
3. You can't fake passion and enthusiasm. If you don't love what you do, you will never be able to work the long hours it takes to achieve excellence.
4. The pursuit of a team's success is most often dependent on passion and commitment.
5. The most productive members of a team are the ones with the most passion and enthusiasm.
6. Passion for the team should be reflected in the team mission statement. This document should be printed, posted, and reviewed.
7. To have teams that compete with passion, build them around people who have fun doing what they do. Build them around people who love the other people on the team and seem to enjoy life in general.
8. If a team has passion and desire, it will have the dedication and determination necessary to achieve excellence.
9. It has always been true that an athlete must be learning, growing, and improving if they are going to win and enjoy the game. Winning is fun.
10. If you don't love what you are doing, find another sport, another job, or another passion. If you do love what you're doing, enjoy the grind, be a better teammate, and have some fun.

–CHAPTER NINE–
NEVER, NEVER, NEVER, SURRENDER

"Never give in, never give in, never, never, never, never—in nothing, great or small, large or petty. Never give in except to convictions of honor and good sense."—Winston Churchill

Photo of Matt Kaulig courtesy of Kaulig Media

Bio Box: Matt Kaulig- Executive Chairman, Kaulig Companies, and Founder of LeafFilter

Background: Matt Kaulig was born on October 19, 1972, in Columbus, Ohio. He has a twin sister, Melissa. He also has a younger brother, Mark. Matt's father, Bob, was in sales and marketing with Raybestos Brakes, and his mother, Debbie, worked in merchandising for Mars.

Athletic Achievement: Matt was a three-sport athlete at Crystal Lake Central High School near Chicago and earned a Division I football scholarship to Akron.

Scholastic Achievement: Kaulig graduated from Crystal Lake Central High School in 1991. He earned a business degree in marketing/management from the University of Akron in the summer of 1996.

Professional Achievement: Kaulig is a Harvard Business School entrepreneur of the year, a business owner, and philanthropist. He is executive chairman of Kaulig Companies Limited, his single-member family office, known for offering a diverse spectrum of businesses, which include sports and entertainment, marketing and events, private equity, real estate, and philanthropy, with a focus on children and families. Kaulig is the founder of Leaf Home, a contractor business he started out of his home in 2005 that is now the largest direct-to-consumer home-products companies in the United States and Canada, noting $1.8 billion in sales in 2024. His sports ventures include Kaulig Racing, a multicar NASCAR Xfinity and Cup Series team. He is a minority owner of the Cleveland Guardians baseball team and runs the Kaulig Companies Championship, a PGA Champions Tour Major at Firestone CC in Akron. He has received the NCAA Legends and Legacy Award and was named Entrepreneur of the Year by Ernst & Young. He was inducted into the Cleveland Business Hall of Fame in 2022. Matt is an Akron Children's Hospital Champions for Children honoree, and his charitable giving programs have provided philanthropic support to more than three hundred 501(c)(3) organizations. He won two consecutive Championships with the NASCAR team Kaulig Racing Inc.

To understand my relationship with Matt Kaulig, it might be best to understand the landscape in which we first met.

I got my first head coaching job at the collegiate level in 1995. I had been an offensive line coach for three years at Ohio State, and after the 1994 season two job offers were floated, one from Ohio University, the other from the University of Akron. Both were dreadful programs. As Urban Meyer noted when he accepted the position at Bowling Green in 2001, "That's an awful job." His mentor, Earle Bruce, assured him he was right. "Of course it is. Why do you think they're interested in you?"

Entering the final game of the 1994 season, Akron and Ohio University were both winless, with the Zips earning a 24-10 victory over the Bobcats at Akron's Rubber Bowl. I figured Akron was closer to the metropolitan areas of Akron, Canton, Cleveland, and Youngstown, fertile recruiting grounds. Most importantly, I really liked Mike Bobinski, the athletic director at Akron. Mike convinced me that Akron had great potential and together we could turn the program around, so that's the job I chose.

Unfortunately for me and the University of Akron, Mike was destined to become a superstar in college athletic administration. He left Akron for Xavier and then moved on to Georgia Tech. As of this writing, Mike is the athletic director at Purdue.

So I inherited a team coming off a 1-10 season that had just fired its coach, Gerry Faust. Only four seniors decided to stick around for their final campaign. Frankly, that wasn't a concern, I was much more interested in bringing in my own players.

I eventually realized this was a mistake for several reasons. Perhaps the biggest mistake of all was underestimating the leadership of a returning quarterback who didn't figure into my plans, Matt Kaulig. Matt had been one of Coach Faust's recruits and had entered the Akron program when it was in a far different place.

To this day, Gerry Faust is considered one of the greatest coaches in Ohio high school football history. He built a dynasty from nothing. Faust coached at Cincinnati Moeller from 1962 to 1980. The Crusaders compiled a record of 178-23-2 with twelve Greater Catholic League championships, seven undefeated seasons, five

Ohio state championships, and four national titles. His Cincinnati Moeller program ripped off a fifty-eight-game winning streak, produced twenty-five all-Americans, and sent nearly three hundred players to Division I college football programs. Faust was charismatic, emotional, deeply religious, and easily voted into the National High School Football Hall of Fame.

He became the subject of a story in Sports Illustrated when he was hired as head coach at the University of Notre Dame in 1981. It was a huge gamble. Not since Ohio State hired Paul Brown from Massillon High School in 1940 had one of the blue bloods of college football hired a coach directly from the high school ranks. Brown won a national championship in his second year at Ohio State and was well on his way to constructing a dynasty when World War II ended his tenure at the school after just three years.

Notre Dame had never hired a coach from the prep ranks. Unfortunately, the Fighting Irish would not find success under Gerry Faust. Although, like Brown, Faust was widely considered the best high school coach in the nation, he lacked the background needed to prepare him for the magnitude of the job at Notre Dame. He took over for Dan Devine, who had gone 9-2-1 in 1980 and finished ninth in the final Associated Press poll before retiring. Faust had charisma, spiritual will, and the proper respect for the job. He just couldn't make it work, compiling a 30-26-1 record in five years. He resigned after the 1985 season and landed at Akron in 1986.

"People listen to me because I'm not all about success," Faust told Sports Illustrated. "They'll listen to someone who failed, because most people fail at something in life."

The Zips had experienced a fair amount of success under coach Jim Dennison, but in Faust they now had someone with big-time experience, a strong familiarity with Ohio recruiting grounds, and a household name in the coaching community.

At that time, Akron was a Division I-AA school that played football in the Ohio Valley Conference. Faust's first team went 7-4, 4-3 in the league. By the time he recruited Matt Kaulig out of Chicago, the Zips were a Division IA school and about to enter the Mid-American Conference.

THE SPIRIT OF A TEAM

Matt redshirted his true freshman year but played a bit at quarterback in 1992, when the Zips went 7-3-1, 5-3, in their first season in the Mid-American Conference. However, the program turned steadily downward from there. Akron was 5-6 in 1993 and 1-10 in 1994. Coach Faust was fired after compiling a 43-53-4 mark in nine years. That's when I came on the scene and first met Matt. The Akron football team was in an awful state, and my mindset was that it had to be restarted almost completely, and in every facet.

Matt had shown promise all the way back to high school, where he bounced from Chicago to Philadelphia and back to Chicago as his father was transferred multiple times in his job.

Still, the recruiters found Kaulig, even though he had played only five games his senior season. An injury midway through that fall wiped out his basketball and spring sports seasons too. Coach Faust still offered him a full ride when others, including Illinois and Syracuse, were frightened off the trail by the injury.

Matt played sparingly throughout his career at Akron, but it wasn't so much from a lack of ability. He just could not stay healthy. He played forty-four games in his career, completing 87 passes for 950 yards and a touchdown. But it was the grit he showed, that Never Surrender attitude, that impressed me later, and I really should have given it more weight while it was happening.

Matt had no reason to stick around. He knew he was going to be delegated to the scout team as a senior. But Matt and his roommate, Chris Counahan, led this small group of four seniors who refused to quit. Today, Chris Counahan is still Matt's best friend and his chief sales officer for Leaf Home.

"I had played a little bit as a freshman, and we were pretty good, had a winning record. I mean, we didn't go to a bowl game, but it was interesting. Then, my sophomore year, I tore my hamstring in camp, or I would have played a lot more," Matt said. "My junior year I was a starter, but in the fourth game I tore up my shoulder, separated my AC joint, and had to have surgery, so I was done for that season too. Then Coach Faust gets fired, and suddenly I'm fourth or fifth on the depth chart. I mean, if you want to talk about personal adversity, that was it.

"Here I am a fifth-year senior, I've played some, and now I'm on the scout team? I mean, I'd be lying if I said I didn't think I was better than the guys in front of me or that I didn't need to be doing this anymore. But that's what I was doing, and to be honest, quitting just wasn't an option for me. I just made up my mind that I'm going to help the team as much as I can, do whatever I can. You just keep your head down even in a job like that and do the best you can."

Akron took some fierce beatings my first year, and one of the worst was at Kansas State. They were ranked nineteenth in the country and beat us 67-0. Their coach, Bill Snyder, came to our locker room after the game and told our kids not to hang their heads, keep working hard. Now most people would have thought that was gracious of Coach Snyder, a gesture of sportsmanship. Matt didn't take it that way at all. His competitive juices wouldn't allow it.

"I'm sitting there and I'm thinking, as a competitor, this really pisses me off," Matt said. "I couldn't believe a coach from another team would come in there and do that. I mean he wasn't apologizing, but it felt like we were being treated like little kids by someone who had just beaten our ass for three hours. I had played football my whole life and never had another coach come in and done something like that."

Matt didn't take much to being pitied, and nobody had to tell him to keep his head up, his chin strapped, and to hit the practice field again next week, hard. That was the person he already embodied.

"Anyway, Coach Owens made a big deal about me that week in practice," Matt said. "Talking to the team, you said, 'Here's a guy that's not even playing anymore, and look how hard he goes. He was the starting quarterback last year, and he's not even playing, and he's as into it as anybody. He has the best attitude out here.' That really stuck with me."

Matt had just been so banged up in his career, and we had a couple of hotshot freshmen quarterbacks we had recruited, so I wanted to see what they could do. Looking back on it, Matt was our quarterback. He was a leader. He was tough and gritty and had great character; that's what you want in your quarterback. He had a Never Surrender personality. I realize now I should have done things differently. Still, that situation didn't deter Matt Kaulig.

Matt knew the NFL wasn't part of his future, His scholastic career took a couple of turns, as he switched majors from business to psychology and then back again to business. But he got his degree, with a focus on marketing, and this is where he really found his niche.

Matt Kaulig is among the most successful players I've ever coached, maybe the most successful. And it has absolutely nothing to do with his performance on the field or his academics. Matt was not a quitter, and regardless of any circumstances or adversity, he was going to find a way to win. Matt Kaulig was a warrior, and people rally around warriors.

Matt met his wife, Lisa, a cheerleader, at Akron, and they soon married. She was from nearby Copley, and Matt also liked the community. They decided to stay and make their home in Northeast Ohio.

Matt went to work at Erie Construction and rose through the ranks. He started as a sales representative and advanced to sales manager. For nine years at the company, he was learning a business that would become his life's work. But he also saw some gaps, opportunities that he believed the company was missing.

"I was making a bunch of money, but I was also used to being in charge and leading people," Matt said. "I was getting older, in my early thirties, and I'm starting to question some of the things that the company is doing, the way we were marketing some things. I just thought we could be way more efficient. I had gotten enough tenure and was old enough that I started to talk about it to the owners and my managers. 'Why are we doing it this way? Why don't we use this script?' And the answer was usually something like 'Well, we've been doing it like this for fifty years, and that's just the way we do things.'"

So Matt would go home at night and ponder, What if I was in charge? How would I approach the business?

"Part of me was like, listen, these guys have been doing this for way longer than I have, and even though I have these thoughts or these opinions, they're probably right," Matt said. "But eventually I just got to the point where I'm like, you know what? I'm right. I think I can do this."

It was that quarterback in Matt coming out at just the right time. In particular, he was selling a product in LeafFilter that utilized the latest technology, a surgical-grade stainless steel screen. LeafFilter kept everything except water out of the gutter; pine needles, debris, those pesky little helicopters, nothing sticks to it. Matt certainly had the experience too. He believed in the product and sold it passionately for nine years.

"I had sold this stuff in construction, and there was nothing like it. I just felt like, man, this is an opportunity. I could sell this stuff out of my house and make more money. That was the genesis behind the whole company," Matt said. "I just wasn't really happy at my current job, and I thought I was talented enough where I could just quit my job and sell the stuff out of my house, so that's what I did."

Matt noted that he was in a solid financial situation, and Lisa was a professional too. As a marriage and family counselor, she was making a decent income. The couple did not yet have children, and Matt never lacked courage. The time to jump out on his own was upon him. So he became one of ninety-one national LeafFilter dealers.

"I figured with such a great product, and nobody in Ohio was really selling it, I could make more money if I just started my own business," Kaulig said. "I didn't start the LeafFilter company. I started as a contractor, and my company was called LeafFilter North. You would sign up as an authorized dealer, and they would sell you the product. I was good at selling it, and what happened is we started expanding. We started getting bigger."

"It wasn't as big a risk as it might sound. It's true I started it in our basement, but we weren't scratching and clawing or anything like that. If this didn't pan out, it wouldn't have been like we were broke. I could've gotten a sales job somewhere else. But I think that's probably what I'm most proud of. When I started with LeafFilter, it was with no money. I mean, I put no money into it at all. I didn't have to take out a loan. I didn't have investors or anybody to come in and help. I literally started it by renting out a booth at the Hartville Flea Market for seven dollars a day, twenty-one dollars for three days. I had to pay for our booth, a backdrop, a water display to show how the filter worked, the water pump, and that was it. I had a cell phone, and that was the number I used on our brochures and ads.

"I would make the appointments, drive out to the house, sell the job, and I made all the money. I didn't have to pay a commission to anybody because I sold it. I had to buy the product and have an installer install it, but those two things weren't expensive. So when I would sell a $3,000 or $4,000 job, I would make most of the money. Then I would take that money, do more marketing, and it grew from there."

"Grow" isn't a big enough word for what happened with Matt's operation—"exploded" is more like it. In his first year in 2005, his LeafFilter office accumulated $350,000 in sales. In 2006, that number mushroomed to $750,000. In 2007, it rocketed to $1.7 million. Matt moved out of the basement and into office space as LeafFilter enveloped Northeast Ohio.

"It took off here, and then I just thought, Hey, I can scale this. I can do this in other cities. So then I expanded to Pittsburgh, to Columbus and Toledo. I opened three offices in 2008, and we made $5.4 million. That's when I knew I had something. I mean, I wasn't even running the offices in those cities, and we were making money."

So, Matt figured, why not expand to even more cities? Still, he needed to be measured. Growing too fast might overwhelm good employees, whom he now counted on to follow his lead. He had the Never Surrender attitude, but he had to implement it in others personally. So he limited himself to opening three new offices per year. The offices followed the same script, down to the same office furniture. Drawers would be organized the same way. The reason was that an employee could be trained in Pittsburgh and yet plugged into an office in Cincinnati with little to no learning curve.

The operation followed the same pattern. Matt turned perhaps the most challenging era for the home-improvement business into one of his greatest triumphs. The housing crisis in 2008 hit, and it impacted mortgage companies, builders, and especially home improvement operations. Kaulig estimated half his competitors went out of business. Others were too scared to do anything but survive, purging their marketing budgets altogether. LeafFilter North went in the opposite direction.

"I know that you either continue to grow or you begin to die," Matt said. "You just can't sit stagnant. That's a big philosophy I've always had in business and in life. I just made the decision that 'Hey, trees aren't going to stop dropping their leaves. They don't know there's a recession.' I had heard that government jobs are still good when the economy is bad. So that year I put in two offices, one in Baltimore and one in Manassas, Virginia, near the DC area, surrounding the U.S. Capitol. I just felt like with everyone else shutting down, this is our chance to really grow."

Matt took another step that may seem unconventional. He didn't want his people paying attention to the radio or TV. Social media was beginning to emerge too. And in that time frame, the news was mostly bleak.

"I just said, 'Look, we'll have a fifteen-minute conference call every day, and I'll tell you anything pertinent about the news that you need to know. But I don't want to hear about or talk about anything negative.' I mean, that's all it was, morning, noon, and night, gloom and doom. I just didn't want them worrying about losing their jobs. Our attitude was that we were going to thrive. And you know what? We did."

LeafFilter North sales erupted from $5.4 million to $11.6 million in 2009, more than doubling its business when others in the same situation were folding. The company blossomed following Matt's leadership and courage.

Then came his next key step. In 2009, Matt wanted to expand to Chicago. However, there were already four LeafFilter dealers working in the Windy City, and the manufacturers didn't want to disrupt their sales. Yet Matt didn't want to be locked out of the biggest city in the Midwest. So in January 2010, Kaulig started a distribution business where the manufacturer sold to him. In turn, he sold it to the contractors.

"You know what that was about?" Matt said. "Attitude and the will to win made something special happen."

By 2016, Matt Kaulig owned all of LeafFilter, including the manufacturing, the patents, the trademarks, and the stores. He was able to take charge of all the dealerships. Today there is only one

LeafFilter dealer, meaning the customer has only one point of contact. Matt streamlined the business to shore up efficiency problems that plagued some of his competitors.

In addition, LeafFilter began development of new products, which meant the establishment of a development team. Different parts of the country require different types of gutters for different building styles and various weather conditions. LeafFilter has grown to include Leaf Home Solutions, Leaf Water Solutions, and Leaf Home Enhancements.

In September 2016, his growing business led him to branch out in yet another new direction. Kaulig closed an investment deal with Gridiron Capital of New Canaan, Connecticut. The private investment firm specialized in partnering with middle-market companies, providing strategic, marketing, and operational expertise as well as capital infusion.

"We did $112 million in revenue [in 2016]," Matt said at the time. "These guys came in and supercharged our business, and we will do $180 million [in 2017]."

In 2019, Leaf Home Safety Solutions was launched, a direct-to-consumer business geared toward senior citizens that transforms homes into safe and stylish environments through quality solutions, including walk-in tubs and stair lifts. In 2021, Leaf announced three more residential direct-to-consumer businesses, Thiel's Home Solutions, Storm Tight Windows, and Miracle Windows and Showers.

Those entities fed a growing revenue stream and allowed Kaulig's portfolio to expand. In time, Kaulig Capital became its own private equity firm, with investments in media, technology, health, food, and sports. Matt noted that those pursuits were established with shared values and strong partnerships.

Today LeafFilter is the largest gutter guard company in North America. The parent company, Leaf Home, is an international home-improvement operation that did $1.8 billion in sales in 2024 with offices across the continent.

All the while, Matt has long maintained his interest in sports. In 2016, he founded a NASCAR racing team. In 2020, he was chosen as a Comcast Community Champion of the Year finalist in recognition of his philanthropic efforts within the NASCAR industry.

As a philanthropist, Kaulig wanted to focus on the well-being of children, so the partnership with the NASCAR Foundation was an ideal one. Both share the goal of impacting communities they love by helping children in need live happier, healthier lives. The NASCAR Foundation and Kaulig Giving bring hope, opportunity, and plenty of love and care to children in need who reside in race markets across the country. To date over ten thousand teddy bears have been delivered to children in hospitals across the country, and over one thousand bikes have been built for nonprofits.

The attention to children's issues came to the forefront after a private challenge for Matt and Lisa. When the couple decided they were ready to start their family, they ran into fertility issues. The Kauligs sampled multiple potential solutions, including in vitro fertilization. It was costly and frustrating. After years of struggle, they finally had a daughter, Samantha. The experience shaped Matt's philanthropic pursuits, frequently based around charities for children.

"You don't know how many couples go through that until you're going through it," Matt said. "I think it's tougher on my wife. She's the one going through it physically."

One will notice that Matt Kaulig's many charitable interests are inspired by his daughter, frequently focused on aiding children and/or on adults struggling to raise a family. Matt and Lisa Kaulig are also the founders of and donors to Samantha's Gift of Hope, a monetary award presented quarterly to couples who have joined the Reproductive Gynecology & Infertility's IVF 100% Success Guaranteed Plan in the Northeast Ohio office locations.

Kaulig Giving is one of the top charitable organizations in Northeast Ohio. They support the well-being of children and families through direct giving from Kaulig Companies, community involvement and service, and partnerships with like-minded nonprofits. Kaulig Giving strives to make a lasting impact on Northeast Ohio and beyond.

Some of its most notable partners include the LeBron James Family Foundation, Cavaliers Community Foundation, CC's Sabathia's PItCCh in Foundation, and the NASCAR Foundation. Matt believes it's his duty as a successful businessman to give back to the community that has supported him.

"I have a philosophy that the more you make, the more you give," Matt said. "I think we have a corporate responsibility as well as a personal responsibility to give back to the community. We give responsibly, though. The vice president of our charitable giving program oversees vetting organizations. You've got to know who you're giving to and that they're a legitimate organization."

Every year Matt gives $1,000 to all of his employees to donate to a charity of their choice. Then the employees were given a crash course in how to judge a charitable organization worthy of their generosity.

To date, nearly three hundred charitable organizations have benefited from Matt Kaulig's generosity. He's still approaching his role as the quarterback of his company with courage and that Never Surrender attitude. Indeed, Matt Kaulig's motto at LeafFilter is "Today, not Tomorrow."

Jason Taylor: Fighting Adversity
"Success is measured not so much by the position that one has reached in life as by the obstacles which he has overcome while trying to exceed."
– Booker T. Washington

My first season as the head football coach at the University of Akron was the greatest challenge of my life. Matt Kaulig told the story of our early season, 67-0 loss to Kansas State. By the final game of the season, it wasn't any better.

We were scheduled to play against a very good Miami team in Oxford, Ohio. Miami was coached by Randy Walker, who went on to coach in the Big Ten at Northwestern. We were beat up and had some discipline problems. We had a difficult time filling the bus with 55 players who could travel and play. We lost the game 65-0.

I assembled the team after the handshake and spent several minutes just looking into their eyes. They were hurting both mentally and physically. But they didn't quit. They fought hard to the end.

I told the players I wanted a quiet bus ride back to Akron. No talking. No movies. I said we were going to start the offseason program as soon we got back to campus. I asked the players to consider their commitment to the program. I told the team the results of this game would be much different the next time we played Miami if we all committed to a great offseason.

Losing the last game of the year is like taking a bite out of an onion, the taste stays in your mouth for a very long time. And, with this loss we were never able to spit that bad taste for Miami out of our mouths.

The team made a big-time commitment in the offseason, and we were all excited for the 1997 campaign to begin. No one was more excited than Jason Taylor. Like so many others, Jason had considered leaving the team the year I was hired. Fortunately, we were able to put a plan together to keep Jason on the squad.

When I was hired, Jason was attempting to play both basketball and football for the Zips. This was a commitment made to him when he was recruited. But it wasn't working out for the football team or for Jason. He was having a hard time keeping up with his football training and his grades. Jason had fought hard with the NCAA for his eligibility after being recruited as a home-schooled athlete, and he didn't want to lose his scholarship.

We wanted Jason to commit 100 percent to only football and his books. After watching tape of Jason as an outside linebacker, we believed he had the speed, quickness and athleticism to put his hand down and come off the edge as a defensive end. At first, he would be a bit undersized, but with him making a full-time commitment to the weight room that would change.

Before the 1996 season, Jason committed 100 percent to this plan. His decision to stay on the team changed his life. Jason Taylor ended up being a first team all-conference defensive end his final year. More importantly, he was a third-round draft pick for the Miami Dolphins and eventually a member of the Pro Football Hall of Fame in nearby Canton.

When asked about the adversity he had faced early in football Jason said, "I overcame adversity by keeping my sights on my goals. There was no barrier that I couldn't run through. Life is like football, after every dark night there is a bright day."

I was honored to have the chance to coach Jason Taylor. When we traveled, he would sit in the front of the bus, close to my seat, often reading his Bible. He was a smart player, and he loved his teammates.

"In football all I really have is my team," Jason said. "These are the people I trust. When I step into the huddle and grab my teammate's hand, I know my back is covered."

Jason was an emotional player and loyal to his coaches. There was a trip our family made to Florida, and at the last minute we decided to stop at the Dolphins training camp in Davie to see Jason. My oldest daughter had a crush on Jason Taylor long before his stardom on Dancing with the Stars. We were having an issue with security getting into practice. Jason saw us two fields away and immediately made sure we were taken care of.

Jason faced lots of adversity in his family life. In Canton at his Hall of Fame induction, I listened closely as he talked about not knowing his father and growing up in Section 8 housing. His shared how his mother, Georgia, worked to keep the family together. Jason concluded his speech by telling his three children, "There is no better job in the world than being a father."

The fall of 1996 was my second season at Akron, and Jason was a senior. He was elected a captain, and his leadership was apparent in our home opener versus Virginia Tech. The Hokies were coming off a Sugar Bowl victory over Texas with players like all-American Cornell Brown and quarterback Jim Druckenmiller. No one gave us a chance to win this game. I remember seeing the local newspaper headline that Saturday morning, big, bold, letters: "Mismatch of the Century."

This was a game we would have lost the prior year by sixty points. But on September 7, 1996, we went toe-to-toe with Virginia Tech, and they could not knock us out. Eventually, the Hokies earned a tough, 21-18 win over Akron. But it felt like we just ran out of time. Jason Taylor had 12 tackles, 3 for a loss; 2 sacks; and 2 fumble recoveries and was the National Defensive Player of the Week.

Several weeks later, on October 19, we had our rematch with Miami. The Redskins (as they were called then) again were loaded and competing for a MAC championship. We were at least a four-touchdown underdog. Ever since the loss the year before, this was the team we most wanted to beat. We adopted the slogan "Hate Red. If it is red, and it is moving, hit it."

The game was played at the Rubber Bowl, our home stadium. Miami had the ball first. On their first drive, we were called for three personal-foul penalties. Jason Taylor was called for two late hits. The officials called a timeout and came over to my sideline to ask me to calm my team down. I told the officials we had a very slim chance to win the game, but we had no chance to win if we didn't play the entire game like our hair was on fire. The team played its hearts out for sixty minutes, and we won 10-7.

Our victory over Miami cost them the conference championship. Their players left the field without shaking hands.

"Revenge," Samuel Johnson said, "is an act of passion, vengeance of justice"

Getting Fired
"There are two types of coaches: coaches who have been fired and coaches who are going to get fired."–Popular Saying

In year two of my tenure at Akron, we were a much more competitive team, but the progress was far too slow. It seemed like we were building a team from scratch while playing in the highly competitive Mid-American Conference and at the same time playing one of the most difficult nonleague schedules in the country.

For example, in year three we started the season at number six Nebraska, number thirteen LSU, and, two weeks later, at Miami. After year three and year four at Akron, I felt fortunate to still have a job.

But I knew we were close. We had completely changed the culture. Our team graduation rate went from 17 percent to over 70 percent. We improved our recruiting and our retention. Most importantly, we recruited two talented quarterbacks, Butchie Washington and Charlie Frye, both of whom had toughness and character. In our last five years at Akron, Butchie and Charlie led us to three winning seasons, a winning record in the MAC, and a first-place finish in the East Division.

Charlie's final game as a junior in 2003 was a 35-28 victory over Ohio University. The week before that, we beat Central Michigan 40-

28. Earlier that season we suffered a 38-37 loss at the University of Connecticut and a 48-31 defeat at number eighteen Wisconsin in a game that was much closer than the score indicated. We finished the year 7-5, and I still had three years to go on my contract. We had a team of upperclassmen returning that was stacked with great players, including Charlie Frye, Chase Blackburn, and Domenik Hixon, all future NFL players.

And yet, after the Ohio University game, when I returned to campus from the Rubber Bowl and went into my office, there was a letter on my desk from the athletic director notifying me that I had been fired.

It's not fair, I thought. I was bitter. People get fired all the time, but in most cases it's not headlines on the front page of the newspaper or running for the next twenty-four hours on an ESPN ticker. I felt sorry for myself, and it was never more apparent than at the team meeting on Sunday. I was informed just before the meeting that I had to be out of my office by the next day, and I was upset.

Our team chaplain, Knute Larson, stopped by the office to provide his support, and I invited him to attend the meeting. Pastor Larson asked to visit with me after the meeting ended. He was quick to point out how poorly I had handled myself to the team.

"Football isn't fair. Life isn't fair. Stop feeling sorry for yourself. There are players and staff hurting just as much as you are hurting; being bitter is never the answer. Ultimately, you will be judged in life on how well you handle the adversities of life!"

His personal sermon that day was a lifesaver. In less than a week after being fired, I found another team to coach, at Ashland University. Several of the coaches on the staff joined me at Ashland. I did all I could to help all the Akron coaches find jobs and to support the players who stayed at Akron.

I'm no longer bitter about being fired, and yet some wounds never completely heal. The athletic director who fired me wanted his own coach. He has that right. He was the fourth athletic director I had worked for in my nine-year tenure at the University of Akron, and sooner or later I was going to get fired. But as Knute Larson told me that day in my office, "This isn't about you." This was about "the team."

Even with the addition of an indoor facility and a new stadium, in the twenty-one years since our staff was fired, no Zips team has finished with a better record. Also, in the thirty-two years that the University of Akron has competed in the Mid-American Conference, only six conference teams have finished with a winning record. Three of those teams played in our last five seasons, and two of those teams played in the two seasons right after we were fired.

I only make this point to honor the players and the coaches we recruited to the University of Akron who believed in and committed to the process and the culture of winning football games that we built there.

IF YOU START YOU FINISH
Don't Quit
When things go wrong, as they sometime will,
When the road you're trudging seems all uphill,
When funds are low and debts are high,
And you want to smile, but you have to sigh,
When care is pressing down a bit-
Rest if you must, but don't you quit . . .
Success is failure turned inside out,
The silver tent of the clouds of doubt.
And you will never know how close you are,
It may be nearer when it seems afar.
So stick to the fight when you're hardest hit,
It's when things seem worst that you mustn't quit.
—Edgar A. Guest

More than four hundred times I've led a team out of the locker room and onto the field. Right before leaving the locker room, each one of those teams would take their helmets off, thrust them in the air, and shout after me, "Never, Never, Never, Surrender!" These were displayed in our locker room for more than thirty years. Only one other word, "TEAM," had a similar place, always hanging over the exit door from the locker room.

These words evoked Winston Churchill's famous "Never Surrender" speech to the Allied Forces during World War II, which became the battle cry for victory. No matter what happens, we just don't quit.

A football game is four quarters and sixty minutes, not three quarters or fifty-eight minutes. For sixty minutes, regardless of the odds, regardless of adversity, a team can never lay down. A commitment to excellence is a commitment to play your hearts out for sixty minutes. There is no greater indictment of a team leader than to lose his team and have them quit on him.

Quitters are good losers, and quitting quickly becomes a habit.

As a child I had only a few rules, but number three on the list was always "If you start something, you finish it." I could always read the body language of an athlete who would hesitantly come into my office to quit the team. I would ask why. The most common answer was "It's just not fun anymore." So, I would follow up, "What are you going to do when your job or your marriage or being a parent is just not fun anymore? Quit?"

Today the transfer portal in the NCAA is an easy out for many college athletes facing adversity. What has happened to work harder and compete harder? What about team loyalty? These have always been some of the best lessons learned in sports and some of the most important characteristics of team excellence.

Persistence and Perseverance

"Nothing in the world takes the place of persistence. Talent will not. Nothing is more common than unsuccessful men with talent. Genius will not. Unrewarded genius is almost a proverb. Education will not. The world is full of educated derelicts. Persistence and determination alone are omnipotent."–Ray Krok

The greatest quality of excellence is not talent or skill but the persistence to keep going, to be able to fight off defeat and discouragement and never give up.

Persistence and perseverance define what it means to overcome odds. I met David Ring when he spoke at the Fellowship of Christian Athletes breakfast at the Citrus Bowl in Orlando, Florida. His story is about a young boy with cerebral palsy who loses both parents. He stops and asks the audience, "So what is your problem?" And yet despite all his adversities, he goes on to become one of the most successful men I have ever met.

David Ring's message was a reminder that no odds are too big to overcome. All things are possible if you don't give up or make excuses or feel sorry for yourself. If any of the teams I coached were looking for sympathy or making excuses after a tough loss, I reminded them that our competitors would show them no pity.

I'm reminded of a player I coached at Massillon High School, Ryan Sparkman. Ryan and I were both inducted into the Massillon Tiger Football Hall of Fame in the Fall of 2024. This seemed only appropriate considering the great respect I have for Ryan not only as a player but also as a person.

During Ryan's senior season, I took him to the Touchdown Club, where I was going to recognize him as the player of the week. On the way, Ryan and I were talking about some of the racial issues we were dealing with as a team and as a community. Ryan stopped me and said, "Coach there will always be prejudice and discrimination no matter where I go or what I do. It's not right, and it's not fair, but I refuse to use it as an excuse that makes it okay for me to fall short of my goals in life."

Excuses are crutches. Excuses rationalize losing and quitting. One Sunday night I took my Akron football team into the woods on top of the Rubber Bowl hill. In one hand I had a shovel. My father gave me this shovel when I left home to start college. He told me if I didn't make it, I could always use the shovel to find some unforgiving backbreaking work. I'm pretty sure he didn't want to hear any alibis from his kid who had a chance to do something special in life.

In my other hand I had a shoebox designed as a casket. I told the team the time had come to bury all the excuses that supposedly were keeping our team from winning. We are too young. We are too slow. The coaches call the wrong plays. The coaches practice us too hard, and we meet too long. There was bad food, bad weather, bad facilities, even bad pregame movies.

We put all these excuses in the box. The seniors dug the hole, dropped the box in the hole, and shoveled dirt to cover up the box.

From that point forward, whenever anyone on the team started to complain or jumped offsides or dropped the ball or fumbled the ball or threw an interception, we just pointed to the woods. We called it the "Loser's Lap." They would have to run up the stadium steps to the top of the hill, around the burial site, and then back to the practice field. Excuses are for losers.

Once we stopped using excuses and started to realize that all teams face adversity, but winning teams refuse to give in to adversity, we started winning.

Perseverance requires courage and hard work. Perseverance requires goal setting, planning, and belief. Perseverance requires a positive attitude and a commitment to fight to the end. Team excellence takes perseverance. Be prepared; to overcome some adversities takes a lot of perseverance. But for those who do persevere, the rewards of team excellence are life-changing.

Let Go of Defeat
"Forgetting what lies behind, looking forward to what lies ahead, I press on."–The Apostle Paul

How many times has it been said that if God wanted us to see where we have been and not where we are going, he would have put eyes in the back of our heads, not in the front?

Many times, overcoming adversity means letting go of defeat. Great teams have the mental toughness to let go of defeat. I believe all games in college football should be left behind after Sunday's practice. In 1996 at Akron, we were upset in a big rivalry game versus Kent State, and because we couldn't let go, it cost us an embarrassing loss the next week at Central Michigan. I believe there were several losses to Michigan when I coached at Ohio State that led to losses in the Bowl Game. And I always believed at Massillon the hardest games on the schedule were games nine and eleven. We always played Canton McKinley in week ten.

When we first started building the football team at Ashland University, we struggled like most teams in Division II football to beat Grand Valley State. At one time we had lost six straight games to Grand Valley and then lost to the next team on the schedule six straight times. We let Grand Valley beat us not once but twice.

So after a tough loss or a bad play, we worked hard to build a "Turn-the-Page" culture. The next play and the next game became the focus. Simply put, learn from our mistakes but don't dwell on them. Don't pout about them. Move on. The most important play in the game is the next play. The most important game of the season is the next game.

Learning to replace the anger, frustration, pain, and embarrassment on a team that has been defeated is not easy. The only way this can happen is when the team's focus and concentration are totally in the present. A team's focus can never be in the past or in the future. "This Game, This Week." Keep the focus on where we are right now, and remember it's W.I.N. (What's Important Now).

After winning the Ohio Division 2 State Championship in 1985 I was invited to speak at Louisville, Kentucky as the Ohio High School Coach of the Year. Before my address, Coach Grant Teaff of Baylor was the speaker. Coach Teaff is one of the greatest keynote speakers of all-time. He ended his motivational speech that night by reciting the poem *Winning is How You Play the Game*.

I was so inspired by these words that I had Coach Teaff send me a copy of this poem and copied the way Coach Teaff memorized the words and used them to conclude a motivational speech.

WINNING IS HOW YOU PLAY THE GAME
Winning is how you play the game each and every day
It is in your attitude and in the things you say
It's not in seeking wealth or fame, but in
Reaching goals you hope to claim
Winning is having faith and giving confidence to a friend
It is never giving up or giving in
It is wanting something so badly you could die and if it doesn't happen
be willing to give it one more try
Winning is being clean and sound of mind
It is being loyal and serving all mankind
It is in your teammates, friends, and family

And what they can learn from you
Winning is having faith and hope and love in
Everything you do.

Key Points for Never, Never, Never Surrender

1. Matt Kaulig said, "You either grow or you die, you can't stay stagnant. All teams either get better or they get worse; they never stay the same.
2. In the face of adversity, make a commitment to doing what needs to be done to overcome failure or defeat.
3. Life is not fair. When we are facing adversity, self-pity and bitterness are never the answer.
4. Make "Never Surrender" a battle cry for victory.
5. Quitters are good losers, and quitting quickly becomes a habit.
6. Persistence and perseverance define what it takes to overcome adversity.
7. All things are possible when not making excuses. Excuses are for losers.
8. Persistence and perseverance are needed to achieve team excellence.
9. All teams face adversity. Winning teams refuse to give in to adversity and fight to the end.
10. To overcome adversity, learn from your failures and defeats and then let go.

PART FOUR:
SUSTAINABLE EXCELLENCE

The Blueprint for Building Team Excellence concludes with the question "Are you strong enough to survive success?"

A team that commits to excellence and not success is a team that will stand the test of time. Excellence is a team that always gives their best shot, their best effort. Excellence is a team of eighty-five brothers taking the field hand in hand, playing to one heartbeat. Excellence is a team that stays humble and never forgets where they started or who helped them along the way. Excellence is a team that will use their strengths and gifts to benefit others. The players understand their responsibility to pay it forward.

Pay it forward was a theme often repeated by Ohio State Coach Woody Hayes as he quoted poet/philosopher Ralph Waldo Emerson. Emerson wrote: "Pay every just demand on your time, your talents, or your heart." But he reminds us we can seldom pay back those who have given us much. So we "pay it forward."

To "pay it forward" motivated me to complete this book.

–CHAPTER TEN–
SHARPEN THE EDGE

"Excellence is not an act but a habit."—Aristotle

Photo of Dan Niss courtesy of CNG

Bio Box: Dan Niss, President of Charter Next Generation
Background: Dan was born October 5, 1970. He grew up in Fairmont, Minnesota. His father, Jerry, worked in a machine shop, and his mother, Judy, worked in a department store. They'd both grown up on farms and instilled an appreciation for a farmer's work ethic in Dan and his siblings.
Athletic Achievement: Dan played three sports—football, basketball, and baseball—at Fairmont High School. He led his team to the state playoffs and was the all-Central quarterback in 1989 in the state of Minnesota. He went on to play football at Moorhead State University, which today is known as Minnesota State University.
Scholastic Achievement: Niss graduated with a degree in engineering management.
Professional Achievement: After starting on a blown film manufacturing floor as a teenager, Dan rapidly progressed through the industry to become president of Charter Next Generation, one of the biggest plastic film manufacturers in North America.
Personal: Dan and his wife, Brenda, have a son, Garret, who was recruited by Ashland University and played football there under Lee Owens.

Dan Niss has a background right out of a Norman Rockwell painting. One can practically envision his childhood in the small town of Fairmont, Minnesota. His parents, Jerry and Judy, both grew up with farming backgrounds and a strong work ethic. Those fundamentals were imprinted heavily on Dan and his siblings.

"You know, some people, it's just handed to them, or they're born with a silver spoon in their mouth," Dan said. "Other people, they've got to find a way to do it on their own. I grew up in this small town where bailing hay and detasseling corn [a process that involves removing the tassels from corn plants to control pollination and produce high-quality corn seeds], none of that was automated."

Dan recounts working every summer, even before he was old enough to drive, on the floor in manufacturing plants, the grunt work that would teach invaluable lessons from the very base of an industry where he would later flourish.

But it wasn't all work and no play. Dan was athletic and played football, basketball, and baseball at Fairmont High School. One of his proudest achievements is becoming the school's starting quarterback in his junior year, a rarity for someone of his background.

"Sports created in me the competitiveness and wanting to win in everything I do," Dan said. "I was the first quarterback in my hometown who wasn't a teacher's kid in a minimum of twenty years. That was one of my pure motivations [for succeeding]."

At Fairmont, Dan played for Tom Mahoney Sr., the winningest high school football coach in Minnesota history when he retired following the 1989 season. Mahoney compiled 256 victories in his legendary career.

Dan was the backup quarterback when his junior season began, but the opener did not go well, and in the second game, he got his chance. As his future would prove, an opportunity was generally all that Niss needed. He jumped into action in that second game and never let go of the position. He led his team all the way to the state playoffs. From that point forward, he was the unquestioned starter, good enough to play at Moorhead State University (known today as Minnesota State University). Dan was on the team for three years, but his summer internship at ExxonMobil was far more enticing, and before his senior football season he could see business, not athletics, was where his future was turning.

Upon graduation, Dan took a job with a small packaging company, the same place where he had worked every summer since he was fifteen. He started at the very bottom, dealing with scrap. Learning manufacturing from the floor level, literally, would prove valuable going forward. Dan gained a variety of experiences along the way, including a stop at Carlisle Plastics, which allowed him to travel and network. He then began work at a company called Optimum Plastics. Those experiences taught him about the equipment and manufacturers he would be dealing with going forward. He developed an extensive understanding of operations, raw materials, and sales. He also fostered an ability to relate to and lead different types of people stemming from his genuine appreciation for unique personalities.

At this point, Dan crossed paths with Dave Frecka, a young man with similar hustle and ambition. Dave founded Next Generation Films in 1994 in Lexington, Ohio. The film in the company's name refers to flexible polymer-based film for packaging. The business was in production for a few months when Niss joined.

Dave Frecka was reared by a family molded in the industrial revolution. His grandfather, Harold, was the blast furnace supervisor at Detroit Steel Company in Portsmouth, Ohio. Dave's father, John, was president of the Empire Steel Corporation in Massillon, Ohio. Dave Frecka founded his first company, Ultra-tech Plastics Inc., in Mansfield, Ohio, in 1985. It grew into a $20 million business before being sold to Ultra-tech in 1993. Next Generation Films was the next step for Frecka.

"I pay off fast and reinnovate," Frecka told the Plastics News trade site in 2008. "That's how you do this business."

Dan and Frecka became a powerful combination. Their company blossomed as a manufacturer of specialty plastic films for fresh-cut produce and quick-freeze food packaging.

"I knew the owners of the plastics companies through the equipment end of it," Dan said. "I had traveled to Germany when I was working at Carlisle, and they just recognized that even though I was just a kid, I knew the equipment and the manufacturers and the presidents of those companies. That's how I got involved with everybody. I was really fortunate to meet a lot of the executives in the flexible packaging business, and I think they thought, He's an up-and-coming guy. I was in the right place at the right time."

Dan was learning to Sharpen the Edge. His work ethic quickly became legendary at Next Generation Films. In addition, something even more important happened. Dan met Next Generation Film's customer service manager, Brenda Sinclair. It wasn't long before she became his wife.

"I remember the day we got married," Dan said. "Some friends of mine in the industry still tell this story. We got married in our house. It was a Friday afternoon, and we only had maybe six extrusion lines at the plant, and one of them broke down. So I'm sitting there working on the line, and I'm supposed to get married at five o'clock. [The plant in] Lexington is about twenty minutes from my house, and it's four thirty, and someone says, 'Aren't you getting married at five?' I had just been thinking, We've got to get this line up."

Dan combined single-minded purpose with torrid drive, and the company grew slowly but surely. However, it had its share of setbacks along the way.

"There were many, many times when I was like, 'We don't have a chance. We're never going to get this piece of business.' I remember talking to Dave once when I was out in California. I was like, 'Man, we don't have a chance in this business. These guys are so tight.' But he was like, 'You just must give it time. You'll get it.' He always gave me a lot of confidence."

By the time I came into the picture, Dan was flourishing. Next Generation Films was growing, and Brenda had given birth to their son, Garret, who was a standout football player at Ontario High School, about fifteen miles east of Ashland University. Garret was a four-year two-way starter. He was a big, strong athlete who was tough and looked like the kind of player we had always recruited to play fullback.

Reggie Gamble was our tight end and fullback coach. Reggie had grown up in Mansfield and attended Mansfield Senior High School. Early in my tenure at Ashland University, Reggie was one of our top recruits, and he quickly became one of our best players and an all-conference player at left tackle. Because he was from North Central Ohio, Reggie knew all the schools and was highly respected by the coaches in the community. Naturally, he was responsible for our local recruiting. The proximity of Ontario meant that Reggie was the recruiting coach for Garret Niss, and once we landed him, he became his position coach too.

Reggie developed a strong relationship with Garret, and with his parents. He was excited to sign Garret. But we were frank about the situation. I told Reggie we really didn't have any scholarship money left to sign a fullback, but if Garret committed to the Eagles and did everything we asked of him in the classroom and on the field, he would earn a scholarship.

I asked Reggie how Garret and his parents would feel about this offer. Reggie told me he thought they would agree as long as he assured them I would keep my promise. Garret, like so many of our athletes, did earn a scholarship. He got the job done in the classroom and on the field.

After Garret joined our team, I had the opportunity to meet his parents. I knew Garret's mom as Brenda Sinclair. She was a student at Galion High School when I was the football coach for the Tigers. Her brother Bill Sinclair was the tailback on my first Galion team. I also discovered that Garret's dad, Dan Niss, was one of the most successful industrialists in all of Ohio. Dan was, and is, one of the biggest investors and philanthropists in the region.

Dan and Brenda came to all the football events in support of Garret. Dan asked me once if there was one thing the athletic program at Ashland needed to separate our program from our competition. I shared with him that one of our biggest boosters, Jack Miller, was working with me to find a way to build the indoor Niss Athletic Center. Dan told me to get back to him when we knew what our costs would be and what we would need as a lead gift.

I will never forget the dinner hosted by Dan and Brenda at their home that cold January evening. After most of the guests had left, Jack Miller and I stayed to talk with Dan and Brenda concerning the questions Dan had about our indoor facility. Jack had written down all the information on a wrinkled page off a yellow legal pad. Jack had all the numbers: the costs, all the other donations, and the amount we needed for a lead gift. Dan looked at Brenda, and Brenda back at Dan. They both nodded their heads. At that moment, the dream of an indoor facility that would benefit so many athletes in so many ways became a reality with the Niss Athletic Facility.

Dan and Brenda have supported many of our needs since that initial lead gift. But even more importantly, Dan has employed many of our athletes after they graduated from Ashland University. Dan talks about when he first realized the potential pool of quality student athletes he might hire. He and Brenda attended our Gridiron Club Gold Dinner at the Troop Center. At these events, I would always have the senior football players and accountability captains introduce themselves to our lead donors. I would also have one player speak on behalf of the team.

At this event, sixth-year senior Austin Phillips was the speaker. Austin had missed four full seasons in his Eagles career because of an original redshirt, two injuries, and the COVID year. But he never quit. He stayed with the team and was picked for the All-State Good Works Team his final season. Dan was impressed by Austin, who has become one of his top hires. Another one was Mike Schweitzer, who was also one of our captains.

"They are superstars," Dan said. "They are winners, hungry, intelligent, and most of all competitive. They want to win everything. Austin hadn't been with us a year and he was already making six figures. When I met him and listened to him, I knew within minutes that he's a leader. He's a winner. When someone stands up [in front of a banquet crowd], 24 years old, and talks about how he's been part of a college football team for six years, had all these injuries, I just listened to his maturity, how he articulated himself, and I thought to myself, he HAS to be on my team."

Dan and Brenda have not only become great friends but also my golf partners at many of the AU outings. Meanwhile, Dan's company was flourishing. In April 2019, Charter NEX merged with Next Generation Films in a $1.07 billion deal. The acquisition took two companies with complementary products but different markets and knitted them together. Dan, who had risen to president of Next Generation, was now president of Charter Next Generation, with a new tagline, A Better Way.

Now, in 2024, CNG is one of the top ten film producers in North America. It operates eighteen production plants with more than 150 lines in Ohio, Wisconsin, South Carolina, and Massachusetts. Now that he had climbed the mountain, the trick for Dan was sustainability.

"We are a very large company, but we started with nothing," Dan said. "Our success, and most of it has been organic, has been about the people. That's our number one asset. It's not that we have patents on our structures. It's not like we have some secret sauce. The competition can call on our customers, and they can use the same equipment and our recipes. But the reason we succeed is the people, getting the right people first and putting them in positions where they are going to be successful."

The COVID pandemic crippled numerous businesses across the country, and clawing back from that situation was a monumental effort. At Charter Next Generation, it took some creativity. While the demand for plastic products was even more pronounced, the search for dedicated personnel to fit that need became critical. So the company began an employee ownership program, which essentially makes each worker a stockholder in the company.

"We knew in 2022, after COVID, after people spent a year at home and were getting free money, that they were going to be a precious commodity. So how do we motivate them? How do we get them back? We had to think a little bit outside the box. The ownership program was one of the decisions we made. That's what differentiates us from other manufacturing companies. Giving [the employees] ownership, we did it because they are our most valuable asset. If we're going to grow, we can't do it without people. That program was a difference-maker."

Niss illustrated the point by explaining that on more than one occasion, a big customer has driven through the CNG parking lot and noted how many nice vehicles there are, obviously driven by employees.

"There's a lot of brand-new vehicles that have been purchased here. That helped this community, and the car dealerships. It's a great compliment to us, and that makes me feel good, too."

Niss noted that Charter Next Gen's core values are being competitive and playing to win. These items are key ingredients in achieving sustainability and sharpening the edge.

"Our business is ever-changing," Dan said. "Who has the [best] technology, the [best] relationships with the customers? It's just non-stop. This is 24-7, 365. Whatever we make on February 7, we must make that same quality on Christmas Day. There's no stop button. We must train people to keep that culture going, and that creates competitiveness."

With his track record of success and financial reach, Dan could live virtually anywhere. Yet he chooses to remain in Mansfield and has become the single most important philanthropist in North Central Ohio.

"First of all, let's be honest, [philanthropy] makes me feel good," he said. "I want this community to be something special, and to be known. When we bought Westbrook Country Club, I called our accountant and I said I wanted to buy WBCC, and he said, 'You mean Westbrook?' And I said, 'Yeah.' And he said, 'I'll be over in the morning.'

"So he comes over and gives me the spiel, and I listen to him for about fifteen or twenty minutes, and he tells me this is the dumbest idea I've ever had. I said, 'I know it is. I know I'll never make money and I'm never getting my money back. But I don't care. I've got a couple of options. I like Westbrook. I just want to go right to the golf course and play with my friends because it beats everything else. I could either spend twenty-five or thirty million on a new house in Florida that I really hate or I could spend the same money here and have a great place for my friends, my family, and just North Central Ohio—and it's a jewel now."

Dan embraces that vision in many of his philanthropic pursuits. He's in the process of modernizing aspects around the local airport in Mansfield. He's also donated to facilities at Ashland University and Ontario High School and contributed to a number of projects around North Central Ohio.

"Sometimes you feel like you have a responsibility," Niss said. "When you give back to the community, you're helping a community that has done so much, played such a big part in the success that you've had. It just feels like the right thing to do."

Bob Sebo-Fellow Philanthropist
"Success is never final."– Winston Churchill

Bob Sebo was born May 22, 1936. He grew up in northeast Ohio and is a proud graduate of Salem High School and a lifelong Quaker fan. His father, John, was a foundry worker, and a QB for the semipro Sebring Merchants football squad in 1933.

Bob was an outstanding high school athlete and scholar and a well-rounded student. He earned eleven letters at Salem, three in football, three in track, two in basketball, and three in band. Bob won the Columbiana County Most Valuable Player trophy in track after winning the 100-yard dash, finishing second in the 180-yard low hurdles, third in the 220-yard dash, and fourth in the discus.

Sebo graduated from Salem High School in 1954. He attended Bowling Green State University and earned a degree in business administration in 1958. He was in the ROTC at Bowling Green and served as a lieutenant in the US Army from 1958 to 1960. He was later appointed to Bowling Green's board of trustees and was selected as a BGSU Distinguished Alumni. Among his many gifts to the school is the $4.4 million Sebo Athletic Center. Bob was honored as a distinguished contributor at the 54th Curbstone Coaches Hall of Fame Banquet.

In 1974, Bob joined founder Tom Golisano to establish a fledgling company called Paychex Inc. of Ohio. They were the only two employees. The company went public in 1983 with Bob as VP. By 2008, Paychex was processing the payrolls of more than 560,000 clients. In 2019, Ohio had more than seven million clients.

Bob and his wife, Linda, have two daughters Julie (Schmelzle) and Christine (Parisi); a stepdaughter, Courtney (Hill); and a stepson, Parker Hydrick.

Bob Sebo and Dan Niss have a very interesting common trait: both wildly successful businessmen have indoor football facilities named after them. In Bob's case, it's the Sebo Center at Bowling Green State University.

Bob loves the Salem Quakers, the Bowling Green Falcons, the Ashland Eagles, the Youngstown State Penguins, the Mount Union Purple Raiders, and the Ohio State Buckeyes, not necessarily in that order. He has long been a great supporter of and friend to all their football programs and a huge booster of the coaches who guide those programs. He counts among his friends Lou Holtz, Jim Tressel, and Urban Meyer. I am proud to call Bob my friend too.

Next to perch fishing—and I have taken Bob on a few such voyages—golf and football are his great loves. Bob hosts friends Tim Baum, Kip Matteson, and me every winter at his Naples National Golf

Club. Bob and I always seem to find a way to win the competition. Like Dan Niss, Bob Sebo absorbed life lessons from the game of football and made them the foundation for his success in the business world.

"Playing as a team member, when you rely on a team member, that's something you have to do in life," Sebo said. "It's a part of life. That's one of the things I learned about cooperation: getting things done with other people."

Growing up in Salem, Bob was groomed in a house geared toward football. His father was the starting quarterback in 1933 for a semipro football team in Sebring, Ohio. Bob remembers donning his dad's spikes and helmet as a youngster. He took part in Knothole Gang football, which got into the high school games for free. He couldn't wait to become a Salem Quaker and make his own mark on the high school gridiron.

Bob started as a sophomore and became the featured back under coach Ben Barrett. He had a fine junior season and was primed for a big senior year when disaster struck. Sebo was a standout in the first two games but was hurt in the third contest against Youngstown Woodrow Wilson in 1953.

"I still remember the play, seventy years later," Bob recalled. "It should've been a ninety-yard touchdown, but I got to about the twenty-five or thirty and my leg just blew out."

He missed the next four games but returned for the season finale against East Liverpool, which suited up an opposing player named Lou Holtz. Bob said Holtz constantly teases him about that game. Salem won 13-2, with Sebo scoring for both teams, including East Liverpool's only points—when he was tackled in the end zone for a safety. Bob also registered a touchdown for the Quakers to clinch his team's victory. Sebo finished the season with 614 yards of total offense in just fourteen quarters of action.

He played basketball and track too and even participated in the band. Bob was approached about college football, even after landing on campus at Bowling Green. But his leg injury simply wouldn't allow him to play at that level. As a high school track athlete in the spring of 1954, Bob won the Columbiana County Most Valuable Player trophy after winning the 100-yard dash, finishing second in the 180-yard low hurdles, third in the 220-yard dash, and fourth in the discus. The latter was a sport he learned less than an hour before that day's competition.

"The tough thing for me was I was a decent high school football player, but I never got to see how good I could've been," Sebo said. "But I learned there are other ways to satisfy your competitiveness. I always call myself a wannabe. I wanted to be a great athlete. Maybe that's why I'm so addicted to sports. It established in me that I would be a lifelong sports fan."

Bob took ROTC in college, and after graduation from Bowling Green, he served as a lieutenant in the US Army from 1958 to 1960. He was a commander at the Nike Missile Air Defense Unit. Sebo left the service and took a job with General Motors. He started as distribution manager of the Cadillac Motor Division in western New York. He advanced to be a business manager and then a district sales manager.

"At that point, I was teaching others how to make money, how to utilize financial statements," Bob said. "But the truth is I was supposed to be teaching when I was really learning about them and from them, how they reacted to what we were telling them."

Sebo didn't know it, but he was Sharpening the Edge, honing the leadership qualities within. It was a trait that would become vital in his future.

"In the business world, if I had a problem or something I agonized over, my first thought was my own father [John]. What would my dad say? He was a foundry worker who became a superintendent later in life. He had this natural wisdom about him. I would relate whatever issue I had to thinking about how he would handle it."

In 1974, Bob took a huge leap of faith. He left General Motors and joined a friend named Tom Golisano. Bob founded a fledgling company known as Paychex. It started by focusing on processing company payrolls for businesses stretching from Salem to Cleveland. Many people who cashed a paycheck in the 1980s in the Midwest were probably cashing those checks through Paychex services.

But the company certainly didn't start that way. In fact, in the

THE SPIRIT OF A TEAM

beginning it was Tom and Bob, two employees.

"I didn't have any money, so I sold my house for $28,000," Sebo said. "I owed $24,000 for it. So, I had $4,000 to start a business. Really, failure was not an option. I had two daughters, so I knew I needed a place to eat and a place to sleep if I didn't make it. I mean, you must have some common sense about it. I had my butt covered. We moved back to Salem to be close to my parents [if things went sideways]. But it allowed me to go full-fledged into it, and it took off from there. I was very fortunate that I picked a business that didn't require a big dollar amount for assets to get started."

Bob readily acknowledges Tom's role as a brilliant tactician whose vision led the company. Sebo served as the "get-it-done" guy. Progress was steady at first, then exploded. Bob said he went out and bought a desk for seventy-five dollars. Then he had to buy a second one when business picked up to the point of needing an assistant.

While working under Golisano's guidance, Sebo again started to Sharpen the Edge. He sat down with a spreadsheet and projected exactly where the businesses needed to grow for the next year, then three years, then five years, and even seven years. He keeps that spreadsheet, and the company did even better than hitting those goals; it blew them away.

"We did extremely well, a lot faster even than I had projected," Sebo said. "But I went into it with no fear, no concern. My mind was on *How quickly could I get to my goals?* I think it's important that you're going to start something, you must have the foresight to ask yourself, 'What is the future of this business? What do I have to do to achieve success?' It has to be more than just this year and next year. When you go all in, you want to know where you're going to take it in three, six, even nine years. That was the fun part of it for me, because I was pretty good at projections."

Paychex grew to provide automatic tax payment, direct deposit, and wage garnishment processing. It evolved into offering 401(k) recordkeeping, risk management, benefits administration, and group insurance management.

In 1982, the company went public, and Bob was senior vice president for Paychex of Rochester, New York. By 2008, it was processing payroll for 560,000 clients while focusing on midsized businesses (those with fewer than one hundred employees). In 2019, the company reported processing the payrolls of about seven million clients, making it the second-largest payroll-processing firm in the United States.

"[Tom] would say, 'This is what we need to do,' and I would say, 'This is what we've got to do within that,'" Bob said. "They say friends don't stay friends if you go into business together. But for us, to this day we are still very good friends. The only difference is he's a billionaire and I'm a millionaire."

Bob reflected on the rise of Paychex and pointed to leadership within the company as perhaps the secret sauce to its development.

"I would be very comfortable managing two employees or two hundred employees,": Sebo said. "I would have no problem dealing with things and applying my philosophy relative to that of a coach. I looked at myself in business as a coach more than a manager. I felt more comfortable doing it that way.

"Your style of leadership, it's how a leader gets the point across to get the job done. There are no specific rules on how to [demonstrate] leadership. You don't have to be a born leader. You can be a developer without necessarily being a strong leader. But leadership is what's necessary to become number one, to win the battles."

Bob's great success led to numerous philanthropic pursuits. He made it possible for many graduate assistants to serve on our coaching staff at Ashland University. Bob is a bigger-than-life person in the world of college football.

On many occasions, Bob would take off from an airport near Salem and fly to Ashland for an early-afternoon Eagles' game and then fly to Bowling Green for a night game.

Bob was at a state high school football playoff game when he heard I was making the announcement about my retirement from Ashland. He immediately asked his friend and driver to travel to Ashland just to show his support for me. That's Bob Sebo. Coaches across the country know that when they have his support, it's a long-term commitment. In 2024, Sebo was honored as a distinguished contributor at the 54th Curbstone Coaches Hall of Fame Banquet.

Bob long ago learned his lessons of teamwork, cooperation, commitment, and leadership in Salem High School athletics and then maintained those principles throughout his business endeavors.

"My experiences underline that," Bob said. "That has always been the thought process. My friend Lou Holtz carries three philosophies: Number one, 'Do the right thing.' Number two, the Golden Rule, which is 'treat others the way you want to be treated.' Number three, 'Do the best that you can.' If you can live by those three things, you're probably going in the right direction and will continue to go in the right direction for a very long time."

The Edge

Former Miami Dolphins Head Coach Don Shula, an Ohio native, described the edge he demanded:

"The whole idea is to get an edge. Sometimes it takes something a little extra to get an edge, but you must have it. The ultimate goal is victory, and if you refuse to work as hard as you possibly can towards that aim, or if you do anything that keeps you from achieving that goal, you are just cheating yourself. I feel that way about athletics, but more importantly, I feel that way about life in general. I demand total involvement from our players. After God and family, the only thing that's more important is what the Dolphins do on game day. What we want to dedicate ourselves to is establishing a standard of excellence in the future, and we are always looking for 'The Winning Edge.'"

You must have an edge to be successful in athletics or in business. No matter the stage of your growth, you must be trying to get the edge and keep the edge. This is at the core of any sustained excellence. If you are working on a skill, you must always try to perform the skill better than your opponent. If working on your strength, you must always try to be stronger than your opponent. If you have a physical limitation, your edge will be your conditioning.

In the first scene of the movie *Gladiator*, Maximus, played by Russel Crowe, returns to his army and prepares for war. The Gladiators have an edge, the sword of Maximus. In the face of a certain defeat, Maximus leads the Gladiators to a great victory. It is after this battle that we see something very powerful. These highly trained warriors know to stay alive. There is no time to celebrate. They must prepare their swords for the next battle and "Sharpen the Edge."

The purpose of team excellence is not only to get an edge but to keep the edge. I never want to compete with a team that has lost its edge. Remember, most team leaders believe it is easier to get to the top than to stay on the top.

These are the characteristics of teams that lose their edge. All these characteristics result from a lack of mental toughness.
1. Teams that become comfortable, complacent, and arrogant.
2. Teams that embrace the outcome and the rewards of success and not the process of getting there.
3. Teams that focus on recent victories and the immediate gratification of success.
4. Teams that adopt the D.I.L.L.Y. plan of attack: Do It Like Last Year. And teams that accept the easy way: "If it's not broken, don't fix it."
5. Teams that listen to all the noise about how good they are and read the clippings about how good they are projected to be.
6. Teams that forget they have competitors that are poor, hungry, and driven—competitors that will do everything they can to unseat the top team. Teams that forget that as the top team they have a target on their back and will get everyone's best shot.
7. Teams that are motivated to win for the wrong reasons and allow the "selfish beast" to take over.

These are the characteristics of teams that keep their edge. None of these characteristics requires physical talent.
1. Teams that were motivated to win for the right reasons and understand that the road to success is always under construction, there is no final draft.
2. Teams that are aware of "where they are now" but look back to "where they started" and look forward to seeing "where they go next." A team that takes time to look back will see and thank those who were there for them and review what they did right

in becoming successful. A team that takes time to look forward will begin to set new goals, reach-up goals, this team will then replace the old plan of action with a new more creative plan and immediately start committing to this new plan.
3. Teams that have established a culture and a tradition of excellence. Tradition is not living in the past but learning from the past, blending and building a better future. Tradition creates a legacy that binds the past and present together. Where there is team culture that takes care of the younger members on the team and celebrates the senior members of the team. Tradition motivates and helps to eliminate the negative aspects of human nature.
4. Teams that want to give back and share their success, leaving a path for future teams to follow.
5. Teams that are always trying to improve their performance and always chasing perfection. Teams that never stop giving more. Teams that realize there is always more to be done, and the team is always capable of doing more.
6. Teams that are always committing to higher and tougher standards and have an alertness where complacency can be checked and there can be no letdown.
7. Teams that stay humble and gracious. Praise their opponent and never praise themselves.

Staying on Top

"Perfection is not attainable, but if we chase perfection, we can catch excellence."– Vince Lombardi

Aron Cramer, president and CEO of BSR, published the book Sustainable Excellence: The Future of Business in a Fast-Changing World. The book addressed a business environment that has rapidly changed in the past decade and is continuing to accelerate. Cramer identified five principles of sustainability that are crucial ingredients of the business strategy needed to navigate our changing world.

From the boardroom to the gridiron, there are far more similarities than contrasts. For both, the only constant is change, and the only

certainty is uncertainty. For teams chasing excellence in both business and sport, the five principles outlined in his book have a common value in their ability to deliver sustainable excellence.
1. Think big.
2. Use sustainability to drive innovation.
3. Set the right incentives.
4. Embrace the transparent world and collaborate.
5. Make consumers your partners.

For teams to get to the top and stay on top, they must try to reach their full potential. In attempting to reach their full potential, they will begin to understand the value of improvement. Improvement is a process that is never complete. No matter what the circumstance, there is always something a team can do better.

Brad Stulberg of the Growth Foundation listed ten rules for sustaining excellence. Rule number one is Be the Best at Getting Better: "The human brain did not evolve to arrive, it evolved to strive. It's critical to find meaning and satisfaction in the path. If you make the ultimate goal getting better the rest takes care of itself."

When teams reach the top, they can't afford to have the imposter syndrome. Your team has earned this position and belongs. There will always be new competition, new ideas, and new challenges making you doubt that your team will stay on top. The confidence of belonging at the top will grow on a team with like-minded people who are committed to staying on top.

Like-minded people who believe in their team.

In 2024, Kansas City's 25-22 overtime victory in the Super Bowl cemented its legacy as the most recent dynasty in the NFL. "Dynasty" is defined in sport as the ability to sustain excellence. I was talking with Los Angeles Chargers Assistant Coach Steve Clinkscale this past season before their game versus Kansas City and asked him, "What makes them great?"

He first acknowledged the leadership and continuity of Head Coach Andy Reid. He also said Reid has never changed his core values, his beliefs, or even his strategies. He is doing the same things he has always done, just with better players and a greater emphasis on making what he does look different each week.

Mike Vrabel, who was at Ohio State when I coached there, played for the Patriots during their dynasty years and was recently hired as their new head coach. I asked Mike once why he thought New England was so hard to beat when he played for them? Of course he mentioned both Coach Bill Belichick and quarterback Tom Brady. But he also told me that to negate all the advances in technology and scouting that Coach Belichick was such a good teacher he could reinvent his team each week.

In college football, I have witnessed dozens of major changes and challenges in the past few decades. None was bigger than the amount of money in the game. When I left Massillon High School to go coach for John Cooper at Ohio State in 1992, I took a pay cut. Twenty years later coaches were making ten to twenty times the amount of money I made at the same job.

I'm not saying they don't deserve it. They are making more sacrifices with higher expectations and risks than ever before. But I believe that kind of money can cloud what we do and why we do it. The same is true for players. Do college players today choose a team for the right reasons or only for the money?

The amount of fame and fortune in our game fosters a win-at-all-costs mentality. Do more teams today cheat and compromise the rules and the integrity of the game? Do more teams today compromise the academics of the athletes? Do more teams today compromise the mental and physical health of their players and staff by eliminating all opportunities to maintain a balance in life?

I believe the sustainability of our sport and its athletics will always be dependent on just a few core values and beliefs. The number one responsibility as a leader in sport is to challenge the players and coaches who are a part of your game—at all levels—to play and to coach the game for the right reasons. To me, the right reasons include love of the game, passion for the sport, and the desire to honor their teammates in the locker room, their families, and their faith.

A coach's job is to be a dealer of hope by using their power of influence to help athletes move in the right direction, putting the well-being of everyone on the team before the win. I also believe we must convince our players and coaches to be the best wherever they are. Convince them that what we did at Ohio State was no more important than what we did at Crestview High School. Our players and coaches at Crestview worked just as hard with far fewer rewards.

Finally, and most importantly, to sustain our game we must give back to our game. Become a member of your coaching association, serve on a committee, attend the clinics and conventions. The year I served as the AFCA president, I had the opportunity to award John Cooper the Amos Alonzo Stagg Award. This award is given each year for "outstanding service in the advancement of the best interests of football."

Talk about full circle. I went to my first AFCA convention the year Coach Cooper hired me to coach with him at Ohio State. Coach Cooper was serving as the AFCA president that year, and his service and commitment to our association inspired me to serve the AFCA my entire college coaching career. By giving back to the game through the AFCA, I had opportunities to network with other coaches, access information, and advance professionally, all while working to advance the best interest of my sport.

Be Strong Enough to Handle Success
"I don't remember too many celebrations. Just pick up the trophy, get home, and get ready for the next season."–Larry Kehres

Excellence is something for which all teams strive, but it brings with it an entirely new set of pressures and problems. Handling the pressure and standing up to the challenge are the keys to sustaining excellence. When excellence is achieved, the feeling can be overwhelming. The most important thing a team can do after a win or after a championship season is get right back to work. The team that can win and then sit down and critically analyze every facet of the championship has a good chance of repeating the championship.

It is as they say, all about the next year, the next season, the next journey. It is the next journey that energizes a team, not last year's success. A championship season must always be the beginning of a new journey.

THE ROAD TO ANYWHERE...

Unfortunately, the road to anywhere is filled with many pitfalls, and it takes a man of determination, and character not to fall into them. As I have said many times, whenever you get your head above average, someone will take a poke at you. That is expected in any phase of life. However, as I have also said many times before, if you see a man on top of the mountain, he didn't just light there! Chances are he had to climb through many difficulties with a great expenditure of energy to get there, and the same is true of a man in any profession, be he a great attorney, a great minister, a great man of medicine or a great businessman. I am certain he worked with a definite plan, and an aim and a purpose in life and will be envied by those less successful.

"To sit by and worry about criticism, which too often comes from the misinformed or from those incapable of passing judgment on an individual or a problem, is a waste of time."— Adolph Rupp

Key Points for Sharpening the Edge

1. Teams must be dedicated to a standard of excellence and always look for the "Winning Edge."
2. The idea of team excellence is not only to get the edge but also to keep the edge. Most team leaders believe it is easier to get to the top than to stay on the top.
3. Teams that lose their edge lack mental toughness, become comfortable, lose their focus, and become distracted by all the noise.
4. Teams that keep an edge commit to all things that require no physical talent.
5. Teams that are motivated to win for the right reasons and have established a culture and a tradition of excellence will keep their edge.
6. Sustainable excellence is more challenging in today's world because of the constant acceleration of change.
7. In business and in sport, there are five strategies that will help to deliver sustainable excellence: Think Big, Use Sustainability to Drive Innovation, Set the Right Incentives, Embrace the

Transparent, Make Consumers Your Partners.
8. For teams to stay on top, they must understand and commit to the process of improvement. Become the best at getting better.
9. Once a team reaches the top, it must individually and collectively believe it belongs and commit to staying there.
10. Handling the pressure of success and the challenge of success is the key to sustaining excellence.

–FINAL WORD–
LASTING LEGACY

"A leader's legacy is only as strong as the foundation they leave behind that allows others to continue to advance the organization in their name." – Simon Sinek

Photo of Sue Ramsey

Bio Box: Sue Ramsey Motivational Speaker/ 2013 Division II Women's Basketball National Champion
Background: Sue was born August 6, 1956, and grew up in Bexley, Ohio, a suburb of Columbus. Her father, Van, owned his own business as a professional photographer. Her mother, Anne, volunteered for a variety of organizations until becoming Van's office manager when Sue was in sixth grade. Both parents were graduates of the Ohio State University, where Van ran track for the Buckeyes. Sue inherited his athletic genes, while older sister Lynn was more interested in music and artistic pursuits.
Athletic Achievement: Sue took part in the beginning of girls' high school athletics at Bexley. She played four sports for the Lions: volleyball, basketball, field hockey and softball. She became the first women's basketball scholarship player at Indiana University and finished her career at Miami University.
Scholastic Achievement: Ramsey attended Indiana University for three years before transferring to Miami, Ohio, as a senior and graduating in 1978 with a degree in education and minors in athletic training and coaching.
Professional Achievement: Sue was the NCAA Division II National Women's Basketball Coach of the Year in 2012. She was inducted into the Ohio Basketball Hall of Fame in 2018. Ramsey is a member of Miami University's Cradle of Coaches. Other honors include the Kay Yow Heart of a Coach Award (2011), the Carol Eckman Award for demonstrating outstanding values and character (2012), the Athletes in Action Hall of Faith in 2013. At Ashland University, her teams racked up a 501-364 mark over twenty years. She led AU to a Division II national championship in 2013, and the Eagles were national runners-up in 2012. Her record was 367-217 at AU.

I wanted this book to finish with a chapter that highlights a career with a lasting legacy and the life lessons of excellence. I gave quite a bit of thought to who personifies inner peace, a well-rounded life, and personal as well as professional achievement. After much thought on a lifetime of experiences with a vast array of incredibly successful people, I landed on a woman who worked alongside me at Ashland University, Sue Ramsey.

What does it mean to leave a legacy? To me, a lasting legacy is the positive impact your life has on other people—friends, colleagues, even strangers. Your legacy is the sum of your personal values, accomplishments, and actions—setting an example for others and a guide for future generations.

Sue built the Ashland University women's basketball program from the ground floor into a towering powerhouse that remains the envy of Division II athletic departments. Yet she's also extremely grounded. Sue can talk about cooking one second and the next describe the run-and-jump defense she played at Indiana University.

Her program at Ashland competed for two national championships, won the first national title in program history, and laid the foundation for a dynasty that exists to this day—well past her retirement. Sue takes great pride in the AU women's basketball program and its continued success under the leadership of one of her former players, who followed one of her former assistants. Meanwhile, she stays busy as a professional speaker, team culture facilitator, and leadership specialist.

"It's my passion to share my life experiences with others to inspire, encourage, and motivate them to pursue their God-given purpose with joy, humility, and gratitude," Ramsey stated matter-of-factly.

Sue's story began in Bexley, Ohio, a suburb of Columbus. She is the younger of two daughters of former Ohio State track athlete Van Ramsey and his wife, Anne. Van became a professional photographer, and Anne served the Bexley community before going to work alongside her husband.

"My parents were amazing people. When they got married, my dad swore he wasn't going to screw up the vows. He practiced reciting 'I, Van, take you, Anne.' Sure enough, on the big day, 'I, Anne, take you,

Van,' tumbled out of his mouth," Sue chuckled. "If you ask people who knew my parents, they would confirm I am a carbon copy of both of them!"

Sue was raised in the core values of faith and servitude while focusing on things that matter instead of material possessions.

"I always said they did a great job not letting us know how poor we were. On Saturday evenings, we'd walk two blocks up to the thrift shop. Mom had a key to sort through the good stuff that came in that day. Monday morning I'd be sitting in class sporting a new sweater, and someone would say, 'Hey, I used to have a sweater just like that.' I'd respond with a smile and gratitude for my twenty-five-cent investment."

Like her father, Sue leaned into athletics, in an era when there weren't many rewards for girls in sports. She would shoot baskets in the alley that separated the homes in South Bexley. The neighbor would flip on the lights as darkness descended so that she could keep going. She dreamed of being on a team someday, but before Title IX legislation, it was nothing more than a dream.

In short, Title IX is a federal law signed by President Richard Nixon in 1972 that prohibits sex discrimination in educational programs and activities that receive federal funding. This meant schools (including high schools) are legally obligated to provide equal athletic opportunities to students regardless of gender. That was the intent. In practice, it can be a struggle to realize those rights. But the timing of that legislation meant that Title IX would play a significant factor in Sue Ramsey's life, because when she reached high school, girls' sports teams were in their infancy at Bexley.

A woman named Charlotte Bassnet was the first to recognize Sue's passion. A physical education teacher at Bexley High School, Bassnet immediately spotted Ramsey's athleticism.

"I was two weeks into high school and not even on a sports team, because at that time it wasn't allowed [for freshmen]," Sue said. "Ms. B approached me and asked, 'Sue, have you thought about what you want your major to be in college?' I just looked at her and said, 'Ms. B, I'm lucky if I can find my locker right now. I have no idea!' Undeterred, she simply said, 'Well, I recommend you choose physical education as your future.' I remember thinking, Cool, I get to wear sweats and play in the gym all day. I'm in! And look at me today: I'm still wearing sweats."

Sue was sold on the idea and all in on playing sports when that door opened the following fall. Bassnet coached her in softball, while Ramsey's other early mentor, Diana Ford, was her coach in field hockey, volleyball, and basketball.

Ford's first move was to change the rule that barred freshmen from competing in athletics. High school sports were to be available to all girls at Bexley High School. In Sue's case, that merely fed her passion. Under the mentorship of her high school coaches, Sue jumped at the opportunities they presented to learn and study all facets of physical education, including coaching.

Sue graduated in 1974, without the opportunity to participate in a state tournament—as girls' high school sports were just beginning from a statewide perspective. She was hoping to continue playing either volleyball or basketball at the next level. The one thing she was set on was playing for a person of faith.

"I had gone to a [girls] basketball camp. There were only two in those days. One of them was Eastern Ohio Basketball Camp, and the coach that was running it was Mary Alice Jeremiah. She was the first Christian coach I had been associated with, and she said, 'Sue, I'd love for you to come and play at Cedarville [College], but I think you can play at a higher level.' I expressed my desire to play for a Christian coach, so she directed me to Indiana University. I went to watch Indiana play Ohio State in my senior year of high school in Columbus. I remember after the game I went down and introduced myself to the coach. I wore my clogs, which propelled me to six foot one, I said, 'I want to play for you.' And she said, 'Okay.' I think there was a handshake and 'We'll-see-you-in-the-fall type of deal.' And that was it."

The woman she spoke to was Bea Gorton, Indiana's first women's basketball coach, who guided the program from 1972 to 1976. Gorton was making a whopping $500 in that position while she toiled as a grad student chipping away at her doctorate. Oh, by the way, Gorton compiled a 79-28 overall record and led the Hoosiers to the Elite Eight of the Association for Intercollegiate Athletics for Women National Tournament in 1972.

Truly it was a different era. Still, Sue was sold on Gorton and Indiana.

"So I committed to Indiana. During move-in weekend, I grabbed my basketball and ventured over to the HPER [Health, Physical Education, Recreation] building to get some shots in. I spotted someone watching me from the doorway. Eventually she comes over and we made introductions. She asked me if I was thinking about trying out for the basketball team. When I said I might try out for both basketball and volleyball, she was quick to set me on the right track. 'No. I think you just want to play basketball.' That person and soon-to-be teammate was Tara VanDerveer—you know, the GOAT?"

VanDerveer would become the winningest coach in the history of men's or women's college basketball. She retired after stints at Idaho, Ohio State, and Stanford with a career record of 1,216-271, for an incredible .818 winning percentage.

But for Ramsey, Tara was an influential teammate as a senior with the Hoosiers. VanDerveer combined with all-American Debbie Oing to give IU a formidable squad that went 18-4 overall, 7-0 in the conference, although the Big Ten was not yet sanctioning a women's conference schedule. The Hoosiers were eventually eliminated after advancing to the National Women's Invitational Tournament.

"My freshman year was so fun because the other guard on our team was Debbie Oing, a first-team Kodak All-American," Sue recalled. "So here's Debbie and Tara in the backcourt, and they're doing run-and-jump [defense] before anybody knew what run-and-jump was. Debbie would turn the ball handler toward Tara to get the steal and Debbie would run down the court. She was an all-American, so you know she's not going to miss the layup, but my job in my mind was to run after her in case she did. I mastered the art of high-fiving while backpedaling back down the court."

Ramsey stayed at Indiana for three years and was the Hoosiers first scholarship women's basketball player as a junior. She enjoyed her time playing for Gorton in her first two seasons, but a new coach proved to be a challenging fit for her third year. So before Sue's senior season, the decision was made to transfer to Miami University in Oxford, Ohio.

"Looking back, my journey proved to be invaluable to my coaching career" Ramsey said. "I had three college coaches in four years and learned valuable lessons from each one of them. Also, making the decision to transfer was the biggest challenge I had yet to face. Pam Wettig, the graduate assistant during my freshman year at Indiana, became the head coach at Miami University. In addition, I already knew several players on the team. After doing my homework, I approached my parents with the news about transferring. No surprise, they supported me 100 percent."

Sue fit in nicely at Miami, where the Redskins went 15-6, and she made a strong impression that would come in handy a few years down the road.

Sue graduated from Miami and then became a teacher, coach, and athletic trainer at Noblesville High School in Indiana for three years. She taught elementary physical education, was the head athletic trainer, and coached cross-country, basketball, and track. After three years, she wanted to focus on coaching at the collegiate level, so she accepted a position as a graduate assistant coach at Illinois State for the 1983-84 season.

Her college basketball coaching journey had begun, and it would take the form of a gypsy's lifestyle in those early stages. She had a brief stint at Illinois State, returned to Miami as an assistant for a year, and then held the same position for two years at the University of Cincinnati. At that point she was offered two head coaching jobs, one at Bradley University (in Peoria, Illinois) and the other at the University of Dayton. She cast her lot with the Flyers, accepting the job prior to the 1986-87 season.

To this point, Ramsey had largely taken on the posture of a coaching student, noting the exploits of Bobby Knight at Indiana University while she was a student there (the Hoosiers won the 1976 national championship). She was also introduced to the teachings of UCLA basketball coaching legend John Wooden, an Indiana native and Purdue graduate. She was most impressed by Wooden's Pyramid of Success and the building blocks he believed were essential to personal and professional development and achievement.

At Dayton, the Flyers were like nearly every other collegiate athletic program. Title IX meant complying with government guidelines and affording women the same sports opportunities as men—but often within the same financial constraints that were in place prior to the legal ruling, when the focus was strictly on men. It was a transitional period for everyone: the schools, their administrators, the coaches, and obviously the athletes themselves. The climb encountered an added hurdle at Dayton when the Flyers advanced from a strong Division II program (that made five appearances in the AIAW National Division II basketball tournament from 1977 to 1981) to the Division I level in 1985-86. That was the backdrop for Ramsey's first head-coaching stint.

"I was hired by Tom Frericks [athletic director], who understood the challenges we were facing. He said, 'Here's what I want: I need you to graduate your kids, run a clean program, and beat Notre Dame every once in a while.' We did what he wanted, graduating every single student-athlete that stayed all four years, ran a clean program, and we beat Notre Dame! It was fun."

Unfortunately, Frericks suffered from prostate cancer and died in 1992. Sue's record wasn't great (95-128 in eight years, a .426 winning percentage), and her first season under the new athletic director became her final campaign as a head coach with the Flyers, going 8-19 in 1993-94.

She transitioned to the education department, where she worked on her educational specialist degree, thinking her future would be in administration, possibly as an elementary school principal. However, God had a different plan.

"I had no idea what I was going to do at that point. I had been called back for a second interview for an elementary principal's job, but it just wasn't feeling right. I was literally down to my last payment for my condo that I'd been trying to sell. It was the middle of September when I received a call from one of my college teammates. She was friends with the sister of a coach at Ashland University [Karen Linder]. The women's basketball job had just opened up, and my name was mentioned as a possible candidate for the position. I remember telling my friend, 'Nah, I'm done coaching.' She countered, 'Sue, you walk through this door until God closes it.'

"Bill Weidner hired me on October 1 as the new women's basketball coach at Ashland University. Bill was happy because he didn't have to take a coach from another program that late. I was happy because I was back in coaching, even though all my coaching in college was at the Division I level and now I was in Division II. That first year I had no assistant coaches. All I had was a fifth-year senior finishing up her degree who was interested in coaching. But I'll tell you, adversity doesn't define you; it refines you. When I got to Ashland in 1995, I immediately knew that is where God wanted me to be."

Ramsey inherited a program that had fashioned decent seasons under Linder and predecessor Melanie Balcomb, but it had never reached the pinnacle. It would take quite a climb for Sue to get there. Her first team registered a 16-10 mark, a nine-game improvement from the previous year, and she continued to hone her craft in varied ways. Her first two teams registered solid seasons: 18-9, 17-12. But then the Eagles hit a lull, 9-18 and 6-21, and like any good leader, Ramsey began searching for answers.

"I had been at Ashland for five years or so when I went to a Women's Leadership Summit sponsored by Athletes in Action. They proposed the question, 'Do you have a PDP?' I didn't even know what a PDP was. They clarified it for me: it's a Personal Development Plan, a philosophy. Affirming that I had a philosophy, I was challenged to write it down. Back in my office, I stared at the wall featuring John Wooden's 'Pyramid of Success' and 'Life Lessons' by Kay Yow, women's basketball coach at North Carolina State. Using their words as inspiration, I began the process of formulating my own vision. Using their words as inspiration, I began the process of formulating my own vision/core values for the program. A ream of paper later, I drew a basketball court and, in the center, wrote the word 'commitment'—because that's where everything starts for us. The end lines followed with the words 'integrity' and 'trust.' Those served as the foundational pieces for AU women's basketball from that point forward."

Sue didn't know it, but she had begun her "Court of Commitment," which became the program's standards:

Around the center circle the word "COMMITMENT" is in all

caps. Across the center jump circle are the words "Determination," "Effort," "Focus," and "Passion." In the left key, where "INTEGRITY" is listed along the baseline, are the phrases "Undisputed Character" and "Consistent Dependability." At the other end, where "TRUST" resides, are the words: "Selfless Love," "Honesty," "Sincerity," "Loyalty," and "Communication."

"Everyone associated with our program, from the coaches to the players, managers, athletic trainers were accountable to the words on the court," Sue said. "Obviously, no one is going to be perfect, so grace and mercy will be extended, but that's what we're striving for.

"I'll give you an example. I had a young lady who was a sophomore on one of our best teams. She showed up for practice and gave her all for two hours. She was a good teammate and was coachable. However, basketball was not her passion. She would be up until 2:00 a.m. designing homes on the internet. That was her true passion, and that was okay. However, if you're part of a team striving to be the best in the nation, you must be willing to commit to more than two hours a day. That's not a difficult ask IF it's your passion. At our end-of-season meeting, I pointed out the obvious. 'You know, I love you and appreciate all you've done. But see this little thing right here? It says 'FOCUSED PASSION,' and I said, 'This is just not for you, and that's okay. It doesn't have to be. But if you're going to play basketball here, FOCUSED PASSION is a requirement.' There were some tears and a little denial. But once emotions settled, the truth was embarrassing. She transferred to a school with an interior design program and called me five months later to say, 'Thank you, Coach. I'm so much happier.' As coaches, we are committed to the total development of our student-athletes. It must be a holistic approach. We're here to help them grow mentally, emotionally, physically, spiritually, and socially."

Likewise, Sue noted something I deal with myself. On the recruiting trail, it's so important to meet the athlete in their home, see how they interact with their family, their siblings. Are they showing respect? Are the parents offering discipline? Is this a youngster with personal accountability? These things can tell you if that individual can handle coaching, and tough coaching if necessary. If there's a concern on any of these issues, then you have to ask yourself if this young person can live up to your program's standards. If they can't, then it's best to take a pass on that particular student-athlete. That can be tough when the talent is so obvious. But no matter what kind of talent the player may possess, recruiting a problem child can become a four-year problem—one that's rarely worth the hassle that an individual can create for the rest of the team members.

By the 2003-04 season, Ramsey's project began taking shape. The Eagles went 23-8, the first of three consecutive twenty-win campaigns. She also developed the ability to probe a team's performance for strengths and weaknesses that led to some interesting self-reflections.

One lesson she incorporated and implemented within her program might seem counterintuitive to some. On many teams, freshmen are given grunt work: collecting uniforms, cleaning up the locker room, hauling the ball bags, sweeping the gym floor. Some coaches consider these chores a rite of passage for freshmen. Dean Smith famously noted how it was freshman Michael Jordan's job to carry senior James Worthy's gym bag at North Carolina.

But Ramsey approached these chores in a very different manner, inspired by one of her athletes. After the 2009-10 season ended with a 14-14 record, Sue challenged one of her key returnees, Rachel Poorman, to read Bruce Brown's book titled Captains, 7 Ways to Lead Your Team . . . Be First Be Last. Sue sought Rachel's opinion as a player who would be a captain the following year on what she could take from the book, how to absorb it and apply it to the Eagles. This exercise became a revelation to the coach too.

"Rachel read the book over the summer, and when she reported back, she said, 'Coach, I agree with everything I read. That being said, there's something we have to change. No longer should the freshmen carry the dirty laundry. We need to start looking at serving our teammates as a privilege, for those of us who have been here the longest. The seniors need to serve and take care of the younger players.'

"I appreciate Rachel so much because she carried the laundry her freshman year and was willing to do it again her senior year. That simple act changed the mindset, changed the culture of our program. Teammates started looking for ways to serve each other, and it caught on.

"In my last year of coaching, we were playing in the regional championship game. We came up short but accomplished a great deal with a young team. Following the handshakes, Taylor Woods, our only senior, and I walked off the court together—both having finished our careers. Following the press conference, Taylor went to the locker room. About thirty minutes later, I vividly recall looking down this long corridor to see my team walking toward me. In the middle of the pack was Taylor carrying both bags of laundry over her shoulders. One of the freshmen came up to me and said, 'Coach, we offered to carry it for her, but she said, "No. This is my last chance to serve you as my teammates."' What a powerful message. She just played her last game, and what's she thinking about? How can I serve my teammates one more time?"

When the 2010-11 season began, Sue's sixteenth at Ashland, the Eagles were prepared to take flight. They finished that year 19-10, good enough to attract a transformative talent in six-foot-one swing player Kari Daugherty, who transferred in from Dayton. Daugherty's grandfather Dave Mast was a longtime high school basketball coach. Her mother, Caroline Mast, was an all-Ohio player who led her team to a 1982 state championship at River View High School in Warsaw, Ohio. Caroline went to Ohio University and was selected the Mid-American Conference Player of the Decade in the 1980s. She then became a state championship coach, also at River View High School, and coached her daughters, Kari and her sister Kristin. Kari was Ohio's Co-Player of the Year as a senior and played on state title teams in 2006 and 2007 and a state runner-up team in 2009. While Kristin went on to Dayton and was an all-Atlantic Ten player there, Kari decided to transfer after her sophomore season with the Flyers. She became the missing piece to Ramsey's puzzle in the quest for a national championship.

"I came to Ashland for my faith," Kari said in a story posted on the Ashland University athletic department website. "I became a Christian when I was at Dayton, and I wanted to be at a place where I could grow more in my relationship with God. I didn't want to come to Ashland when I visited, but I felt like this is where He wanted me to be. And He was right. He was right in how I've been able to grow in my faith here, how it's shaped who I am. I know I wouldn't be where I am today if it wasn't for being here and the people that surrounded me and helped me grow in my faith during my time here.

"I felt like God wanted me here so that Coach Ramsey could mentor me in that way, because she is such a huge part of who I am and who I've become."

In 2011-12, Kari Daugherty had the greatest season of any women's basketball player in Ashland University history. She averaged 21.4 points and 14.3 rebounds per game while leading the Eagles to a 33-2 record and an NCAA Division II national runner-up finish. Daugherty was chosen a first-team all-American by Daktronics and the Women's Basketball Coaches Association, was the WBCA National Player of the Year, won the 2011-12 Honda Sports Award, and was chosen the NCAA Division II Female Athlete of the Year.

"Kari is the most competitive person I've ever known," Ramsey said. "She would rip the soul out of you to get that rebound. But then she's the kindest soul after the game. One of the things that Kari did when she became the head coach at Ashland University was to make 'Have Fun' one of her program's core values. That's a very important point for Kari in particular because when she competed, she was very intense. She's a serious person, and you must be true to yourself. But as a coach, she wants to make sure the team is having fun. I love that self-awareness!"

In 2012-13, Daugherty was even better, and so were the Eagles. Ramsey guided that bunch to a 37-1 record and the Division II national championship. Daugherty was again the Division II National Player of the Year and led the Eagles to a 71-56 beating of Dowling College (New York) in the championship game at San Antonio.

"If you're going to lose, lose to the best team in the country," Dowling Coach Joe Pellicane said. "They're a great team, great coach. We were thoroughly beaten."

It was sweet vindication for Ramsey and the Eagles, who had fallen to Shaw 88-82 in overtime in the NCAA finals the previous year. That stinging setback ended a thirty-three-game winning streak.

"My young ladies, I couldn't be more thrilled, happier, with the performance, not just today, but for the last 365 days, because they've been a determined bunch of young ladies since we left here last year as the runner-up," Sue told the NCAA Division II women's basketball tournament website after that game. "They've worked hard to make this transition and make this season everything it was. It's a great celebration right now. It's a mixture of smiles, laughter, and tears. Everything is full circle, and it's real times two. When it soaks in, I think they'll realize, as do I having coached thirty-four years, that this is a once-in-a-lifetime accomplishment. They deserve every bit of it."

Sue retired after leading the 2014-15 team, with Woods as the lone senior, to a 25-9 record. But she left a full cupboard that her capable assistant, Robyn Fralick, immediately rolled with to a 31-2 record in her first season. The next year, AU went 37-0 and claimed another national championship.

No one was more proud than Sue Ramsey. Fralick's achievements validated a decision Ramsey had made to bring on the new assistant in 2008. At the end of that season, Fralick was an assistant coach at the University of Toledo when the women's basketball staff under Coach Mark Ehlen was fired. Ramsey, on the search for a new assistant, called Ehlen.

"Without hesitation, Mark said 'I've got a young one . . . I think she's going to be really good,'" Sue told the Lansing State Journal. "That was all I needed. I trust Mark 100 percent. And I said, 'Okay, let's figure out a way to get her here.'"

On the surface, it might have seemed like a step back for Fralick, who dropped down to Division II, albeit a very successful Division II program. But now Ramsey could lean on another vibrant mind to take the Eagles to heights the program had never reached. Naturally, when Sue stepped down, she immediately endorsed Fralick for the top job. Another national championship proved that was the right move too.

"Robyn told me that her core values might look a little different than mine, but the foundational pieces were still in place," Sue said. "What a huge blessing. I was able to make sure Robyn would take over the team she helped to build, and then Kari after her. Knowing the program would thrive under both of these amazing women and coaches gave and continues to give me great joy."

Fralick led the Eagles to a 36-1 record in 2017-18 and another national runner-up finish. She then took a job at Bowling Green and later became the head coach at Michigan State. In her introductory press conference with the Spartans, Fralick quoted a Ramsey axiom: "Take care of people, and take care of details."

Fralick's departure led Ashland University to hire her assistant, former Division II National Player of the Year Kari Daugherty (now Pickens), for the top job in the women's basketball program. Pickens knew her task inside and out. She had already influenced the program more than any player before her. Now she would impart the lessons Ramsey had imprinted on her.

"One of the things I took away the most as a player was you win a national championship and then you come back and you're still expected to go to class the next day; the world doesn't stop," Pickens said. "As great as it is for us to try to do what we've done, winning a national title is small [in the grand scheme of things]. It must be about so much more than just the end product of a national championship.

"Those earlier championships really taught me that and helped me keep things in perspective more as a head coach."

Kari's task was perhaps even tougher, because she took over a program that Ramsey built and Fralick maintained. It was up to Pickens to continue that level of play. The standard was incredible.

In Kari Daugherty Pickens's two seasons as an AU player, the Eagles posted a combined 70-3 record and back-to-back appearances in the national championship game. As an assistant under Fralick from 2015 to 2018, Ashland went 104-3 and again reached back-to-back national championship games. Those teams also set a Division II record with seventy-three consecutive wins, a whopping twenty-two victories longer than any other team has ever recorded.

"They could have easily opened this job and gotten a ton of applicants, but I think people believed in our program and what I was going to try to continue on with. A ton of credit goes to Coach Ramsey for establishing a program that people wanted to be a part of. I'm just thankful that Robyn [Fralick] believed in me enough to be able to advocate for me to take over and even giving me a position as an assistant to begin with."

Kari attacked her job with a purpose and posted a perfect 31-0 record before COVID thwarted a march to the 2019-20 national championship goal. No worries: Pickens led AU to a third national championship in 2023, with a perfect 37-0 record. Pickens said her time playing under Ramsey taught her to never get too high or too low as a coach. She also noted that much of her practice planning and structure comes from Ramsey's influence.

"There are tons of things I still do the same that we did [when I was a player]," Pickens said in a story for Ashland Source. "Obviously, some things have to change and evolve, but people know. They can ask current players, they can ask former players, and they can ask different people who have known our program; they know what they're going to get."

That is the foundation Ramsey built over the course of two decades and is now resonating through another related coaching regime—one that thrives under Sue's immense shadow.

"I talked about it in my workshops . . . being part of a team is like a jigsaw puzzle. Each member of the team has his/her unique talents and abilities. Whatever that looks like, it is essential to understand that all roles have equal value, and each team member is needed in order for the 'puzzle/team' to be complete. I then implore those I am working with to not be the missing piece of the 'puzzle/team' to be complete. Bring your best every day and you will have no regrets."

Ashland University Legacies

"If you are going to live, leave a legacy. Make a mark on the world that can't be erased."–Maya Angelou

Coach Ramsey left a powerful legacy for the women's basketball team at Ashland University.

During my tenure at Ashland, there were many others who, like Sue Ramsey, would leave lasting legacies.

When I left Crestview High School to go to Galion High School, I was young, confused, and uncertain about the move. My athletic director at Crestview was Larry Rader, and he had been a true mentor for me early in my coaching career. He told me this about leaving a school I loved for another opportunity: *"There is good and bad everywhere you go; it is all about what you make of it."*

After making several moves in my coaching career, I experienced the wisdom of Larry Rader's words, although after spending the last twenty years in Ashland, I felt the good far outweighed the bad. I believe this was because there were so many good people working to make Ashland and Ashland University a good place.

To me the greatest legacies are those people who have lived life fully and honorably. They are people who have enjoyed the richness of life and dedicated their lives to being the best they can while making the most of their impact on the world.

I have met and worked with far too many Ashland University Legacies to list. But there are a few who quickly come to mind when I consider their significance to Ashland athletics and how much they inspired me and made a positive impact on my life.

Bob and Jan Archer are two of the biggest fans of AU women's basketball. They are also two of the biggest fans of all Ashland University athletics and academics. It seems only appropriate that these two high school valedictorians would have the Ashland University library named in their honor.

Jack and Deb Miller compete with the Archers in their support of AU women's basketball. The Ashland University Chapel is named in their honor. Jack was recently honored in Wayne County for his leadership and philanthropy in building youth, high school, and college athletic facilities, including the six thousand-seat Jack Miller Stadium at Ashland University. Jack said this at the event, "Deb and I like to see long-term needs for athletic facilities that can help groups of people for generations."

In a recent *Ashland University Accent* story, it was reported that Ralph Tomassi and his wife, Betty Jo, continue to uplift and support others in their retirement years. Ralph Tomassi has become a legend at Ashland University. "His heart is made of gold, the blood that pumps through it is a shade of Ashland purple," that story noted.

Don and Kathy Graham live in Willard, Ohio. Don was a highly successful high school football coach who is now the president and CEO of Don Graham and Associates. His company is a financial services firm that employs several Ashland graduates. Don has been president of the Ashland University Gridiron Club since 2006, when it was founded. Coach Graham's legacy to Ashland University football is best summed up in this *Ashland Accent* story, "Graham's contributions to Ashland University and its football team have been immeasurable. His involvement has not been limited to mere financial support. He's also dedicated his time and effort to the cause, helping shape the team and the university into what they are today—a source of pride for alumni and current students alike."

The Mary C Miller Student-Achievement Center was opened in 2019. Mary served thirty years as a professor in the Dauch College of Business and was an academic adviser for many of our athletes. Mary was also one of our best recruiters. Mary and Stan Miller have always been strong advocates for the successful integration of athletic and academic success.

Jud Logan won a gold medal in the hammer throw at the 1987 Pan American Games. Jud also competed in four Summer Olympics starting in 1984. Jud served Ashland University as the head track and field coach for seventeen years, leading Ashland to three consecutive national championship titles. After he passed away on January 3, 2022, the *Repository* wrote these words to honor his memory: "His greatest achievements though were not of world records or championships, but how he impacted people's lives in such a positive way. He believed in finding and then becoming a 'Light Giver,' mentoring and instilling belief in those around you. Being a Light Giver is the torch of his Legacy he would want all to continue passing on."

These Ashland Legacies are lives that matter. They are lives of personal excellence and social significance. They go above and beyond the limits of their own lives to reach out and help enhance the lives of those around them. Legacy is positively affecting other people's lives and leaving a mark on the world that matters.

Giving Yourself to Others
"It is more blessed to give than to receive."–Apostle Paul

Excellence in life will never be measured by wealth or fame. All we can take with us when we leave this world is that which we leave behind for others. That is our legacy. This is why it is important to invest in the things that will still be around when we are gone.

I believe excellence in life is measured by our relationships, specifically our relationships with family and friends. We were not meant to live selfishly on our own and to go through the motions in life simply to be alive and nothing more.

Two of the greatest things in life are to love and to be loved. Therefore, excellence in life will always require that we work hard to cultivate and to maintain meaningful relationships.

Every religion and philosophy in history has started with the basic concept that the highest calling in life is to give yourself to others or to serve others. To live a life where you help others reach their full potential and to be there for others when they are in need.

There is little difference in achieving team excellence and excellence in life. After all, we are all on the same team, "God's Team." For every team and every individual, each day is a new day. The importance of each new day and the choices we make within it will determine our excellence in life.

BEGINNING OF A NEW DAY
This is the beginning of a new day,
God has given me this day to use as I will,
I can waste it or use it for good.
What I do today is very important because I am
Exchanging a day of my life for it.
When tomorrow comes, this day will be gone
forever,
Leaving something in its place I have traded for
it.
I want it to be gain, not loss, good not evil,
Success, not failure in order that I
Shall not forget the price I paid for it."
Dr. Heartsill Wilson

LEE OWENS WITH LARRY PHILLIPS

—ACKNOWLEDGMENTS—

I would like to start by acknowledging Team Owens. The group participation in Chicago during Thanksgiving was a big help in picking out the cover for the book. No matter how busy or how distracted I seem to be, family has always been most important in my life. I love you all, especially the twelve grandchildren: Benjamin, Natalie, Matthew, Laney, James, Henry, Emersyn, Willow, Corbin, Raegan, Madison, and Lincoln.

Thanks to Coach Doug Geiser and Ashland University for sharing their facilities with Larry and me for completing the interviews. So much of this book was inspired by my experiences and my relationships in Ashland. I truly appreciate the support I was given by so many Ashland administrators, staff members, and fellow coaches making my tenure at Ashland University most valued. And a final Ashland shoutout to Dusty Sloan for taking time to make sure I had all my Ashland sports information correct in the book.

I never would have been able to write this book without the encouragement of friends—real friends, not Facebook friends. To a great group of guys who like to hang out together and experience my great hunting and fishing skills and my below-average golf game.

This book would not have been possible without the superstar CEOs and coaches featured in these pages and, in several cases, their assistants. I thank this group for their patience and their trust in sharing their stories. I'm sure these stories will inspire the readers and have a positive impact on future team builders.

To our biggest superstar, Coach Jim Tressel, for taking time to write the foreword to this book. I have always been honored to call Coach Tressel a friend.

To Becca Moore and her book with Scott Ryan, *Massillon Against the World*. This book was also published by Tucker DS Press with Scott doing the design and David Bushman doing the editing. After reading this book, Larry and I were convinced this was the team we wanted for our book.

Larry Phillips once told me I had a better chance teaching him to coach Cover 4 defense than he did teaching me to write. I told him I didn't need to know how to write; that was his job. Larry is an award-winning writer who shares my passion for athletics and team excellence.

Larry and I would like to thank our good friend Jon Spencer for his work on our early interviews. We would also like to acknowledge my grandson Benjamin and my daughter Leanne for sharing their computer expertise.

Finally, to a mentor who refuses to be acknowledged, you have always inspired me to find new experiences that challenge me, force me to grow, and require that I give my best. Thank you.

MORE TO READ AT TUCKERDSPRESS.COM

Read more about Massillon in the award-winning book *Massillon Against The World*. The book covers the 2023 Massillon Tigers winning the State Championship for Div. II for the first time on the field. Written by Scott Ryan and Becca Moore, hosts of *Tiger Talk* on YouTube.

MORE TO READ AT TUCKERDSPRESS.COM

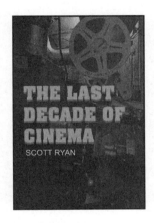

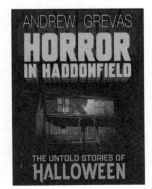